PARALANGUAGE AND KINESICS

(Nonverbal Communication)

With a bibliography

by

MARY RITCHIE KEY

The Scarecrow Press, Inc.
Metuchen, N. J. 1975

Library of Congress Cataloging in Publication Data

Key, Mary Ritchie.
Paralanguage and kinesics.

Includes index.
1. Nonverbal communication. I. Title.
BF637.C45K48 153 74-30217
ISBN 0-8108-0789-0

ACKNOWLEDGMENTS

It would be hard to account for all of the influences and contributions that have benefitted this study. When I roam through the attic and find old college notes on courses I don't even remember taking, I realize again that so much of learning is out-of-awareness. If I have overlooked any bibliographical credits, it is most unintentional. As I have thought about the ideas in this book for over fifteen years, it would be difficult to recall every discussion, every piece of correspondence, and every book or article I have read.

When I first offered a course in Nonverbal Communication at the University of California in 1968, I had not planned to write a book on it. But as I developed outlines, and dittoed material and bibliographies for the course, it became increasingly evident that there was need for publishing. So the dittoed material developed into larger drafts and preliminary chapters which I have used in class for the last few years. Response from students and colleagues has improved my early ideas. It is a commonplace these days for professors to acknowledge the help their students have been in writing a book. This recognition is no meaningless cliché. Many improvements in the study have resulted from responses from students--a good many of them <u>nonverbal</u>!

I first came into linguistics when George L. Trager and his peers were attracting worldwide attention to linguistics by their remarkable discussions on language. And, as in every cumulative venture, the work of today is in debt to the work of yesterday. I am grateful to George Trager and Dell Hymes for their helpful responses to my first drafts. I want to thank André Martinet who was responsible for seeing that I did the 1970 article, which was written from an early draft of this book. I am grateful to my professor Archibald Hill, who suggested the term "paralinguistics" a generation ago and who has encouraged me to explore further.

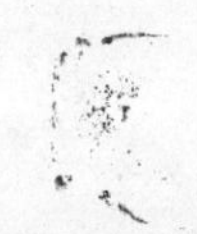

When I started out on this project, I didn't realize there was as much material as there actually is. In a library research project, librarians, in the final analysis, are one's best friends. I am grateful for the help the librarians on my campus have been in locating items in my working bibliography which numbers around 2500 references. Deanna Spehn, former student, helped in many concrete and encouraging ways. My niece, Anna Margaret Miller, performed many loving acts in the way of proofreading, typing, and indexing.

In the course of producing a newsletter on nonverbal communication I have corresponded, literally, with dozens of colleagues working on various aspects of interactional behavior. Though most of this book was written before I started the newsletter, I have tried to include information that has come to me as a result of correspondence. The bibliography, especially, is richer because of the cooperation and helpfulness of many, many colleagues.

I also want to acknowledge the help of my scholar son, Tomás, whose diverse background and wide reading has brought me in touch with items I would not have seen otherwise. In addition he has spent a great deal of time editing, proofreading, and looking up references. It is a superb gift to be able to be a critical and evaluative reader . . . and at the same time be inspirational and encouraging.

TABLE OF CONTENTS

Acknowledgments iii

Part One

I INTRODUCTION 9

Limitations of Study and Definitions
Structured Behavior
The Blind Men and the Elephant
Interdisciplinary Approach
Cross-Cultural Approach
Learned Behavior and Imprinting
Innate Behavior and Universals
Imitative Behavior
Antithesis
Functions of Communication
Extent and Importance of Nonverbal Communication

II A MODEL for Describing Nonverbal Behavior in Communication 22

Signals
Behavioral Event
Verbal Act
Nonverbal Act
By-Elements of the Nonverbal Act: Artifacts, Clothing, Hair
Paralinguistic Acts and Kinesic Acts
Relationship of Nonverbal Act to Language
Nonverbal Acts and Linguistic Structures

III PARALANGUAGE: The Vocal Sounds of Nonverbal Communication 41

Elements Used in Paralanguage
- Language Sounds
- Language Element Modifications
- Suprasegmental Elements
- Non-Language Sounds
- Non-Language Modifications
- Modification Made with By-Element
- Laugh--Giggle--Tremulousness--Sob--Cry
- Control of Air Movement

Paralinguistic Acts
- Outcries
- Mimicry

IV KINESICS--Body Language 76

Elements Used in Kinesics
- Posture
- Facial Expression
  - Eye
  - Mouth
  - Nose
- Other Body Movement
- Physiology
  - Regular Physiological Functions
  - Spontaneous Physiological Acts
  - Automatic Reflex, Instinctive
- Combinatory--Body Movement and Noise

Kinesic Acts
- Tactile Gestures and Movements
- Autistic Gestures and Movements

V SENSORY COMMUNICATION 107

Acoustical, Optical, Tactual, Chemical, Electrical
The Olfactory Sense
Cutaneous Response

VI THE FUNCTION OF SILENCE in Communication 116

VII THE CONTEXT OF SITUATION in a Theory of Communication 122

Media

Time
Location and Space
Participants
Physical Conditions
Zeitgeist
Style and Function

VIII DIALECTS OF NONVERBAL BEHAVIOR and Special Message Systems 135

Patterned Individual Behavior
Patterned Group Behavior
- Geographic Varieties
- Temporal Varieties
- State-of-Being-Dimensions
  - Age
  - Sex
  - Status
- Cultural Dialects

Language Substitutes

IX SCIENTIFIC METHOD 162

Concepts and Methodology
- Classification
- Interpretation
- Segmentation
- Redundancy
- Order of Events
- Focus and Observation

Applicability of Research

CHAPTER NOTES 171

Part Two

BIBLIOGRAPHY 177

INDEX 237

Part One

Chapter I: INTRODUCTION

The study of human behavior is in a pristine stage and our naïveté about it is evidenced daily in our lack of understanding of people and their actions reported to us on all sides, as well as lack of understanding of ourselves. We have been able to cross oceans, forge through mountains, control rivers and energy. We have stepped out into space and have tantalized ourselves with recording mysterious communications from way beyond. But all too often we haven't been able to understand or to be understood by the person sitting next to us.

One aspect of human behavior, communication, takes place primarily by verbal means. Verbal communication may be expressed in Hindustani, Apache, Swahili, or English. But whatever language, or whatever the purpose in communication, informational or expressive, emotions and attitudes always project themselves in an overlay of superimposed patterns. Kingdoms and democracies topple, marriages are sealed, and minority groups discriminated against because of emotions and attitudes--not intellectual reasoning and facts. The "myths" and the "what everyone knows" direct the actions of human beings and often result in conflict between human beings. We think we know how we behave and we have definite ideas about the behavior of other people: "Latins are more emotional"; "women gesture more than men"; "black people have better rhythm." But in fact we know very little about human behavior, or to put it another way, we have such a long way to go to understand us. One would hope that through rigorous treatment, systematic observation, and rejection of the myths, one could attain insights into the most baffling of the secrets of the universe, those of human behavior.

Nonverbal communication comprises a very large area of human behavior, but the discussions in this book will be limited, for the most part, to paralanguage and kinesics, with some reference to time and space dimensions, sensory communication, and cutaneous experiences. These are common to all people. I have a feeling that these latter should take a larger part in our discussions on nonverbal behavior, but so far little is written on the subjects in terms of communication devices, and it is difficult at this point to see how they fit in with language in the way that paralanguage and kinesics do. For these reasons, they are handled differently in this study. The study will not include nonverbal events such as music, painting, and writing, except in reference to paralinguistic and kinesic acts. Nor will it include such mental states as motivation, intention, thought processes, symbol response, and belief systems, which are all important studies which must be dealt with eventually in reference to nonverbal communication, but are beyond the scope of this book.

For the most part I will avoid technical terms, but there are times when discussions are enhanced between disciplines and between different segments of society by having some terms in common. In this study, "paralanguage" and "kinesics" will be used frequently.

Paralanguage is some kind of articulation of the vocal apparatus, or significant lack of it, i.e. hesitation, between segments of vocal articulation. This includes all noises and sounds which are extra-speech sounds, such as hissing, shushing, whistling, and imitation sounds, as well as a large variety of speech modifications, such as quality of voice (sepulchral, whiney, giggling), extra high-pitched utterances, or hesitations and speed in talking. Ostwald calls these "nonverbal acoustic signs." Kinesics is articulation of the body, or movements resulting from muscular and skeletal shift. This includes all actions, physical or physiological, automatic reflexes, posture, facial expressions, gestures, and other body movements.

The term paralanguage was first used in publication in 1954 by Welmers. The 1958 article by George L. Trager (see Bibliography) is best known for introducing the term to linguistics. Trager states (p. 275 of the Hymes edition) that the term was suggested by A. A. Hill. In his introductory paragraphs, Trager tells something of the discussions and seminars from 1952 on, during which features of paralanguage and kinesics were focused upon. Ray L. Birdwhistell's 1952 article was the first published use of the term kinesics. Others who made important contributions to the development of ideas in those days were Henry Lee Smith, Jr., Edward T. Hall, Jr., Gregory Bateson, Norman A. McQuown, Robert E. Pittenger. In fact, says Trager (p. 275), Smith, McQuown, and Birdwhistell must be mentioned as virtual coauthors.

The exact definitions of these terms, however, are still nebulous a generation later. In examining the literature I find that hardly any two authors use the term _paralanguage_ with the same perimeters or elements. In conversation Trager confirmed my feeling that it is too soon in the development of a theoretical framework to limit ourselves to too exact a definition. So my definitions and use of terms throughout the book are to be considered as transitory and hopefully useful in encouraging further discussions between disciplines.

The Bibliography at the end of the book is not exhaustive. Many more references can be found in the other bibliographies listed and at the end of the other works cited. The impressive size and number of the bibliographies attest to the interest and curiosity that people have had and continue to have on these aspects of nonverbal communication. On the other hand the lack of theory, the mishmash of the collection, and the hollow ring of some of the works attest to our lack of understanding of the field.

While, admittedly, the subjects of paralanguage and kinesics need further attention in the way of experiments and designed investigation or observation, I feel strongly that in view of the state of the art (discipline?) it is far more important to bring together what _is_ known. Scholars have not been able to profit from other studies, because the publications are from so many different directions, and many are in obscure journals or out of print. Many of the studies reported are redundant, ridiculous, and even inaccurate, simply because the researcher has not done sufficient reading and has not benefitted from what is well known in other disciplines. In some cases the researcher has spent a great deal of time shuffling photographs or charts and running classes of students through experiments to prove something that had been reported a generation ago! So then, this book is an attempt to bring together ideas previously set forth on the subject of nonverbal behavior, and thus reflect the current work, and to provide a framework with which nonverbal communcation can be discussed.

Paralanguage and kinesics accompany and relate to verbal communication in a definable system. My thesis is that all of this nonverbal behavior is structured, as language and other experiences in human behavior are, even though our present state of knowledge is not complete and not even the scholar has a skeletal description of this behavior for any culture or people because of the magnitude of the subject. A native speaker of any language is not able to verbalize about the structure of his language (known or unknown) without linguistic training or studied observation; likewise no one is able to systematically describe the structure of his nonverbal behavioral patterns (even the parts that are slightly known) without concerted effort to analyze that system. At the same time, every normal human being, in whatever culture he lives, responds to and operates within the particular system of nonverbal communication patterns of his society and subsocieties, even as he is able to communicate with words because he automatically responds to <u>that</u> system of <u>verbal</u> communication. The well-known anthropological linguist, Edward Sapir (1927b, p. 556), said, "... we respond to gestures with an extreme alertness and one might almost say, in accord with an elaborate and secret code that is written nowhere, known by none, and understood by all."

The <u>human communication</u> in these discussions takes place primarily between human beings or to oneself but may at times involve other animate creatures who can respond. On a given day, an animal trainer may actually spend more time communicating with animals than humans. A hermit may communicate primarily with non-humans and with himself. Just as important in our discussions is the communication to oneself, particularly as a function of expressive or emotive behavior, or a dress-rehearsal for a future communication to other humans. Whistling in the dark is self-communication. Observations of the communication to self move toward the discovery of "Who Am I?"

The model for describing nonverbal behavior in Chapter II is a tentative outline. The many-dimensional aspects of human behavior defy a single model as a framework for describing such. It is a commonplace that human beings are so complex and the interrelationships so involved that one almost despairs of finding a model even as a starting point of discussion or investigation. It is as though one were attempting to describe a two-dimensional phenomenon with a one-dimensional model, or a three-dimensional experience with a two-dimensional sketch. Over the years in which I have gathered this material and thought about gestures and paralanguage, the story of the blind men and the elephant has repeatedly jumped back into my thoughts. While I am trying to describe the tail, someone is shouting about the ear; when I get engrossed with the leg, voices clamor concerning the side of the elephant. I am somewhat amused by claims these days to "tell it like it is!" The speaker is only able to tell what his part of the elephant is like! And even that part will change as the elephant gets older and fatter! At this point it doesn't seem possible to discuss nonverbal behavior without several possible models.

And in fact, the Bibliography shows that some topics of our study have, indeed, been described from many approaches: the vocal behavior of the noises emanating from the vocal cavities; attitudes in social behavior; functional interpretation of various acts, such as laughter; non-normal behavior, such as mentally disturbed or deaf sign language; systems substituting for language, such as whistle talk or visible gesture language such as is used at the grain market; detailed acoustic studies with precise instruments; the interpretation of behavior by others, seen and unseen; and on and on. Allport and Vernon in one area of our study substantiate that it is essential to focus on several levels and that failure to do so "often leads to restricted and inadequate definitions of personality." Cherry corroborates the idea that to be understood, communication must be approached from a variety of directions.

In the chapters following the model I have tried to present classifications and illustrations from different perspectives. The listings and inventories I am presenting should in no way be considered definitive, but should be taken as suggestive for further development of the theoretical framework and, hopefully, provocative of further research.

In the academic world all too often research and study is presented in such a way that only one's colleagues are able to read the publications. As Cherry said (p. 2), "Too many of us today are scientifically lonely...." Even with all the talk about interdisciplinary involvement, the fact remains in universities all over the world that there are ivory towers within ivory towers, and years stretch by with professors never dialoguing with other professors outside of their own disciplines. I am a linguist. Undoubtedly my discipline, training, and linguistic experiences will heavily influence my outlook on this aspect of communication. But I will attempt to climb down the narrow steps of the ivory tower and write for other persons too. I will try to avoid the jargon of my own discipline and other kinds of gobbledygook. I don't believe that this more relaxed type of presentation obviates a scholarly, carefully thought-out treatment. There is an aura about academic publishing these days that implies, in effect, "If you can understand it, it's not profound!" I believe, along with Robert Coles, that human behavior is so profound, and so sacred, that discussions should be in the simplest kind of prose.

> Our journals, our habits of talk become cluttered with jargon or the trivial. There are negative cathects, libido quanta, 'pre-symbiotic, normal-autistic phases of mother-infant unity', and 'a hierarchically stratified, firmly cathected organization of self-representations'. Such dross is excused as a short cut to understanding a complicated message by those versed in the trade; its practitioners call on the authority of symbolic communication in the sciences. But the real test is whether we best understand by this strange proliferation of language the worries, fears, or loves in individual people. As the words grow longer and the concepts more intricate and tedious, human sorrows and temptations disappear, loves move away, envies and jealousies, revenge and terror dissolve. Gone are strong, sensible words with good meaning and the flavor of the real.... [1]

The subject of human behavior merits--demands--discussion across disciplines. But I realize that an attempt to bridge interdisciplinary crevices is traveling a precarious path--I am subject to critical exposure. I choose to live dangerously. I welcome any observer of human beings to scrutinize the discussions here and further contribute to our knowledge of nonverbal communication.

In addition to an interdisciplinary approach I am also treating the subject with strong emphasis on cross-cultural perspectives. Goethe has said, [2] "Wer fremde Sprachen nicht kennt, weiss nicht von seiner eigenen" [who does not know another language does not know his own], and, indeed, one can say the same for nonverbal communication. All people, in any society, have emotions and needs which are common to all of mankind. All people participate in the same physiological functions, want to be loved, need to have many kinds of relationships with other members of society, need to communicate learning and emotional feelings, and share common physical acts of eating, sleeping, and living.

In investigating the panhuman aspect of gestures and paralanguage, one becomes more convinced of the fact that most of it is learned behavior. See Hess (1958 and 1959), and Salk regarding the concept of imprinting. Probably most of the system of nonverbal communication is learned out-of-awareness. Tiny children learn to sit, or squat, or kneel, because they are excellent mimics and copy their models, the adults. Usually parents don't concern themselves with explicit instructions on how to fold the arms, how far to tuck the hands in, and how to accommodate the shoulders. There are, however, some aspects of behavior which are overtly taught. Young ladies might be trained rigorously not to cross their knees--and when to wink (or, more often, not to!)--and who they should shake hands with.

It is still an unanswered question as to how much of behavior is explicitly taught and how much is learned below the level of conscious awareness. In fact, it might even approach the impossible to try to articulate the teaching of every behavioral act. Consider the act of teaching a person to ride a bicycle (Miller, Galanter, and Pribam, p. 87):

> Almost no one--including physicists, engineers, bicycle manufacturers--can communicate the strategy whereby a cyclist keeps his balance.... 'Adjust the curvature of your bicycle's path in proportion to the ratio of your unbalance over the square of your speed.' ([--fn 3:] from Michael Polanyi, Personal Knowledge (University of Chicago Press, 1958). Chapter 4 in that remarkable book emphasizes the importance of our inarticulate skills for all branches of knowledge and the extent to which we blindly accept a frame of reference that we cannot justify when we acquire a skill.)

If we think of a child learning a language, we realize that most of language learning takes place out-of-awareness, as far as the structures of the language are concerned. A parent or teacher may teach more items of vocabulary or make a few corrections in grammatical structures: "Don't use double negatives" or "Say 'feet,' not 'foots'." But compared to the enormous number of grammatical rules, these explicit instructions seem to be relatively few. It is unheard of that a parent instructs a young child, "Now direct the apex of the tongue to the alveolar ridge and emit a certain amount of aspiration from the first air chamber, the lungs" (to teach a child to pronounce a "t"). And it would be impossible to imagine a parent teaching the child to articulate a sentence by instructing, "The auxiliary structure must modify the verbal item which follows the noun phrase. And of the components of this auxiliary the tense rule is obligatory; the modal is optional and may be followed by rules governing aspect. The adverbial of manner may occur with a transitive verbal type but never occurs with the verbals of the V-mid type." No, these structural features are learned out-of-awareness. (In these illustrations, the language is English--they would be different for a speaker of another language.) It would seem that most of the patterns or structures of nonverbal communication are also learned without conscious attention. To test this, one can observe the points of interference when living or visiting in another culture or society. Or, in one's own society, try doing something differently, or leaving out something.

In either case, whether unconsciously or consciously learned, behavior patterns are passed on from one generation to the next, with every generation contributing its own set of changes. For a long time people have recognized that learning starts to take place very early in life. De Tocqueville (1835) believed that learning began in the cradle:

> We must watch the infant in his mother's arms; we must see the first images which the external world casts upon the dark mirror of his mind, the first occurrences which he witnesses; we must hear the first words which awaken the sleeping powers of thought, and stand by his earliest efforts--if we would understand the prejudices, the habits, and the passions which will rule his life. The entire man is, so to speak, to be seen in the cradle of the child.[3]

Margaret Mead (Sebeok, Hayes, and Bateson, p. 43) suggests that this learning starts to take place at least at birth, and perhaps before:

> ... All of this behavior is patterned from the moment of birth and probably--although the evidence is not conclusive--from the moment of conception, and that we are dealing with the fact that from the moment something occurs once and there is a response to it or a non-response to it, it is changed. One cannot speak of simple spontaneous events that occur more than once. We have to keep this whole pattern of systematic types of behavior characteristic of different cultures very clearly in context.

Eibl-Eibesfeldt corroborates (1964, p. 297), "... an animal ... is always put in an environment which acts upon it, and it might even learn in utero or in the egg."

An important aspect of the study of paralanguage and kinesics is the study of innate behavior patterns and universals of behavior. Charles Darwin (p. 13) suggested six areas of research, "in order to acquire as good a foundation as possible, and to ascertain, independently of common opinion, how far particular movements of the features and gestures are really expressive of certain states of the mind...." He suggested the study of infants, the insane, photographs, paintings and sculpture of great masters (who are close observers), all the races of mankind, and animals. He was concerned with other non-normal situations, the deaf (pp. 61-2), and the blind (pp. 196-7, and other references to Laura Bridgman). Ekman, Sorenson, and Friesen approach learned and innate behavior with cross-cultural studies. The distinction between culture and nature is a matter of discussion and speculation by many.

Eibl-Eibesfeldt (1964, p. 304) lists some innate behaviors:

> A number of observations show that man, too, although most of his behavior is learned and formed by tradition, has a given outfit of innate behavior patterns. In detail they have been studied in the neonate. Innate patterns are the sucking response, the breast-seeking automatism, smiling, crying, and a number of reflexes. The fact that babies, born deaf, start to burble like normal ones at a certain age indicates that the urge to use the vocal apparatus is inborn, too. The uniformity of many mimical expressions throughout mankind of different races and cultures and the finding of

> homologous patterns in anthropoids indicate that they are fixed action patterns, although the proof has been given only for the smiling response.

Eibl-Eibesfeldt cites Lorenz' study of the blind reaction of mimical expression to crude dummies. He further mentions the cross-cultural similarities in greeting ceremonies, submissive postures, and display behavior. See also Tylor, 1878, Chapter III. It *is* curious that certain gestures, while perhaps not identical in meaning from culture to culture, have a range of similar semantic interpretation. Shrugging the shoulders, for example, might mean indifference, carelessness, rejection, or disdain, but this act has never been reported meaning anything in the range of joy, eagerness, or hopeful delight. Likewise, pinching the nose indicates feelings in a range of negative reaction, "it stinks" or other repugnant response. The attitudes of rejection and humility appear to be universally portrayed by turning away and bowed head, respectively. But of course, none of these suggestions are documented yet.

Morris (1967, p. 94) lists as *instinctive* expressions, the smile, the grin, the frown, the fixed stare, the panic face, the angry face. He further suggests that the scream, the whimper, the laugh, the roar, the moan, the rhythmic crying, without training all mean the same in all cultures. Some studies would take issue with some items in his list, but there do seem to be enough similarities across cultures to merit further study.

The theme of Ostwald's book, *Soundmaking*, is that vocal articulation "is an activity as necessary to human survival and comfort as are breathing, feeding, sleeping, and other vital processes ..." (p. ix). He believed that Darwin also maintained that "soundmaking is a biological activity allied to procreation and the preservation of communal life" (p. 9). It is worth mentioning, too, that Darwin often spoke of "inherited gestures." In the way of future research, Ostwald suggested that "Soundmaking might prove to be a useful intervening variable for future studies of the relationship between genetic patterns and human behavior" (p. 48).

Imitative behavior is another aspect of group behavior that relates to communication. Yawning is often cited as an act of imitative behavior. Coughing is another well-known example. Is this group communication? Sometimes directed toward a single person, for example, the dull speaker or the boring teacher?

Antithesis in human behavior is another concept to consider in nonverbal behavior--the opposites: pain-pleasure; idiot-genius; cry-laugh; love-hate. They are a constant part of life. The interpretation of nonverbal events is curiously antithetical. Tickling is a kinesic act of hateful aggression and of love-making; spitting is done in contempt and the exchange of spittle is an act of love; urinating is done at the enemy's house to show hatred and it is a culminating expression of satisfaction among the Japanese and certain peoples of Africa in sexual intercourse. Darwin (p. 50) speaks often of the antithesis in human behavior. La Barre also (1947, pp. 56ff.).

Artists have often been quoted as exceptional observers of human behavior (Efron, e.g.). Sir Joshua Reynolds remarked, "It is curious to observe, and it is certainly true, that the extremes of contrary passions are, with very little variation, expressed by the same action" (Darwin, p. 28). His examples are the frantic joy of a Bacchante and the grief of a Mary Magdalen.

The functions of communication in nonverbal behavior are probably much the same as they are in verbal behavior. At least it seems useful in the discussion to follow a skeletal outline which is generally used (and often expanded upon) in discussions of the functions of verbal language:[4] (1) Informative, (2) Directive, and (3) Expressive. Informative language is propositional language; it supplies information and is a vehicle for ideas. In nonverbal events, this is illustrated by lexical sounds and gestures which convey information, such as counting gestures, and a nod of the head to indicate "yes."

The second function is directive and effects behavior in the respondent. A good deal of this persuasive communication is handled in nonverbal ways. A look can quiet and control a child. A speaker raising both hands to shoulder level can bring the audience to attention. A hand gesture gets the door closed. Nonverbal events from the audience, such as yawning, coughing, chair squeaking, looking at the watch, direct the speaker to look at his watch and end the speech! Quality of voice also controls and directs the consequent behavior of the one spoken to. A weak, tired, and pitiful voice says, "Poor little me--don't pick on me!"--a subtle form of socially acceptable tyranny. Distance and space are used to control relationships with others. As someone has said, "Moving away from a person to get closer...." Among the Eskimos, the nonverbal event of silence is used to punish children and control their behavior (Salisbury, pp. 81-2).

It is unlikely that any behavioral event has a single function, but rather contains overlapping functions. Jakobson (1960) believes, however, that one function is dominant. A directive gesture may be used for social control in which case it has a highly emotional impact as well. It seems that it would be difficult to say which of the functions is dominant in a gesture such as "V for Victory." During World War II this gesture was intended to provoke action: "fight!" (Schuler). The evolution of this gesture is interesting. From a directive to agitation, it has become a symbol of PEACE--don't fight!

The extent of nonverbal communication is probably not fully realized--nor is the importance of it. This is graphically illustrated in the formula:

Behavioral Event ⟶ (Verbal Act) + Nonverbal Act

which is presented in the Model in Chapter II. In any instance of a communication item occurring as a behavior event, nonverbal communication is obligatory, while speech, or verbal communication, may or may not occur concurrently. Note further discussions on this in Chapter II. It will probably turn out to be true that the Nonverbal Paralinguistic and Kinesic Acts carry the heavier load in communicating emotions and attitudes. In some way that we don't understand completely yet, the Nonverbal Act seems to be more important in interpersonal relationships than language itself. William Austin (1972) supports this idea. Mehrabian (1968, p. 53) even presents a formula, but he does not indicate how he got his figures.

It is worth noting, too, that psychologists and psychiatrists, who deal largely in human emotions, have contributed a significantly large proportion of the studies in these aspects of human behavior. And just in passing, we can recall that in describing some items, for example, a spiral, gestures are much more eloquent than speech. Define a spiral without using your hands! In Pidgin languages it is reported that paralinguistic and kinesic behavior carry a heavy load of communication because, of course, these languages are reduced languages and therefore the verbal event is limited.

History--and Time magazine--give many examples of people being put in jail or otherwise punished for making a gesture--or for not making a gesture. Time (April 9, 1965) reported on gestures of insult in Italy. A truck driver was fined $50 and court costs for doing the corna (or mano cornuta) at a motorist. And in Rome, a butcher was jailed for placing a bull's horns in the corner of his shop nearest that of another fellow widely known to be frequently cuckolded!

During World War II the United States Congress passed a law which made the flag salute obligatory. Francis Hayes (1957, p. 298) gives references to the court problems of the Jehovah's Witnesses before the law was declared unconstitutional. Hayes cites other experiences which were drastic to the person(s) who did not conform to the nonverbal behavioral patterns of society. A Chinese who did not bow to the portrait of Sun Yat-sen was liable to punishment (p. 231). "The Chevalier de la Barre was decapitated (July 1, 1766) on two counts, one of which was failing to doff his hat as a religious procession passed by" (Hayes, p. 283, who quoted D. Mornet).

Arthur M. Schlesinger, Sr. reports that in the early days of establishing our country, "People were punished, usually in public, for scandalmongering, cursing, lying, name-calling, even for flirting, jeering, 'finger-sticking' and making ugly faces."[5] A linguist colleague in Germany recounted to me the unhappy fracas in Leipzig in 1928 that worked its way through the courts clear up to the supreme court because of an insult caused by "the way he said it." The actual words involved were innocuous, something to the effect of, Das ist ein feiner Herr! "That's a fine man!"

We started out by saying that it isn't the rational verbal language that moves human beings to action, but the great, underlying force that actually causes interaction between people and nations is the emotional, attitudinal communication. If this is true, and if it is also true that the great weight of emotional communication is handled by paralanguage and kinesics, then a deeper study of those aspects of human behavior is indicated if we are to understand the world today.

Chapter II: A MODEL For Describing Nonverbal Behavior in Communication

> "Science is the attempt to make the chaotic diversity of our sense-experience correspond to a logically uniform system of thought. In this system single experiences must be correlated with the theoretic structure in such a way that the resulting coordination is unique and convincing.
>
> "The sense-experiences are the given subject-matter. But the theory that shall interpret them is man-made. It is the result of an extremely laborious process of adaptation: hypothetical, never completely final, always subject to question and doubt." --Albert Einstein[6]

In order to discuss nonverbal acts and to see them in their relationship to language and other communicative signals I have outlined some simple formulas (Key 1970). The first formula of a communication experience is as follows:

$$\text{Communication Item} \longrightarrow \begin{bmatrix} \text{(Signal)} \\ \text{(Behavioral Event)} \end{bmatrix}$$

Signal color, flag, flowers, incense, road sign, bent twig...

The formula means, "A Communication Item is to be read as--or is defined as--a Signal and/or a Behavioral Event." The arrow indicates that anything on the right of it is equal to or defines that which is on the left. Parentheses enclose optional elements. The Signal may or may not occur; the Behavioral Event may or may not occur. It is assumed that at least one of them will occur--otherwise there would be no Communication Item. The three dots (...) mean that the inventory given here is not complete; other items can occur as signals. Direct communication is expressed in the Behavioral Event, and indirect communication is expressed in the Signal.

Signals

Indirect communication by Signal may be expressed by artifacts or accoutrements, such as flags and jeweled crowns, or other experiences, such as smoke signals, incense, dots and dashes, or a raised flag on a mailbox. Bram points out that "Anything at all that can be perceived by the senses of man can be used for purposes of symbolization." He gives some examples:

> gestural (a handshake)
> alimentary (a birthday cake)
> architectural (a pyramid)
> graphic (stars and daggers referring the reader to the bottom of the page)
> musical (college songs; "Happy Birthday to You")[7]

Other than a brief mention of these elements of communication, signals (or symbols) will not consume a large place in this study. Many other studies discuss this element of communication.[8]

Signals also include flowers and colors. Flowers have played an important part in interpersonal relationships throughout the ages. "Rosemary for remembrance." On Mother's Day, a red rose for a living mother--a white one if she is not living. Japanese flower arrangements carry a particularly significant load of communication. Colors also "mean" something: white for mourning in China and in some South American Indian tribes; purple for royalty among Western cultures, but purple flowers for the dead in Mexico; yellow for cowardice among English-speaking people, and yellow for royalty among the Manchu rulers. In the United States colored combs are for women; black combs are for men. Anyone using a comb of a color other than that indicating his/her sex is either a foreigner or an individual!

Behavioral Event

The next formula moves closer to the main concern of this book:

Behavioral Event ⟶ [Nonverbal Coded Language Substitute / Verbal Act / Nonverbal Act]

The Behavioral Event concerns itself with three aspects of direct communication: (1) language; (2) paralanguage--vocalizations and prosodic features; and (3) kinesics--gestures and motions. George Trager (1965) started his discussions of these aspects of communication with this outline in his pioneering work on paralanguage.

The Verbal Act can be identified with Language, and the Nonverbal Act and the Nonverbal Coded Language Substitute can be identified with Paralanguage and Kinesics. Note that the formula indicates (by parentheses) that the Nonverbal Coded Language Substitute and the Verbal Act are optional--each may or may not occur--and the Nonverbal Act <u>must</u> occur--it is obligatory. In other words, a human being may communicate something to himself or to another without words, but some kind of body stance, movement, facial expression, or some noise is always present. These components usually have not been accounted for or even recognized by linguists--in fact, the subject has appeared to be taboo. Even when a Nonverbal Act seems neutral or passive, it is still a part of the communication process. An extreme lack of movement or expression is, of course, of concern to the psychologist or psychiatrist.

<u>Nonverbal Coded Language Substitutes</u> are those systems rich enough to substitute, in some degree, for natural language. Stern has used the expression "speech surrogates" to cover drum and whistle "languages."

Nonverbal Coded Language Substitute   Gestural Sign Language, Paralinguistic Language, Combinatory Language...
Gestural Sign Language   Deaf Sign Language, American Indian Sign Language, Australian Sign Language, Trappist Monk Sign Language...
Paralinguistic Language   Whistle Language...
Combinatory Language   Drum Language, Gong Language...

Of all these nonverbal coded systems, the deaf sign language is by far the most complete. Stokoe refers to it as American Sign Language, and his recent studies based on linguistic principles are of significant interest to scholars investigating the syntactic and semantic relationship of surrogates and natural language.

Verbal Act

The next formula outlines the Verbal Act and its concomitant paralinguistic features:

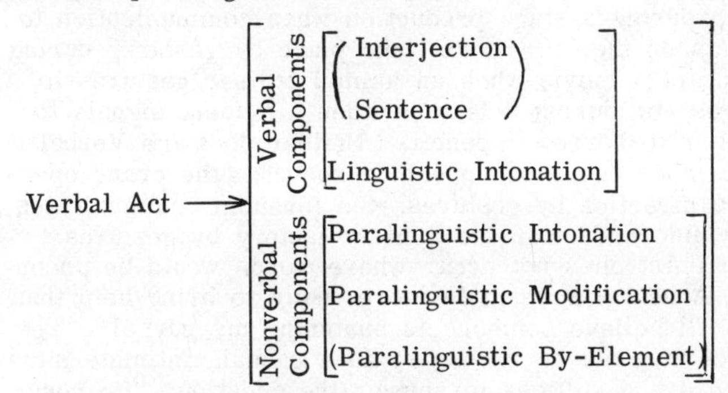

Interjection Whee! Help! Damn it...
Sentence NP + VP
Linguistic Intonation 2-3-1, 2-3...
Paralinguistic Intonation Extra-high, Extra-loud, Extra-long...
Paralinguistic Modification Shrill, Rough, Smooth, Whiney...
Paralinguistic By-Element Grass Blade, Membrane, Paper on Comb, Electronics...

Interjections comprise a class of utterances such as are illustrated on the right side of the arrow following "interjection." The three dots ... mean that the inventory given here is not complete. Sentence is that group of word(s) which is traditionally known as a sentence, with subject and predicate--or in some languages only a predicate. It is not further analyzed or described in this presentation. Nor will other grammatical structures be treated. For further information on the structures of languages, per se, the reader is referred to linguistic descriptions. Linguistic Intonation includes combinations of features such as pitch and stress which linguists speak of as suprasegmentals. Intonation features will be discussed in more detail along with paralinguistic features--they often overlap and coincide.

Speech may be modified by adding paralinguistic effects. An example of a Paralinguistic By-element is the vibrating membrane stretched across a tube or hollow container. This instrument disguises the voice and is used as a secret language in ritualistic or mystical performances in Africa and India.

The Verbal Act does not occur in certain definable situations. It does not occur when silence is necessary: at a funeral, during a stage production when communication to participants on the stage must take place by gesture, during the filming of a movie when an animal trainer gestures to his charges, or during a lecture when a student signals to his neighbor to borrow a pencil. Neither does the Verbal Act occur when conditions preclude speech: the crane operator gives direction by gestures, the foreman communicates necessary information inside a noisy factory by gestures. The Verbal Act does not occur where words would be unconvincing. A hearty scream is more likely to bring help than a speech, "I believe someone is snatching my purse!" The Verbal Act may not be necessary in a casual, intimate situation where a nod suffices to answer the question, "Do you want more coffee?" To a coworker, a nod of the head or a wink may answer a greeting more readily than would spoken words, whereas in a more formal situation the Verbal Act would probably occur. A Verbal Act does not or cannot occur when intensity of emotion precludes speech: an obscene gesture usually occurs without its lexical equivalent. And, finally, a Verbal Act is unlikely to occur when spoken words would shatter the tenderness of a precious moment.

Nonverbal Act

The Nonverbal Act is further explained:

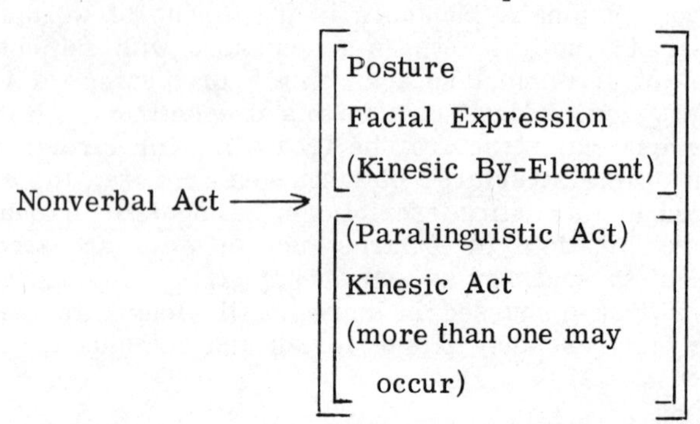

Posture ⟶ Bent Knees, Lying Down, Standing
Bent Knees ⟶ Sitting (on furniture), Squatting, Kneeling...
Lying Down ⟶ ?
Standing ⟶ Approach, Withdrawal, Expansion, Contraction...
Facial Expression ⟶ Neutral, Relaxed, Tense, Uplifted, Droopy
Kinesic By-Element ⟶ Artifact, Clothing, Hair
Artifact ⟶ Cigarette, Pencil, Fork, Eye Glasses...

Posture is the manner in which the body is held or the arrangement of the different parts of the body at the time of the Communication Item. Other features of posture and facial expression will be discussed in the chapter on kinesics.

By-Elements of the Nonverbal Act

Artifacts, Clothing, Hair

At times it is necessary to mention relevant artifacts or inanimate objects manipulated during the Behavioral Event. It would be difficult to describe Churchill's idiomovements without mention of the cigar. The modifications of speech caused by a cigarette reshaping the mouth might be interpreted in bizarre ways if the cigarette were not identified. Unless, of course, the language were one of those unusual ones that has a significant lack of bilabial articulation, such as Iroquois. It is said that an Iroquois speaker "can smoke his pipe while he talks without producing any distortion in speech."[9] It might be necessary to account for the cigarette in certain hand gestures--compare the differences in the manner in which men and women hold it. Ruesch and Kees (p. 89) call these artifacts "object language." It is necessary to differentiate between artifacts which are extensions of the hand used to communicate by gesturing and artifacts such as pieces of furniture which are not intimate with the Communication Item.

Status and geographical dimensions (see Chapter VIII) must be considered in interpreting the use of by-elements of nonverbal communication. Toothpicks are offered in the best of society in Europe, but the use of toothpicks in public is deemed ungainly in the United States. History tells us that the use of and response to artifacts can be of very long standing. Newell (p. 106) discusses the medieval custom of drawing blades of grass or straw, a practice recognized by law to decide controversies. Nowadays children use this method to decide who is to be "it" and university professors draw straws to determine office space!

Efron speaks of "gesturing with objects" (p. 93): " 'Traditional' Eastern Jews are prone to use in the guise of an arm-extension any inanimate object (whether pencil, cane, newspaper, package, table utensil, etc.) which they happen to be holding in their hands while gesturing." This they are likely to use, with profit, "as an additional weapon of gestural persuasion." Efron notes the dexterity with which these objects are manipulated, as for example, the meatball on the end of a fork, "gracefully defying the laws of physical equilibrium." But, he says, this artifact manipulation "is wholly absent in the gestural behavior of the 'Americanized' Jew."

Playing with rings or bracelets communicates information about the personality or immediate circumstance. The string of beads, "worry beads," carried by men in Greece is a commonly accepted release of tension. The Oriental fan and the European fan of earlier times provides (provided) an exquisite way to exercise direction over behavior--others as well as one's own. It afforded opportunities for delicate and magnetic movements, and a rich gestural language grew up around it in various places, for example, in Spain.

Grooming is another way of communicating something to oneself or other persons. Beards, depending upon the time and place, mean: scholar, hippie, religious sect, or a particular fashion. Barefoot means: poor, hippie, religious sect, beach party, child, relaxing at home, and more recently, a college student.

Body hair, or lack of it, elicits different feelings of appreciation or repugnance or status in interpersonal relationships in various cultures. The Chacobo Indians of the Amazon rain forest carefully trim and groom their head hair, but feel that other body hair is not attractive, e.g., they methodically eliminate eyebrows by completely plucking. Note also that the Mona Lisa doesn't have eyebrows, apparently evidence of grooming for beauty. Eyebrows may be shaved for mourning; for example, the Mingrelians of the Caucasus do this, according to Frazer (1919, pp. 275-6). In some societies widows have their heads completely shaved.

And, of course, shaving the head for religious purposes is well known. Concerning other body hair, in Western societies, at least some men are adversely affected by chorus girls who are too closely shaven. Playing with one's own hair or that of another, usually a beloved person or a child, is an often-occurring act in autistic and interpersonal communication. Rubbing of the scalp figures in tactile communication.

A kinesic description of the flowing body movement in Eastern European and Scandinavian dancing could not be appreciated without mention of the wine bottle and the candle held serenely on top of the head. Movements of the Highland Fling open up the pleated tartan in an effective display. In order to appreciate certain classical gestures and movement of the Asian people, it is necessary to observe clothing. The movement of clothes in Asian dancing, especially sleeve movement, is a highly developed art. Older Japanese art shows that in a love affair the partners are often at least partially clothed[10]--this in a culture accustomed to mixed nude bathing. In contrast, in classical art in Western cultures the nude figure is considered highly artistic while in pornography the figure is partially clothed. The nonverbal language expressed by the toga in Ethiopia is discussed by Messing. Clark (p. 412) reports American Indian gestures with the blanket.

Clothes can enhance, control relationships (the judge's robe), frighten (the uniform in a police state), seduce, or be unobtrusive (which also <u>says</u> something). Clothing has often been a subject central in discussions of human types, personality evidence, and other aspects of human behavior (see Flugel, for example). The manner of wearing a hat has been a favorite topic. Tylor (1878, pp. 41-3) discusses the removal of clothing, such as head coverings, body coverings, and foot gear in terms of status relationships. He calls this "reverential uncoverings of the body ... the subject presents himself naked, defenceless, poor, and miserable before his lord...." Krout (1942, p. 298) discusses disrobing as a ceremonial; for example, a Hindu testifying in court, or as in many cultures, walking barefooted during mourning.

Paralinguistic Acts and Kinesic Acts

Paralinguistic Acts and Kinesic Acts are of several types: <u>Lexical</u>, <u>Descriptive</u>, <u>Reinforcing</u>, <u>Embellishing</u>, and

Incidental. The Lexical type constitutes a class of nonverbal episodes that have meaning in themselves without the aid of speech. They can substitute for the Verbal Act. A hand gesture in a prescribed movement means "come here!" In English, "shhh" means "be quiet!" "Tsk-tsk" means warning or disapproval. "Uh-huh" means "yes." Lexical gestures and noises are arbitrarily learned items, and the inventory of these lexical types differs from culture to culture. Spanish and Italian seem to be relatively rich in the range of lexical types. Lexical acts, either paralinguistic or kinesic, can be listed and accurately described in a lexicon of a particular language just as words are listed and defined in a dictionary.

The Descriptive types of Paralinguistic and Kinesic Acts are by nature illustrative. They may be pictorial--for example, drawing in the air to indicate size or shape. They may be symbolic, such as two fingers to the mouth for "cigarette." A pointing gesture or a gesture indicating position would be descriptive. Descriptive Paralinguistic Acts would be noises such as imitation of a bang, a splash, or a knock. The description type of noises and gestures are onomatopoeic, reflecting features of the item described. They supplement the dialogue in ear- and eye-catching ways, affecting the senses more dramatically than speech could alone.

The Reinforcing types of Paralinguistic and Kinesic Acts are episodes that emphasize or highlight the Verbal Act. The kinesic reinforcing type could be illustrated by pounding a fist on the lectern to emphasize a point being made in a speech, or clenching the fist to accompany an angry statement. Reinforcing gestures augment the speech act--make it more forceful and worthy of response.

The Embellishing type is another kind of accompanying body language or paralinguistic behavior. It is not needed to reinforce or describe, but simply, and often eloquently, to enhance speech. This would include the interesting body movement that invites response and attention to the Communication Act. Without the Embellishing types of body language, speech would be dull and unattractive. The Embellishing Acts coordinate with personality types and other individual features.

The Incidental type is that nonverbal behavior that does not contribute in definable ways to the lexical event of the moment. It is quite incidental to the lexical item (either verbal or nonverbal). For example, one might say shhh and cross the knees at the same time or shift position in some other way. But this is not to mean that this feature is incidental to the total behavior of the individual expressing it. It is somehow related to a larger communication or juncture of a behavioral event. It might be thought of as unintentional or involuntary communication. As far as the lexical meaning of the dialogue in question, the incidental act might be considered random activity.

A Paralinguistic Act and/or a Kinesic Act may occur concomitantly with speech. The vocable "yes" may be articulated along with nodding the head in an affirmative gesture. In Yiddish, Efron (pp. 71, 180) cites "... the peculiar vocal inflection of the word, 'Nu', which often goes together with a kind of 'question-mark' or 'exploratory' sinuous little gesture."

There are some co-occurrence restrictions and constraints. For example, raising the index finger to the lips would co-occur with "shhh" but not likely with "be quiet!"

Likewise, combinations of Paralinguistic and Kinesic Acts may occur in a Nonverbal Act without speech. The above illustration of "shhh" in addition to the raised index finger is such an act. A whistle may accompany a wave of the hand. "Goodbye" may be communicated by a hand gesture alone, or a nod of the head, or both. The Nonverbal Act meaning "no" among the Levantine Arabs consists of three features (any one alone also communicates "no"): (a) jerk head up slightly, (b) raise eyebrows and purse lips, and (c) click tongue against alveolar ridge (Brewer, p. 235).

The lexical types of Paralinguistic and Kinesic Acts are independent of language and can act as a substitute for language. The remaining types are accompanying behaviors that combine with a lexical item (either verbal or nonverbal) or accompany a more eloquent silence in between sentences or phrases of a dialogue. They do not have meaning in themselves and could not be listed in a lexicon as such. Rather, they add dimensions (another kind of meaning) to the lexical behavior. They are indispensable complements--adjunctive in nature. It might be useful to note that in listing the types, the progression moves away from semantic value. That is, the lexical type has full semantic value; the descriptive type has a measure of semantic value; the embellishing type is neutral to the semantic value of the speech act it accompanies; and the incidental type is quite apart and separate from any semantic value of the Behavioral Event in question. There seems to be a continuum of intentional to inadvertent--or, instituted to spontaneous.

The Paralinguistic Act--some sort of vocalization--may or may not occur in the Nonverbal Act. More than one of the Kinesic Acts always occurs. The hands are of primary concern and can figure in any of the types of Kinesic Acts. For example, a lexical Kinesic Act articulated by the hand may be illustrated by the gesture indicating "come here"--the index finger raised and motioning toward the speaker. A descriptive Kinesic Act articulated by the hands would be "drawing in the air"--making a circle, or indicating length, or curves, or size. A reinforcement Kinesic Act would be something like pounding the fist to emphasize a point, or clenching the fist to accompany an angry statement. An embellishment Kinesic Act could simply be a graceful or jerky movement of the hands accompanying the respective rhythmic movement of the speech act. An incidental Kinesic Act would be exemplified by the hands moving to reach for a cigarette, quite incidental to the sentence being spoken, but perhaps a marker of a larger structure.

It is not clear yet how other parts of the body might be of concern in the various types of Kinesic Acts. For example, should shoulder movement be considered as a Kinesic Act or as a feature of Posture? Should a head nod be a feature of Facial Expression, which moves along with it, or a feature of Posture, or still yet, a Kinesic Act? Ekman and Friesen have made a thoughtful study of the various types of Kinesic Acts, exploring still further the dimensions, relationships of gestures, and their functions.

Relationship of Nonverbal Act to Language

In order to understand nonverbal communication, one must consider it in relationship to language itself--the interplay between verbal and nonverbal. I believe that the reverse is also true: in order to understand language, one must consider the non-verbal components. In a Behavioral Event the Verbal and the Nonverbal Acts are usually in correlation with each other, whether in accordance with or contradictory to each other. This is assuming that there is one Behavioral Event taking place. It can also happen that two (or more) communicative sequences may be taking place at the same time. For example, a restaurant conversation may be in progress with intermittent instructions and requests to the waiter. The gestures and facial expressions directed to the waiter are not part of the conversation act, but rather are part of the communication with the waiter and would not correlate with the conversation. Likewise, parents may be in conversation and to the side be communicating to the children. A telephone conversation may take place with side comments to another. The second Behavioral Event may take place entirely by nonverbal means, or there may be a mixing of both verbal and nonverbal.

When the Verbal Act and the Nonverbal Act of the Behavioral Event are correlative, the Nonverbal component may act in two ways: in <u>accordance</u> with the verbal message and the situation at hand or in <u>contradiction</u> to it. Nonverbal Acts which are in accordance with a speech act or other behavior situation enhance and contribute to communication in a harmonious way. There is no disagreement of message and delivery. In contradictory behaviors, on the other hand, there is a discrepancy between the words and the real feelings held by the speaker, and this disharmony shows up in paralinguistic and kinesic acts. A typical reaction is: "It isn't what he said, it's how he said it!" The <u>real</u> message is conveyed, not by the content of the speech act, but rather by the nonverbal events which contradict what is said.

In 1667 Cordemoy spoke of this contradictory behavior: "The pains which everyone finds in conversation ... if not to comprehend what another thinketh, but to extricate his thought from the signs or words which often agree not with it."[11] Psychiatry has long recognized these contradictions, "When the postural tensions and the spoken word contradict each other it is plain which should be given credence."[12] And we are reminded of Freud's observation, "He that has eyes to see and ears to hear may convince himself that no mortal can keep a secret. If his lips are silent, he chatters with his finger-tips; betrayal oozes out of him at every pore."[13]

Kinesic and paralinguistic acts are specific manifestations of meanings supposedly hidden by words. Criminal investigators and lovers search for these contradictory expressions of the real self. "Does she really love me?" In some ways this kind of investigation is like the <u>ordeals</u> or tests for truth observed in aboriginal societies. Scrutiny of these features is the "lie detector test." Some contradictory behaviors are socially acceptable and considered less offensive than telling the truth. One might say, "yes," with hesitation and a certain negative facial expression in answer to "May I smoke?" if the smoking is not desired. The nonverbal features are contradictory to the Verbal Act, but in cases like this they are considered acceptable etiquette.

There is another kind of behavior when the Verbal Act and the Nonverbal Act are in correlation with each other and also seemingly in accordance. This type has to do with motivation and the person's relationship with himself and society. This includes such acts as lying and even little "white lies" which may be an acceptable form of behavior within the society. Some rituals of etiquette fall into this class. "Come and visit us any time!" is not really intended to be taken literally. This also includes communication that was intended to be true at the moment spoken or written, but some other event changed the situation and the person changed his mind. It could include the naive promises made in the politician's speech and not able to be fulfilled because of the time element or budget problems, as well as those promises which were not naively made. It includes any deliberate attempt to deceive. It could also include the cross-cultural interpersonal relationships when the speaker from another culture tries to please: "I said what you wanted me to say." It would include those verbal episodes of a society where lying is considered a virtue in order to save face for another. Analysis of this kind of behavior has to be from some other frame of reference; it involves human behavior beyond the scope of these discussions.

It may also happen that components within the Nonverbal and the Verbal Acts may be <u>incongruent</u> with each other and may thus be neither in accordance with nor contradictory to the Verbal Act, but confusing or meaningless. An example of a Verbal Act which contains incongruent statements is, "She bundled up in furs because it was so hot outside." In James' experiment with postures, when the facial expression and body movements were not congruent, the observers reported the total as "incongruent, unnatural, meaningless."

Incongruent behavior may also occur when the participant is thinking of something other than the message spoken to him; another experience is intruding and the communication is aborted. The receiver may not be aware of the interfering experience in the sender's mind and may receive the message as canceled out or confused because of incongruent behavior.

The matter of responsibility might be considered in connection with contradictory accompaniments to language. Perhaps there is less realization of responsibility towards that which is conveyed inadvertently by nonverbal behavior than that which is conveyed by the explicit Verbal Act. For example, a chief of police might seem actually to believe himself when he says that he has no racist feelings, even though his nonverbal behavior, in the way of hesitations, misplaced stress, pitch distortions, facial expressions might clearly communicate deep-seated discriminatory feelings. Or the parent who declares vehemently that he understands his offspring and feels no generation gap may indicate by nonverbal behavior that he is pretty far from communicating. It is these communications that the minority person and the youngster receive--not the Verbal Act.

Nonverbal Acts and Linguistic Structures

The interdependency of the Verbal Act and the Nonverbal Act can be seen on many levels, some more obvious than others. It is only recently that these interrelationships have been explicitly brought to the attention of students of language and behavior. Ekman and Friesen (1969b, p. 53) note that "the nonverbal act can repeat, augment, illustrate, accent, or contradict the words."

Starting with the sound level, or the production of the sounds of language, it is evident that with some twisting of the body, change of posture, or tilting the head, the voice quality is affected (Lieberman 1968, p. 37). One can experiment with perceiving these effects by trying to guess the posture of the person on the other end of the telephone. An opera singer learns to control the voice production even while assuming rather ungainly postures. This mechanical effect on the vocal cords must be differentiated from emotional effect which changes voice quality, also. Dwight Bolinger tells me that he used to experiment with vocal articulation and postural affects in class. Out of sight of the students he repeated sentences with identical intonation. During one utterance the postural stance was of eagerness, with the head jutted forward; on repetition of the utterance, the stance was of rejection and disapproval, with the head pulled back. The students were able to tell the difference.

Other kinesic behaviors affect articulation of the Verbal Act: pouting and smiling produce very different sounding sentences; sucking the thumb modifies speech. By-Elements also affect vocal production; drawing on a pipe in the mouth, chewing on a pencil, holding nails in the mouth. A Nonverbal Act may substitute for a complete Verbal Act. In the United States one knocks on the door to announce one's arrival. In certain American Indian villages, one calls out upon arriving; to knock would be rude--and might entail danger because of supernatural beliefs!

A Nonverbal Act may substitute for only part of the Verbal Act. One might express, "It tastes terrible!" by merely saying, "It tastes ..." with a facial expression and twist of the head or shoulders to convey the bad taste! Such incompleted sentences constitute one of the most striking differences between speech and written exposition. An obscene gesture may finish a sentence or substitute for an exclamation in contexts of strong emotion, such as hate and frustration.

Birdwhistell (1966) has done extensive observation and analysis of the relation between body language and verbal language. He finds markers for such grammatical features as pronominals, "I, she, he, it ..." and "that, then, there ..."; pluralizers, "we, us, they, those ..."; markers indicating space and distance, tense, change of direction, "I went to the house" and "He gave it to me"; manner markers, "a short time, slowly, jerkily, roughly, smoothly ..."; area markers, or location phrases, "Put it behind the stove" and "Put it in the can." He notes no body language marker with "behind" and "in" in expressions such as "He arrived behind time" and "He arrived in the nick of time."

Movement of the head, eyes, and hands in conjunction with sentence junctures was demonstrated by Birdwhistell (Scheflen 1964, p. 320). Three basic types of intonation contours have typical corresponding body language: rising contour, indicating a question; falling contour, indicating completion; and level contour, indicating that the speaker will continue. For example, an American speaker (this might not be true of other dialects of English) generally raises his head slightly at the end of statements to which he expects an answer. Scheflen suggests that it might be possible to abstract some theme that would designate each category. For example, the sentence types, explanation, interruption, interpretation, and listening, each occur with a particular head movement--a theme, so to speak, which is identifiable in analysis.

There is some evidence that body language coordinates with markers of units larger than the sentence. Obvious accompaniments are initiators and closures. A definite postural stance and facial expression begin the text, "Once upon a time ..." and a concluding body language terminates the discourse, "And they lived happily ever after." It is possible that the analysis of the junctural features of the postural-facial-gestural components could lead to segmenting paragraphs and units in discourse. Scheflen (1964, p. 320) notes changes of position of head and eyes "every few sentences" and believes that these shifts mark the end of a structural unit within a discourse. He calls these observable shifts, the Point, the Position, and the Presentation, which seem to be roughly equivalent to what we might call the paragraph, the section, and the chapter. Dittmann and Llewellyn have found that certain head and hand movements are related to phonemic clauses in speech; and head nods, vocalizations, changes in glance, and brief smiles have a potential as markers of units.

The Siona language of Colombia[14] has precise enclitic markers in the discourse which appear to have concomitant body language. There are certain grammatical markers which signal the subject and object/goal relationship and the focus, that is, the central or peripheral role of the nominal element. These enclitic markers occur in sequenced text but not in isolated sentences. In dialogue the occurrence of these markers is often accompanied by kinesic behavior, such as focus of vision or pointing with puckered lips.

The one-leg resting position in Australia appears to be a discourse marker, according to remarks by Elkin. Natives may stand on one leg without movement for up to fifteen minutes. Observers say that they rarely change from one leg to the other; they are more likely to finish the conversation and move on rather than take up a fresh stance.

Linguists have observed that the body language repertoire shifts when a speaker changes languages. Birdwhistell (1964) noted that Mayor Fiorello La Guardia spoke Italian, Yiddish, and American English, and with each shift of language, he also shifted his kinesic and paralinguistic behavior.

When working with George Trager, Birdwhistell noted the same phenomenon with a Taos informant speaking English and Taos. I had a similar experience with a blind person who knew my voice well. I had previously conversed with him only in Spanish, and when I approached him one day speaking in English, he did not recognize me!

In the recent literature on linguistic theory, there are hints and comments on verbal language suggesting possible relationships with nonverbal language that might prove to be intriguing areas of research in the future. Ambiguity, for example, is a much-discussed enigma to linguists describing language or formulating theories for such descriptions. The arguments would be somewhat diminished by considering the nonverbal coordinates in ambiguous structures as well as other "context-of-situation" components. Scheflen (1963, pp. 128-9) gives some examples:

> Reduction of ambiguity in spoken language is accomplished by means of supplementary information carried in stress patterns, junctures, paralanguage, and kinesics. For example, a phrase that would be hyphenated in written English might be indicated in speech by a shift in the stress pattern and by a sweep of the head, eyes, or hand. In kinesics there are 'area markers' to indicate the object of ambiguous references--for example, hand sweeps accompany ideas of direction in phrases like 'here and there,' and head nods are used for pronominal reference. Another type of ambiguity reduction has been described as metacommunication--that is, a communication which instructs how a message is to be taken. An example is the use of a smile to indicate that an epithet is not to be taken literally.

Nonverbal behavior might comprise one or more of the semantic domains which are part of the concern of constraints on grammar. But it is by no means clear just how these semantic rules might be formulated in conjunction with syntactic rules; linguists have only begun to discuss them. In "Types of Lexical Information," Fillmore[15] speaks of semantic properties of the vocabulary items of the lexicon, e.g., "biologically given notions as identity, time, space, body movement, territory, life, fear, etc." He treats tactile verbs such as knock, strike, contact, impinge, and smite in his discussion of the notion of surface-contact.

Space and movement are implicit in certain verbs. Vertical position is implied by *leap* and *jump*; position-change along a surface by *slide*; movement across a surface by *scuttle*; rapid sudden motion by *dart*. Verbs of motion are associated with properties rclating to direction, speed, gravity, surface, etc. In discussing *arguments*, Fillmore observes that *silence* can replace certain *predicates*. He notes that some verbs identify events without specifying the entity involved; doff the hat (from the head), slap (open hands), kick (legs/feet), kiss (lips) "and the target of an act of spanking seldom needs to be made explicit!"

Gruber[16] investigates verbs of motion and proposes such features as *Motional* and *Positional* in the description. In an article on the functions of the lexicon in formal descriptive grammars, he mentions verbs which cannot take the passive transformation. The verbs in his third column are: *seem*, *appear*, *resemble*, *look*, *taste*, *feel*, *smell*, *sound*--representing the visual, auditory, chemical, and tactile channels of nonverbal communication. Gruber later states that the factors regulating the restrictions could be traceable to underlying categories in the base, which he regards as equally semantic and syntactic. It might not be out of place here to mention a study done by an earlier scholar, Hopkins, on the sniff-kiss of ancient India. (He also mentions its counterparts in Asia, Alaska, and Africa.) Throughout the article, Hopkins shows the relationships of: *kiss*-*taste*-*lick*-*touch*-*stroke*-*sniff*-*smell*-*breathe in*, all having a similar semantic base. He also observes that the same root in Sanskrit means "caress" and "injure," both deriving from the simple notion of *touch*, as applied for good or for evil (p. 133).

Ross[17] suggests a distinction of [+Linguistic] and [-Linguistic] in his feature analysis of verbs. Verbs such as *said*, *declared*, and *asserted* would be considered [+Linguistic] and verbs such as *frowned*, *smiled*, *shrugged*, and *roared* would be considered [-Linguistic]. These latter verbs denote nonverbal communication, and they seem to have different restrictions from the former class of [+Linguistic] verbs. He notes that Paul Kiparsky has pointed out the need for distinguishing syntactically between verbs such as *groan*, *snort*, *laugh*, *quip*, *grumble*, and verbs such as *say* and *claim*. Ross states that sentences with [-Linguistic] verbs have never been studied by generative grammarians, but acknowledges that there are some strange restrictions on whatever rule it is that produces such sentences. For example, the possessive pronoun which modifies the abstract noun in the object must refer back to the subject. Tom frowned his displeasure. Not permitted is the construction, *Tom frowned Ann's displeasure. Another restriction seems to be in the relationship between the main verb and the abstract noun in the object. Thus,

*Tom scowled his { mirth / gaiety / willingness / eagerness / bonhomie }

"are certainly odd." Ross notes the "mental state" involved in these examples and further observes that the constructions contain "only those nouns which denote mental states which can be behaviorally manifested."

In conclusion, the study of sound and movement must be integrated before an understanding of either verbal or nonverbal behavior can be made more complete.

Chapter III: PARALANGUAGE
The Vocal Sounds of Nonverbal Communication

"Speak, that I may see thee!"
--Socrates/Ben Jonson

The human ear can discriminate among a few hundred thousand sounds. Out of this awesome number of sounds a few thousand can be produced by the vocal apparatus of the human being (apart from pitch differences which would increase the number exponentially). Of the few thousand articulatory possibilities that a human being has, only a relatively few sounds are actually used in language. Learning a second language extends an individual's range of production. Most of the elements used in paralanguage are also used in language systems, but in addition, there are a few non-speech sounds which never occur in the linguistic system of any language of the world, so far as is known today.

People in all walks of life recognize that the human voice communicates something beyond language. These effects are referred to by impressionistic descriptions such as "tone of voice," "voice quality," "manner of speaking," or "the way he said it." All of the sounds discussed in this chapter are produced by the vocal apparatus. Other noises used in nonverbal communication (such as finger snapping, clapping and tapping, and such as are produced by some physiological act such as a sneeze, a cough, or hiccups) are discussed in Chapter IV in connection with body movement.

First are listed the physical elements of paralanguage and following this are some examples of paralinguistic acts which comprise the elements listed and which may occur concurrently with language in any culture of the world. It seems useful to distinguish between paralinguistic elements which are punctiliar in nature and those that are modifying or can be extended in their articulation. Punctiliar acts occur independently, such as "shhh," the "Bronx cheer," "tsk, tsk" or a whistle. Modifying features change the quality of speech, as noted by such impressionistic terms as gruff, sweet, shaky, twangy. There are also modifying features which can occur independently, such as crying and laughing, groaning, and whining. These are Trager's (1958) "vocal characterizers" which one "talks through" when they accompany language.

Language Sounds

The sounds used in language are very often referred to as segmental sounds or phonemes. They are produced by the articulatory organs of speech and each has a particular articulatory phonetic description. With the "scientific" analysis of language that has blossomed in this century have also come many useful and excellent linguistic writings which deal with the areas of phonetics and grammar. For a full description of these elements of language, one should refer to those publications. Most of the examples given here are from the paralinguistic system of English, simply because more data are available from this language than any other.

Certain consonants have been observed in paralanguage. The stop consonants p and t occur in psst! meaning a call to attention. The stop g occurs in ugh! meaning disgust. The glottal stop ʔ occurs in combination with vowels: Ohʔ Oh an exclamation; Uhʔ Uh meaning "no"; Ahʔ Ah! meaning a warning.

Fricative sounds occur frequently in paralanguage, perhaps because of the air expired, and as we will see later, air movement is of much importance in paralinguistics. The sibilant fricatives, such as the s and the sh [š] sounds occur in hissing and hushing sounds of paralanguage. The meaning of these events differs from language to language; the hiss in English, for example, means rejection or contempt but in Japanese it means dignified approval. Even in our own culture there are different uses of the hiss. At a concert, for instance, the polite audience might hiss an absurd piece of experimental music, but probably would not hiss even a badly performed composition by Bach or Beethoven.

Other fricative sounds used in paralanguage are the nonsibilants. The sound [ɸ], made by blowing air out between the two lips, does not occur in the English language system, but is frequently heard in paralinguistic behavior. In literature it may be written *phew!* The fricative h occurs in combination with nasals m or n, or with vowels as in *hmmmm*, a sigh; *mmhmm*, meaning "yes"; and *aha!* meaning a teasing exclamation. In French it is used in expressive utterances to add emotive meaning to the lexical item.

The *nasal* sounds m and n occur in sighing or hesitation, or sounds of delight (*mmmmmmm* "good!"). A voiceless variety--that is, with the vocal cords not vibrating--results in a kind of snort, in English meaning disgust. It may be written with capital letters M or N. A nasal sound ñ, which is like the sound in "onion," is used by children in a teasing refrain with the tune known to all of us and occurring in many parts of the world: "nya nya-nya nya nya!"

A surprising amount of paralanguage makes use of sounds which might be considered more dramatic and exotic than the language sounds such as those mentioned previously. These sounds are *trills* and *clicks* and sounds modified in exotic ways, which without the modification might be considered ordinary. Proportionally these sounds are used less in language systems than in paralanguage systems. *Trills* are a kind of iterative articulation; that is, repetitions of a flap articulation by the movable parts of the speech mechanism. Any part of the speech apparatus which can move may be involved in a trill, whether it be the lips, tongue, cheek, uvula, velic, or vocal cords. The lips produce the bilabial trill, [b̃, p̃], which occurs in English and in Chinese when a person is trembling with the cold temperature. It is usually spelled "b̃rrrr" though the paralinguistic act has no r sound in it. It also may occur as the "raspberry" or the "Bronx cheer"; sometimes this event involves the tongue also. As a language sound the bilabial trill occurs rarely: among the Isthmus Zapoteco of Mexico, the Mewtn of New Hebrides, and I have observed it also in the Pacas Nova Indian language in Brazil near the Bolivian border. Examples in this language are not plentiful, but the sound occurs often enough and in the same way that other consonants occur so that it must be interpreted as part of the alphabet. The word for "chicken" is [tb̃otb̃owe]; "good to drink" is [toktb̃otb̃onda].

The trill r̃ produced by the tip of the tongue tapping against the roof of the mouth is the well-known sound in Spanish, as in *perro* "dog." It may be written *rrrrrr* in the funnybooks, and is often used to represent noise mimicry. Children, for example, play car and airplane with a roaring rrrrrr! Singers may be taught to articulate a trilled r̃ while singing in English, which has no trilled r̃ in speech. The uvular trill [ʁ] is produced far back in the mouth, with the back of the tongue approximating the uvula enough to cause it to vibrate with the flow of air. It is often articulated for sensuous effect, something like "ou-la-la!" and often occurs on entertainment shows. It is a favorite sound of Tom Jones and Zsa Zsa Gabor.

The click sounds are made by causing a suction of air in the mouth cavity. These percussive-like sounds are well documented as speech sounds in several languages, but, like the kiwi bird in New Zealand, they occur in only one geographical area of the world, i.e. South Africa. Miriam Makeba has demonstrated this sound from her Xosa language to audiences around the world and has recorded it in a wistful little folk song, called "The Click Song" by the English. The click sounds do not occur in the English language system but are often used in the paralinguistic system. The alveolar click, made by the tip of the tongue [t←] is used for commiseration or "for shame!" and is often spelled "tsk-tsk." This alveolar variety also occurs among the Greeks and the Arabs to indicate "no" and is pronounced in a single articulation along with other head movements. Click sounds also occur involuntarily among English speakers, for example, in tense moments before the public when the mouth goes dry and embarrassing click noises occur in the speech.

The lateral click tɬ← which is used to encourage horses is not even attempted in script and is usually explained or written "giddyap." The third click used in English is the bilabial variety, better known as the kiss, and since it is not a language sound in any of the languages of the world recorded yet, it will be discussed later with the non-language sounds. Linguists used to joke about the use of clicks in English when they observed that the alveolar click made dogs come, the lateral click made horses go, and the bilabial click made the girls stay!

In summary then, English paralanguage is comprised of sounds which occur in the English language system, such as p, t, g, s, š, h, m, and n; and some sounds which do not occur in the English language system, such as ʔ, p̶, M, ñ, b̃, p̃, r̃, ʁ, t←, tɬ←. It is very likely that most languages of the world follow this pattern of paralinguistic use of language sounds as well as use of additional sounds outside of the language system of each particular language.

The stops in English paralanguage occur only in combination, and for obvious reasons--they cannot be sustained. Those resonants, fricatives, and trills that can be articulated over a longer period are used more in paralanguage. Many illustrations show combinations of sounds used in expressive speech. In English, as so far observed, the combinations which occur are permissible combinations in the language structure. For example, the sequence of consonants in psst! occur in final position in "glimpsed" [glimpst]. The sequence in ouch! occurs in "couch"; the sequence in ugh! occurs in "ugly." Vowel sounds also occur in paralanguage, but they can be discussed more advantageously from the point of view of the modifications which change the quality of the vowel sounds in syllables.

Language Element Modifications

The modifications discussed first are the kinds of things which might also be found in language structures around the world. Later, along with non-language sounds, non-language modifications will be treated. When any of the parts of the speech apparatus change position the resulting sound is different. It doesn't take a linguist to hear the difference in the sentence, "Mary had a little lamb," when spoken with a smiling face and when spoken with a pout. The type of modification when the lips are involved, or puckered, is called labialization, and in speech sounds is used in French, German, Scandinavian, and many other languages. In English, this type of rounded lip modification over the whole discourse, results in "baby talk." In Hungarian labialization is a component of the emotional intonational pattern of "tenderness" (Fónagy and Magdics).

Palatalization is a kind of modification made by the blade of the tongue in contact with the palate. It occurs very commonly in Slavic languages. In addition to use in language structure, it is reported to be used as an expressive device (or a paralinguistic act) in the first words of Czech children. Among English speakers, it can be observed occasionally in the speech of the eager-beaver who grasps at higher social standing and fancies elegance by feigning the speech of certain Eastern dialects of the United States which naturally use palatalized consonants ("P^{y}ark your c^{y}ar in the g^{y}arage").

Nasalization is a kind of modification which permits air to escape through the nose while pronouncing an oral sound. Nasalized vowels occur in the language structure of French, but in English occur only in paralanguage. An overall nasalized effect is heard in some dialects of the South in natural speech. In other contexts nasalization occurs when either a snarling or an uncouth effect is desired--for example in speech mimicry of a gangster or an otherwise unpleasant person or a country bumpkin. Nasalization also occurs in strong emotions of love and hatred due to the swelling and shrinking of the nasal membranes in these circumstances.

Pharyngealization is another modification and is produced in the back of the throat. It results from opening up the area of the pharynx by tongue movement. Pharyngeal sounds are noted in Arabic languages. In English paralanguage it occurs in speech mimicry. Edgar Bergen used this effect in ventriloquism for his character Mortimer Snerd. It can also be used in English for scoffing.

Muscle constriction is a tightening of the vocal apparatus which produces sounds known as "fortis" in language systems, in contrast to sounds made in a relaxed manner, which are known as "lenis." These modifications have been verified in the language systems of some languages in India and in Mexico. Constriction of the vocal cords is said to occur in a special kind of speech among the Amahuacas of Peru (Gumperz and Hymes, p. 16): "... the drinking, questioning, answering in which Amahuaca men are joined by the class of supernaturals known as yoshi associated interestingly enough with a specific form of chant and use of the vocal channel (vocal chords tightly constricted)...."

Sound Placement--Fronting and Backing is a manner of producing sounds with slightly different articulations. A t, for example, may be articulated very far front--even between the teeth--or with the tongue in the center of the palate. A k may be articulated with the back of the tongue hitting the center of the palate or the back of the soft palate. In English paralanguage, fronting may produce a lisping effect, used in baby talk, or other "cute" effects in speech.

The dramatic event of seeing the vocal cords in actual vibration first took place in 1854, when Manuel Garcia, son of a famous opera singer, rigged up some mirrors in conjunction with the light of the sun (Kaiser, p. 149). He observed that when these delicate membranes vibrate, a voiced sound is produced. When the two vocal folds are open too far to vibrate, the result is an unvoiced (voiceless) sound, a whisper or simply breathing. If the vocal cords vibrate and in addition are caused to trill, the resultant sound has a creaky quality called laryngealization. It has the effect of a stick being drawn along a picket fence; children use it to imitate a machine gun. In adult use it occurs frequently for various effects, for example stalling or laziness, as one talks when one hates to get up in the morning. It occurs as a hesitation feature when one is thinking of what to say next and it also occurs for sensuous effects. Molly's famous soliloquy (Joyce's Ulysses) was pungently recited recently by actress Anna Manahan, with frequent laryngealization over whole utterances.

The unvoicing of sounds is simply producing the same sounds without the vocal cords vibrating. This modification can be applied to vowels or consonants. When it extends over the complete utterance it is known as whispering--the sounds are articulated as usual but all unvoiced. As a contrasting feature in language structure, it is rarely used, but has been reported for the Comanche language of Oklahoma. In natural language it is quite common--it is simply the trailing off of syllables at the end of utterances into voicelessness. The "stage whisper" is voicelessness with added friction for further carrying power.

As will be seen later, much of the emotional effect of language is conveyed by pitch--the highs and lows of the speech melody. And since pitch is a concomitant of voiced sounds, it has been a matter of curiosity with linguists as to how the pitches are conveyed when the utterance is whispered. Tone languages, such as Chinese, some American Indian languages, and some African languages, are of particular interest, in that they depend heavily upon pitch for lexical meaning. Nonetheless, whispering occurs apparently in all languages of the world, even the heavily tonal languages.

Whispering, of course, is well known to be the medium of secrets. In embarrassment, the voice may dwindle to a whisper. As a sign of respect it is reported in other areas of the world. In one of the Naga tribes of India, where the ceremonial marriage is very formal, all the talking must be in a whisper when the bride and procession enter the bridegroom's house.[18] Sir James Frazer (1919, pp. 72-3) reported instances in British East Africa and among the California Indians, where a newly widowed woman, if she could speak at all, was permitted only to whisper. This prohibition extended for several months in some cases.

Suprasegmental Elements

Certain elements of language are about us in the sound continuum everywhere: pitch, stress, length, and pause. In discussions of language structures, various terminology have been used to designate these features, such as suprasegmental, prosodic, and intonational. Whatever they are called, they occur in every language of the world. They are superposed on speech; no natural speech act can occur without them, though one must consider, of course, such things as whisper, which, without voice, cannot carry pitch. Pitch, stress, and length can occur as distinctive features in language in the same way that segmental sounds occur; that is, they can differentiate vocabulary items in contrasting ways to give referential meaning. An example of segmental sounds which contrast are the t and d in "tot" and "dot."

This same kind of semantic differentiation can be signaled by pitch in some languages. Chinese is well-known for this feature: mā (hi tone, level) "mother"; má (hi, rising) "hemp"; mǎ (lo, rising) "horse"; mà (lo, falling) "scold." This kind of pitch or tonal contrast occurs in other tone languages, for example, among some American Indian languages, Mazateco, Mixteco, and in Africa. The pitches may be referred to as up, down, hi, mid, and lo, rising, falling, glide, level. Extreme pitches may be referred to as over-hi, over-lo. Paralinguistic pitch must be distinguished from linguistic pitch. While the former is part of the grammar of a language, the latter is a component of the expressive system of a language. Paralinguistic extra-high pitch may be heard in excited speech; paralinguistic narrowing of the pitch range may be heard in bored or monotonous speech.

The feature of stress occurs in many languages as a contrastive feature. Spanish: término "terminal"; termíno "I finish"; terminó "he finished." English has a few pairs of words distinguished by stress: décent and descént; ábstract and abstráct. A shift of stress can shift the meaning of a sentence:

> *He's* giving this money to Peter. (she is not doing it)
> He's *giving* this money to Peter. (not lending it)
> He's giving *this* money to Peter. (not the other fund)
> He's giving this *money* to Peter. (not a check)
> He's giving this money to *Peter*. (not to Jane)

The terminology used in discussing this feature is very profuse. Stress is variously known as "accent, intensity, loudness, force of articulation, articulatory force, amplitude of sound waves." The degree of stress may be referred to as strong and weak, or loud and soft. Extremes of stress may be spoken of as over-loud and over-soft.

Paralinguistic stress is, again, often heard in emotional or attitudinal situations. The illustration cited previously, "He's giving this money to Peter," may be articulated in any number of additional ways, using various nuances of pitch, stress, and length--they really can't be separated. Loudness of voice is a result of an overall articulation of intensity. This varies from culture to culture and within a culture depending upon the situation. Contrast the force of articulation needed at an outdoor athletic event with the quiet articulation to be used at the side of the baby's cradle. Once when I visited an American Indian school, one of the lads told me that the teachers (white) talked too loud! In some cases this has been interpreted by the Indian students to mean anger or that the teacher is mean. Hall (1966) discusses the features of loudness of voice in relation to space and different cultures and the interpretation of these features in various ways.

The medical profession reports an abnormal development, acromegaly, which changes the structures of the vocal apparatus enough so that speech becomes unusually loud. This, of course, would be outside of the person's control and could not be considered paralanguage.

Length or *quantity* is also used as a contrasting linguistic feature in a few languages. Aztec is a classic example: *tatastok* "he is coughing" and *tata:stok* "the hen is laying an egg"; *yolik* "he is born" and *yo:li:k* "slowly." Estonian uses three degrees of length as distinguishing features in vocabulary and grammatical items. The length or timing may be spoken of as long and short. Extremes of length may be referred to as over-long and over-short.

The paralinguistic use of length and intensification of consonants and vowels has been reported in some European languages: German *rrrauss*! *Hilllfe*! *Goott*! *ich* *saaage* *ihnen*; Polish *prrrosze* *Paaana*!; Czech *jēžžīs*, *bōžē*, *to* *bōlī*; Russian *tjatjā*, *babuškā* (in the vocative) (Sebeok, Hayes, and Bateson, p. 248). In English the paralinguistic lengthening of consonants gives a dramatic or terrifying effect: the announcer at the races stirs the blood with his stylistic, "Still runnnnnnning ..." and the evangelist spooks his congregation with, "Without faith, we all are lossssst!"

Pause, *juncture*, or *hesitation* are elements of border signals. Juncture makes the difference between "a tall" and "at all." Juncture is a feature of every language. In Spanish "es un hombre" and "es su nombre" mean "it's a man" and "it's his name," depending upon the juncture. The signal may be a barely perceptible space of silence. Juncture may involve lengthening of a contiguous or even a noncontiguous consonant or vowel; it is a disturbance of time.

For several years now the term *hesitation* has been used to refer to those phenomena that are included in paralinguistic acts in this study. Linguists have recognized that the linguistic pauses, or junctures, were somehow different from the hesitation pauses. Psychologists and psychiatrists studied hesitation pauses along with other nonfluencies, such as false starts, repetitions, stuttering, and slips of tongue. The term *hesitation* has come to include all the behavioral acts which might occur in a situation of hesitation. The "unfilled" pauses consist of silence; the "filled" pauses consist of any number and variety of vocal dawdling, er, ah, uh, mmmmm, um. Other effects such as rough breathing--in or out--and modifications such as laryngealization and nasalization might be found in situations of hesitation. Physiological acts such as clearing the throat, swallowing, a belch, a sigh, a sniff, or a laugh may also occur as fillers of a hesitation pause. Hesitation phenomena seem to be highly individualistic. They occur in the stream of speech of a person when he or she is collecting the thoughts for the next phrase; they occur when a speaker has been interrupted--either internally by his thoughts taking a turn, or externally by a door slamming. They are a means by which a speaker can hold the floor while he constructs his next thought. When the listener is not seen, for example during a telephone conversation, a speaker is more likely to use filled pauses, because he cannot use facial expression and gestures to hold the floor. One function of hesitation or pause is euphemistic --a slight pause followed by an innocent word or look substitutes for gossip, a white lie, or an obscene expression.

In combinations and in various mixings, stress, length, and pause make up the rhythm of a language. The rhythm of a person speaking may be referred to as quick or slow; it may be abrupt, jerky, or clipped; it may be smooth. One might think of speed or the tempo of a language in connection with rhythm.

All of the suprasegmental features of pitch, stress, length, and pause operate very actively in all languages of the world. In combinations, these elements may be said to comprise the intonation patterns of a language. It is said that the intonation patterns are the first elements of language learned by the infant, and the last elements lost when the speaker learns a second language. Often the intonation pattern seems to be the first thing noticed in a non-native speaker. Intonation patterns may signal grammatical structures; they can make the difference between a statement and a question: "He came yesterday." and "He came yesterday?"--the former a simple statement, said with a falling pitch pattern, often referred to as the 2-3-1 pattern, and the latter said with a rising pitch pattern, 2-3, and different quantities of stress and length. Intonation pattern marks the difference between, "Would you like tea, or lemonade?" (choose one of the two) and "Would you like tea or lemonade?" (something to drink?).

The statement pattern, 2-3-1, describes English. The statement pattern of Spanish is 1-2-1. This has a narrower range of pitch and may be interpreted by the English speaker as monotonous, and in turn, the Spanish speaker may interpret the English pattern as over-excited. What may be a linguistic intonation in one language may pattern as a paralinguistic intonation in another language or dialect, thereby causing confusion in the interpretation of these events by the various speakers of the languages.

Intonation patterns are not necessarily the same within one language; dialects may vary considerably. British English has significantly different patterns from American English. In a neutral question type, American English would use the common 2-3-1 pattern:

When is he ^{com} $_{\text{ing?}}$

British English would start with a high pitch and drop in pitch with a dip at the end:

When $_{\text{is}}$ $_{\text{he}}$ $_{\text{com}^{\text{ing?}}}$

Differences in intonation and voice quality are nullified in singing. This contributes to the difficulty in distinguishing a British singer from an American singer. One has no such problem of distinguishing between either dialect in speech.

When the intonational features of language and paralanguage combine, we may speak of two systems that exist simultaneously and independently. The paralinguistic suprasegmental features might be said to be an overlay on the linguistic (or language) suprasegmental features. When these features are used in the language system they indicate lexical and grammatical differences; when they are used in the paralanguage system they indicate emotional and attitudinal differences. They might be called, respectively, "the intonation of language" and "the intonation of emotion." In the analysis of nonverbal communication, it is the blurring together and sometimes homophonous results that make it difficult to analyze and describe the two separate systems. In some ways they seem beyond analysis. In any case, it is clearly evident that paralanguage can be analyzed only after the sounds of language have been identified. And this is probably the reason that there is very little documented information on the intonation of emotion in languages of the world. I am aware of only one study which attempts to describe patterns for emotional phenomena in the same way that patterns are analyzed for linguistic intonation. This is a study of the Hungarian language which abstracts ten primary emotional intonational patterns: joy, tenderness, longing, coquetry, surprise, fear, complaint, scorn, anger, and sarcasm (Fónagy and Magdics). The choice of the ten members of this class is significant when compared to the abstractions which researchers have worked with in other languages. This will be discussed further under the section of "Facial Expressions" where emotions are depicted by the movements of the face.

At times the paralinguistic system overrides the linguistic system. For example, the normal stress pattern of "ridiculous" has the strongest stress on the second syllable "ridículous," but when the word is articulated with intense emotion, an emphatic stress can fall on the first syllable, with a falling pitch pattern, "Rídiculous!**##!" Stress on the first syllable of "próbably" can shift to the final syllable, but with a softly rising pitch it becomes a wistful "probablý...." Teen numbers, when said in a series, take the stress on the first syllable: "thírteen, fóurteen, fífteen...." But the stress may change when said with an emphatic, emotional tenseness: "I said fiftéen!" Contrastive emphasis can shift the stress: "He said to ínflate the balloon, not déflate it!"

Interrogators, newspaper reporters, and investigators, depending upon their purposes, may try to question in a "monotone" style of voice. What is really meant is that the questions and comments phrased carry the verbal intonation patterns, but the nonverbal paralinguistic patterns are studiously avoided. Even such well-disciplined, controlled speech behavior as that of the astronauts on duty gave way to very slight paralinguistic speeding up, as they came within a few hundred feet of the moon. Without this very slight evidence of emotional impact, they would have seemed non-human!

Non-Language Sounds

The extra-speech sounds used for communication which are treated here, never occur, as far as has been recorded, in any language system of the world. This group includes such "noises" as the whistle, the kiss, the yell, the groan, clapping of the tongue, various percussive sounding noises made with mouth air articulated by the lips and tongue (but not to be confused with mouth clicks mentioned previously in speech sounds), and a variety of imitative noises, such as the bilabial "pop" when the champagne cork is released!

Whistling

> Now we're married--spier nae mair [ask no
> more]
> Whistle o'er the lave o't [rest of it].
> --Robert Burns[19]

Whistling as a communication device is world-wide, from the spontaneous, expressive whistling for joy, or "whistling in the dark," to simple signals across distances, such as among mountain climbers in the Alps who call for help by whistling. The articulation of the whistle may be uncomplicated, as a call to the dog (or children!) or whistles from an audience meaning, "Let's get the show going!" or the whistle may comprise a very complicated system of sequences comparable to and substitutable for language. These systems of whistle talk will be discussed in more detail in the variations of nonverbal behavior under dialects or special message systems, Chapter VIII. Feldman (p. 249) recognizes whistling as communication:

> When performed melodiously and moderately, whistling and humming can be a kind of art. Children love to be hummed to sleep. Lovers, or friends, like to hum or, sometimes, to whistle together. They may even agree on a special, invented and agreed-upon whistling melody to communicate with or to send messages to each other.
>
> Then, there is the famous 'whistling in the dark,' meaning, 'I am not afraid. I even betray that I am here.' The latter indicates genuine or feigned self-confidence, strength, and firmness.
>
> On the other hand, whistling can be used in a defiant and derogatory manner. One does not whistle at a dignified person in order to stop him or to call him. If he is a friend who will accept such a communication, then it is all right to whistle.
>
> One may have an argument with his wife or husband or with a stranger. To show that he does not give a damn or that he ignores the other and what was said, he whistles or hums a tune. This can be very insulting, upsetting, and aggravating to the situation.

The function of the whistle is much more varied when it is done on an individual basis than on a mass basis as by audiences. In the case of the wolf whistle, the event is an invitation for response. A whistle may also discourage response, as happened in Austria following World War I when girls discouraged persistent followers by whistling the intonation for Ziehe o! "Beat it!" (Stern, p. 503).

Whistling is known to be used for hunting signals throughout the world with even large hunting parties learning a system of locating each other by whistles and receiving instructions from the leader by whistles. Animal herders depend heavily upon varied whistles to control pigs, cows, and geese. In Burma, children of the Chin people spend long hours herding the animals and pass the time by conversing with each other over the distance by whistle language (Stern, p. 503).

Whistling is of concern in etiquette. Among some people, social propriety is strained by whistling. Among Spanish speakers, however, it is considered more polite to call a friend by whistling than by speaking loudly, which would be considered rude behavior. Ostwald (1959), who has put together the most complete account of whistling, mentions status relationships involved. This was exemplified among the Hungarian Huszars where a complicated set of whistle instructions were taught to horses and humans, and although the commissioned officers had to understand the system, they were not allowed to use these signals.

The manner of whistling may be bilabial, dental, in cooperation with one or more fingers in the tongue tip area, or with the hands cupped and the lips pressed against the thumbs. The pitch is raised or lowered by movements of the speech organs and changing the shape of the resonant chamber, the mouth cavity. The Mazateco Indians of Mexico use only bilabial articulation in their fluent whistle language. The whistle language of Gomera, Canary Islands, is articulated by either dental or the finger supplement manner; bilabial whistles do not carry far enough over the ravines--and very great distances are reported for this particular whistle language. The Kickapoo courtship whistling is done by the cupped hands (Cowan, Classe, Ritzenthaler and Peterson).

The Kickapoo Indians of northern Mexico have been recorded as having a rich system of courtship language, articulated by whistling. The hands are cupped and the air is blown into the cavity between the knuckles of the thumbs placed against the lips. The lovers get together and work out their messages, and from then on, they recognize each other by the nature of their whistling.

The Kiss

The kiss is a bilabial voiceless click which is articulated in the manner of the other clicks actually used in languages and which were described previously under specific language sounds. Because it has never been reported in an actual language system, the bilabial click, or the kiss, is listed here with non-speech sounds. The first scientific description, to my knowledge, was made in 1791 (Nyrop, p. 6), when the scholar von Kempelen carefully investigated the sound which follows a kiss and reported his analysis in _The Mechanism of Human Speech_. He classified kisses into three types, according to their sound: (1) the kiss proper, a clear-ringing kiss, coming from the heart; (2) the weaker kiss (from an acoustic point of view); and (3) a loathsome smack. Others have attempted to classify the types of kisses. Nyrop (p. 8) reports,

> The austere old Rabbis only recognized three kinds of kisses, viz: those of greeting, farewell, and respect. The Romans had also three kinds, but their classification was essentially at variance with the Rabbis': they distinguished between _oscula_, friendly kisses, _basia_, kisses of love, and _suavia_, passionate kisses.

The etymological history of the vocabulary items for "kiss" has some intriguing occurrences of bilabial stop consonants, which, it has been suggested might be traced back to the origin of the words. Hopkins (pp. 127-8) cites some examples:

> It is an interesting fact that some English words for 'kiss' have parallels, etymological and other, in the modern languages of India. One of these is the good old English 'buss' and its learned cousin-word 'bass,' which as late as Chaucer appears as 'ba,' 'Let me ba thy cheke.' Those are the Western representatives of the Persian and Hindustāni words bûsa and bôsa, which in the dialects of Northwestern India have gone through similar changes and appear today as bus, bas, bes, bui, bai, and ba.

During the last century it was thought that the kiss was not a universal act of human behavior. Travelers and anthropologists reported that among some peoples nose-rubbing was the substitute for the kiss. There was considerable discussion among scholars, and Tylor (1871, p. 63) reports that a facetious ethnological friend of his argued that the lack of the kiss among savage tribes was a proof of primeval barbarism, for, he said, if they have ever known the practice they could not possibly have forgotten it! Current study, however, seems to disclaim the earlier observations. Eibl-Eibesfeldt (Argyle and Exline, p. 13), in his study of human greeting behavior all over the world, believes that kissing is a pattern common to all people.

The kiss is, of course, used in greetings and in affectionate display. But it has other functions with communicative value. Our forefathers had great sport with the kiss in parlor games and one very proper etiquette book of 1833, which recommended the games as recreations for business men, encouraged the tactile behavior of the games, saying, "These caresses can alarm neither modesty nor prudence, since a kiss in honor given and taken before numerous witnesses is often an act of propriety" (Newell, p. 6).

Public kissing is not always taken so lightly. Goffman (pp. 166-7) cites cases in Latin countries, the U.S.S.R., and many Eastern societies where public kissing is considered an obscene act. An American newspaper in 1970 gave an account of a young couple who were arrested for kissing on the street in a Southern metropolis of the United States. The judge, however, who has updated the interpretation of the "turmoil and public indecency" laws, dismissed the case (*Los Angeles Times*, August 27).

The relationship of the kiss to the olfactory processes, as illustrated in language behavior, is amply documented in the scholarly study which Hopkins made of the sniff-kiss in ancient India. Examples are found in other countries. In the Philippine Islands, Nyrop wrote in 1901, lovers who are separated send one another presents of bits of their linen in order to keep each other in mind by often inhaling each other's scent.

Yells

The *yell*, and variations of it as expressed by the *scream*, *shout*, *roar*, *howl*, *bellow*, *squeal*, *holler*, *shriek*, or *screech*, are effective non-speech communications, difficult to describe technically, and almost impossible to duplicate the effect of in other kinds of communication media.

Cherry (p. 77) says, "It may take a page of finest prose to convey the spine-chilling effect of one piercing scream." Authorities report that the human ear is most sensitive to tonal stimuli above 500 cycles per second. Almost all sounds intended to arouse human beings, such as whistles, shrieks, screams, and sirens, contain a large amount of energy above 500 cycles per second (Ostwald 1965).

In the unpleasant varieties, yells are the result of fear or anger, and components of the startle reflex, or offensive gestures to instill fear, as, for example, the war cries--the Rebel Yell, the Indian War Whoop. Not only did the war cry inspire terror in the "enemy" but such an expression of aggression instilled confidence in the warrior himself. This self-expression was particularly important in the maintenance of the frenzied state of mind requisite for such activities as scalping and attack.

In its pleasant varieties yells occur as exuberant and joyful shouts, spontaneously with party music and dancing--among the Mexican, gypsy, and Scots, for example.

The Rebel Yell, or Confederate Yell, was made famous again, at least among linguistic audiences, when Raven McDavid gave a rendition of it to accompany Allen Walker Read's paper presented at the 1959 Linguistic Society of America meeting. McDavid suggests (in correspondence) that "It was basically an unstructured high-pitched call such as rural Southerners still use to encourage their dogs in chasing rabbits." This ululant yell may have derived from such hunting calls, or, Read suggests, it may have its origins in the Indian war whoop. Read quotes several descriptions in his study: One said that the shout was "something more overpowering than the cannon's roar. It was taken up, and carried along the line for several miles, and they heard the uproar rolling along in its approach like an avalanche of thunder." Another possibility comes to mind, and that is the frightening roar of the Scots fans at a soccer game. A reporter describes the scene at Hampden Park in Glasgow,

> And then there is the Hampden Roar. To me it seems to start as a moan behind one goal and then, within seconds, to engulf the whole stadium. It is terrifying, indescribable. It is like taking a punch between the eyes ... frightening beyond

> words ... no matter how many times you hear it it never fails to affect you.[20]

The Scots have been known to scare the hell out of their enemy with the bagpipes. Why not with a roaring yell? The Rebel Yell was also used during the lynching and torturing of Negroes in earlier times. In this situation it was not so much to terrorize an "enemy" (who had, in fact, already been terrorized almost to death), but to bolster the confidence of the lynch mob itself.

Varieties of yells occasionally are features of animal calls and animal mimicry. Besides the hunting, herding, and magical purposes of animal calls, they may also be used in an exuberant, recreational diversion. At a recent Pioneer Day, held at Knott's Berry Farm in California, for senior citizens, a yelling contest was held in which both men and women participated. Hog-calling became a fad during the 1930's and contests were held at fairs and country gatherings. They are still reported today at county fairs. Full-blown hollers were part of the repertoire of vocal behavior of less-populated regions of the Midwestern and Southern United States. A scholar of American English, Gordon Wilson, has made an enviable collection of hollers and animal calls local to the area of Mammouth Cave. One of his better-known recordings is of a local resident who thrilled the community with his holler every year at the Fourth of July celebration. Frederic Cassidy, of the American Dialect Society, verifies the use of the sustained yell for communication in the swamps of Old Okefenokee. The hunter announces his anticipated arrival from a hunting or fishing expedition.

One type of exotic and expressive yell seems to be disappearing, the Harvest Cry. Sir James Frazer in The New Golden Bough (pp. 251-3) reports wide occurrence of it:

> ... the melancholy cry of the Egyptian reapers, which down to Roman times could be heard year after year sounding across the fields, announcing the death of the corn-spirit, the rustic prototype of Osiris. Similar cries, as we have seen, were also heard on all the harvest-fields of Western Asia. ... [T]hey probably consisted only of a few words uttered in a prolonged musical note which could be heard for a great distance. ... sonorous and long-drawn cries, raised by a number of strong voices in concert.... In Germany cries

> of Waul! or Wol! or Wôld! are sometimes raised by the reapers at cutting the last corn.

And from England he reports:

> Down to recent times Devonshire reapers uttered cries of the same sort, and performed on the field a ceremony exactly analogous to that in which ... the rites of Osiris originated. ... After the wheat is all cut ... the harvest people have a custom of 'crying the neck' ... [in which] all the men forming the ring take off their hats, stooping and holding them with both hands towards the ground ... [and proceed] in a very prolonged and harmonious tone to cry "The neck!" ... three times.... They then change their cry to 'Wee yen!' 'Way yen!' which they sound in the same ... manner as before.... [Then] they all burst out into a kind of loud and joyous laugh, flinging up their hats and caps into the air, capering about and perhaps kissing the girls.

Non-Language Modifications

> I understand a fury in your words
> But not the words. --Othello

Voice Quality

So far, in dealing with sounds, we have discussed sounds or modification phenomena which are found in languages and are fairly well understood in terms of the scientific description of them. The non-speech segmental sounds, also, are rather clear-cut by definition and present no great problem in the theoretical framework of classifying paralanguage with relation to language. Voice quality, however, is still somewhat of an enigma to phoneticians and linguists in general, and though attempts have been made to classify, scientifically describe, and devise notation systems, there is still no satisfactory scientific explanation of what happens to the vocal cords and other speech organs in the production of the seemingly infinite varieties of voice quality. That it does happen is not questioned by anyone. The recognition that voice quality has communicative value is also a commonplace. Lacking precise terminology, then, it seems convenient to use descriptive labels for such non-language modifications as:

raspy	heavy	gruff
shrill	dull	full
robust	throaty	husky
resonant	gravelly	choking
sweet	soft	moaning
smooth	squeaky	groaning
harsh	guttural	breaking
rough	thin	singing
deep	sepulchral	ringing
shaky	open	"whiskey voice"
hollow		

And many more. The difference between these modifications and language element modifications is that these have never been found in contrastive words to make a semantic differentiation as the language element modifications have been; they are not distinctive features which identify lexical items. They are superimposed on the speaking voice. Verbal communication continues; in fact, these features cannot take place without words. One vocal modification which has been identified as far as articulatory description is concerned, is faucalization or faucialization. This is produced by a drawing together of the "faucal pillars" in the back of the throat and the result is a tight and twangy speech. It is seldom referred to in linguistic writings, but is often used by comedians in speech mimicry to imitate the "nasal" twang of the hillbilly speech.

No comparative study has been made among different languages to discover how these qualities are used in different cultures. It recognized that some qualities are used more extensively than others in particular languages, but statements are made in general terms, such as "the speakers use a higher pitch...." The Japanese language is known to have many varieties of articulation depending upon the purpose. The vocal qualifications appear to consist of making "the sounds more hollow through backing and rounding, with accompanying velarization or pharyngealization."[21]

One investigator, working with the tone language, Southern Agaw, of Ethiopia, recognized that voice quality was different.

> The impression I received ... is that for tone-distinction it is not the musical pitch that is rele-

> vant, but the register of the voice in which the syllable is pronounced. It is easy to perceive that different musical levels produced by the human voice differ from each other not only in terms of height, but also in color, owing to the resonance of different cavities involved in the creation of the voice. Thus, Mid-tone syllables are pronounced in a mid register, according to the personal qualities of the voice of the speaker. High tone is pronounced in a higher register that is not only higher but also clearer. Low tone is pronounced in a very low register that gives the impression of groaning or grumbling[22] [emphasis added].

Voice Disguisers

For purposes of entertainment, carrying power, magic, or secret messages, the human voice can be modified in ways that disguise the natural voice of the speaker. Ventriloquism was practiced in ancient times by soothsayers and other mystic personnel (Tylor 1873, p. 268). Certain women who were professional mystics used ventriloquism in giving oracular responses in the time of Hippocrates. The same practice was known in China during the last century--all for a fee. Anthropologists have documented the use of ventriloquism by witchdoctors needing to disguise their voices from their village compatriots.

Falsetto is another manner of adjusting the vocal cords in order to modify speech. This "false voice" involves some type of reduced aperture and consequent diminished air stream. Moving quickly back and forth from natural voice to false voice, or the falsetto, results in yodeling. It is said that few women can produce falsetto, but since many women "cowboys" and Swiss women yodel, one would have to question whether or not this is simply another of the many culturally learned differences between the behavior of male and female. Pike (1944), for example, observes that "some women can 'squeal' or scream in false voice" but does not mention that they also yodel.

Animal calls by males may be articulated in falsetto, "Kitty, kitty, kitty!" or "Chick, chick, chick!" While English-speaking males mimic women in falsetto, not all cultures do. Mohave men do not, for example, but instead suggest nuances of female speech to mimic a woman or a male transvestite (Devereux). Besides speech mimicry, falsetto may be used in other situations. In Asian cultures, men laugh in falsetto. In Africa among the Jabo, falsetto is used for carrying power to give the pitches for signaling over long distances (Herzog, p. 454). In this use, it serves as a speech surrogate in the same way that whistle and drum "languages" function. Among the Black population in the United States, falsetto is used frequently. Laughing in falsetto is typical. Falsetto voice may be heard in happy greetings, and it may also occur in angry expressions. Charles Kiel suggests that its origin is Africa:

> Falsetto singing comes directly from Africa, where it is considered to be the very essence of masculine expression. The smallest and highest-pitched drum in a West African percussion ensemble or 'family' is designated the male drum because its tone is piercing and the role it plays is colorful, dynamic, and dominant. The falsetto techniques of a West African cabaret singer are sometimes indistinguishable from those employed so effectively by Ray Charles, B. B. King, or the lead voice in a gospel quartet.[23]

During the last century a traveler to New Guinea noted a kind of secret language which used falsetto among other features:

> In New Britain, Duke of York, as well as New Ireland, there is a method of talking when [the people] do not wish to be understood by any stranger. It appears to be a different dialect at each place[;] ... it is chanted in a sort of falsetto voice, and is apparently cut up into a rough kind of rhythm, in which all the smaller words are left out, and it is extremely difficult to understand.[24]

One final illustration of the use of falsetto in paralinguistic communication is the incidence of falsetto in the speech of a homosexual, as reported by Ferenczi. The psychoanalyst observes (in 1915), that "This type of boy seems also to supply the largest contingent of lady imitators, who delight the audiences of our variety theatres with the abrupt transitions of their soprano and bass voices."

Humming

The foregoing comments have to do with modification of the speech act. There is another kind of vocal articulation, humming, which at first glance seems to be more closely related to singing than to speech. But, except for the specialized use in choral work and opera, the functional varieties of humming are nonverbal substitutes for language and can be analyzed in the paralinguistic framework as can other paralinguistic acts. Frequent use of humming occurs in the environment of infants and children. Children like to hum and they like to be rocked to sleep with humming. Lovers hum in a special kind of communication. Humming makes work go faster and without the feeling of drudgery. It may be used as a warning or as a soothing measure, for example to a child in an anxious situation when speech is precluded. Humming, like whistling, may be used as a hostile act, to ignore another, or to set oneself off from another. And humming, like whistle and drum and falsetto, can be used as a surrogate for language, as it is among the Chinese of Chekiang (Stern).

There was an occasion for humming which seems to have been lost in recent times, and that is the occurrence in the audience behavior during church services. Tylor (1871, p. 186) reports it from a biography of a 17th-century preacher.

> There prevailed in those days an indecent custom; when the preacher touched any favourite topick in a manner that delighted his audience, their approbation was expressed by a loud hum, continued in proportion to their zeal or pleasure. When Burnet preached, part of his congregation hummed so loudly and so long, that he sat down to enjoy it, and rubbed his face with his handkerchief. When Sprat preached, he likewise was honoured with the like animating hum, but he stretched out his hand to the congregation, and cried, "Peace, peace; I pray you, peace" [Johnson, *Life of Sprat*].

Modification Made With By-Element

Voice modifications discussed so far, are achieved by manipulation of the speech apparatus itself. Normal vocalization, talking or singing, can also be modified by the addition of another element, which I am calling a By-Element (see Model in Chapter II). This By-Element may be a simple thing such as a membrane or a thin piece of paper on a comb, or the element may be highly complex as in electronic effects on the voice. The use of intricate electronic equipment modifies the voice for various effects: (1) for reaching greater audiences, (2) for characterizations in drama, and (3) for emphasizing breathy and sensuous quality in entertainment, particularly singing.

An extensive study on vibrating membranes as modifiers was done by Balfour, who compiled all the information he could find on instruments which were used as voice disguisers. Most of the data he collected was from Africa, though some descriptions are from India, Java, the Solomon Islands, and Europe. The instruments are, in general, some sort of tube or hollow container, variously decorated and shaped, with a thin membrane stretched across a hole. The membrane is cut from the egg-case of a spider, a bat's wing, a very thin lizard's skin, the thin skin of an onion, very thin parchment, or gold-beater's skin. The membrane vibrates as the speaker talks or sings into the hollow cavity, causing a distortion of the voice, harsh or grotesque, or weird and amusing, the interpretation depending on the event in which the instrument is used.

This type of voice disguiser is the means for a secret language in many cases, to enable one to take part in ritualistic and mystical performances. The "voice" may be said to be of the gods or of ancestors and these articulations take place in initiation ceremonies, fertility rites, funeral rites, and other serious performances. In these cases, the trick is jealously guarded and the uninitiated, particularly the women and children, are not permitted to see or know of the instrument. Intimidation of women is the main object in some of the rites.

The earliest description of this membrane and hollow container effect, apparently, is Lord Bacon's (1561-1626) discovery of the responsive action of a drum-head to vocal sound waves. Balfour (p. 52) quotes a translation,

> If you sing in the hole of a Drum, it maketh the singing more sweet. And so I conceive it would, if it were a song in parts, sung into several Drums; And for handsomeness and strangeness sake, it would not be amiss to have a Curtain be-

> tween the Place, where the Drums are, and the Hearers.

For utilitarian purposes, the voice-disguiser instrument is used for animal mimicry in hunting. It may or may not be connected with magic. In recreation and entertainment, children and others young in heart use blades of grass as voice disguisers. Newell (pp. 108-9) reports the use in Germany during the 13th century. Jesters, nowadays comedians, use voice disguisers to amuse. In Western societies a simple buzzing instrument the "kazoo," made of metal is often used at festive occasions or in play by children. Speech can be muffled or stifled with a By-Element such as a dish towel or a blanket, making the sound dreadful, morbid, pathetic or unrecognizable. A sobbing woman can get a better effect of her miserable state by speaking into a dish towel. This modification of speech is, of course, accompanied by vocal cord modifications described earlier. The Hanunóo, mentioned previously, have a rich inventory of voice disguisers. Another of their methods involves a blanket thrown over the head, used as a By-Element in modifying the speech of lovers (Conklin).

Laugh--Giggle--Tremulousness--Sob--Cry

The relationship between laughing and crying was early recognized and discussed. It is worthwhile to remember that tears accompany both excessive laughing and crying, and that in extreme emotion, it is difficult to interpret whether a person is laughing or crying. A recent description by Crystal and Quirk (pp. 42-3) makes possible "five broad divisions in the types of voice qualification which we would include in paralanguage. These divisions have been labelled on the basis of auditory agreement: laugh--giggle--tremulousness--sob--cry." They also say,

> It is not possible to say when giggle ends and laugh begins, or when cry ends and sob begins, though doubtless it would be possible to examine a great quantity of data and obtain some measurements (of pulse speed, air pressure, prominence, for example) which would be of value in establishing more objective gradations. It is doubtful, however, whether the results would justify the time and ingenuity involved.

The acts of laughing and crying are universals, but it is quite clear that different cultures laugh and cry at different things. Laughing is not necessarily a reaction only to joy, and crying is not necessarily a reaction only to sorrow or pain. Darwin (pp. 155, 175, 212) was well aware of other communications possible:

> Laughter is frequently employed in a forced manner to conceal or mask some other state of mind, even anger. We often see persons laughing in order to conceal their shame or shyness.... In the case of derision, a real or pretended smile or laugh is often blended with the expression proper to contempt, and this may pass into angry contempt or scorn. In such cases the meaning of the laugh or smile is to show the offending person that he excites only amusement.

Laughter

> Laughing causeth a dilatation of the mouth and lips; a continued expulsion of the breath, with a loud noise, which maketh the interjection of laughing; shaking of the breasts and sides; running of the eyes with water, if it be violent and continued.
>
> --Francis Bacon (1561-1626)
> (in Gregory, p. 25)

Laughter is referred to by a wide variety of terminology, reflecting the different emotional states that are communicated in this non-verbal act: happy laughter, cynical, sardonic, comical, hysterical, embarrassed, and so on. A laugh may be called, for instance, a chortle, a guffaw, a cackle, a snicker, a titter, or a chuckle. In happy laughter eye contact is increased; in embarrassed laughter it is decreased. Blushing may accompany laughter and other indicative body movements may occur, such as lowering the head. Sardonic laughter has accompanying nasal aspiration and controlled movement.

Herbert Spencer, in 1860 (p. 299), wrote on the physiology of laughter, commenting that "emotions and sensations tend to generate bodily movements and that the movements are vehement in proportion as the emotions or sensations are intense."

An embarrassing result of too hearty laughter occurs rarely, and is known in medical circles as cataplexy--a complete loss of muscular control in body movement. Note the expressions in language related to this: "fell off the chair laughing" or "went limp with laughter."

La Barre gathered references to the occurrence of laughing and crying in other cultures. He quoted comments (1947, p. 52) made concerning laughter in Africa. "Laughter is used by the negro to express surprise, wonder, embarrassment and even discomfiture."

Crying

The terminology of weeping also reflects varied emotional states: wail, bewail, sob, blubber, whimper, mewl, whine, pule. In a cross-cultural study of the emotions of young people from Uganda and the United States it was observed that crying was associated with anger somewhat more with the Ugandan than with the American participants (Davitz, p. 187). Sir James Frazer collected perhaps the largest number of illustrations from cultures around the world on the act of weeping as a salutation, a formal compliance with an etiquette prescribed by polite society. He includes an eye-witness description of the departure and return of friends among the Maoris of New Zealand (1919, p. 84):

> ... a great display of outward feeling is made: it commences with a kind of ogling glance, then a whimper, and an affectionate exclamation; then a tear begins to glisten in the eye; a wry face is drawn; then they will shuffle nearer to the individual, and at length cling around his neck. They then begin to cry outright ... and, at last, to roar most outrageously, and almost to smother with kisses, tears, and blood....

It has been noted that some people can shed tears on a moment's notice. Even when tears appear to be a spontaneous reaction to sorrow, there are still cultural controls and stipulations as to when the tears may be shed, and where, and in front of whom.

The relationship and significance of laughing and crying to linguistic structures of language itself is little understood. The first group of scholars to talk about paralanguage and its place in the total communication system included laughing and crying in the spectrum of paralinguistic phenomena. Hungarian scholars have further identified emotional intonational patterns and have noted that the "melody of complaint is obviously a stylized form of weeping" (Fónagy and Magdics, p. 316).

Control of Air Movement

Of concern in the phonetic articulation of language elements are the direction and source of the air movement, as well as the amount of air aspirated and inspirated. With the exceptions of a few sounds such as the click and some pharyngeal air sounds, language sounds are produced with the direction of air outward. Paralanguage, on the other hand, makes much greater use of ingressive air sounds; that is, the direction of the air is inward. An often quoted example is the Japanese hiss, which is produced with air drawn in, in contrast to the English hiss, where the air is articulated outward. A sigh is produced with egressive (outward) air movement; a gasp is produced with ingressive air movement. Other examples are: French, a casual sound like a voiceless vowel, produced with air drawn in; Chinese [Ss!] with the air sucked in; Scandinavians, especially the women, sometimes say the word ja "yes" with the breath drawn in--often unvoiced. The Maidu Indians use a long inspirated high vowel sound [i:] for an exclamation.

In noise and animal mimicry, the sounds of inspirated air provide a wide variety of possibilities. The donkey's "hee-haw" can be articulated by alternately drawing air in for the "hee" and expelling air on the "haw." The sounds of ingressive air may sometimes be heard in the act of yawning. In snoring, ingressive air produces a trill across the relaxed velic.

Another kind of voice disguise is a modification made not by the vocal cords but by the manner of controlling the air flow which produces the sounds. This can be observed in children's linguistic behavior: when they run out of breath, they inhale and keep on talking! This use of ingressive air also occurs as a voice disguiser in the courtship behavior of the Hanunóo people of the Philippines (Conklin).

All the examples given so far have to do with normal behavior in human beings. The vocal behavior of mentally disturbed patients sometimes shows more use of ingressive air movement during speech. Psychiatrists have noted that a disturbed patient may speak for long periods with only ingressive air.

Almost all sounds from the oral and nasal cavities discussed in paralanguage are produced with the same sources of air that are used in language sounds, i.e. the lungs primarily, and less often the pharynx and mouth cavities. At least one sound, however, which is used in paralanguage, is produced with the source of air initiated from the esophageal region or the stomach. Better known as the belch, this sound will be discussed in the following chapter under Spontaneous Physiological Acts. In non-normal situations, but not recorded for language or paralanguage, esophageal air is used by speakers who have undergone laryngectomy. Pharyngeal air can produce a paralinguistic exclamation which may be articulated in a situation of feigned surprise or shock, a Gulp! Similarly a dramatic sound accompanying an artificial swallow may occur in like situations, thus approximating the natural speech sounds called "implosives" which occur in some American Indian languages, some African languages, and elsewhere.

The amount of air in the air flow is of considerable importance in language activity as well as nonverbal behavior. Control of the amount may be learned unconsciously, as in the articulation of aspirated and unaspirated stops in language. Respiratory behavior may be excited or repressed by emotional situations. Or the amount may be voluntarily controlled for effect, such as the breathy quality of the voice of Elvis Presley, Claudine Longet, and other popular singers of the day.

Scholars who have documented the emotional intonation patterns of Hungarian, which were referred to previously, have noted a breathy component in the patterns of: longing, coquetry, surprise, fear, and anger. At times it even turns into a whisper. In the humorous but descriptively accurate parody of Italian gestures, "heavy breathing exercises" which involve nostril dilation are recommended for the person who wants to imitate the Great Italian Lover (D'Angelo, p. 72). "Women, too, can use the technique on men with devastating effect."

In expressions of insult, the Gbeya people of Africa begin the utterance with great volume and reduce it until the final words are almost unintelligible (Samarin, 1969, p. 326), but by that time, it is clear, the receiver has indeed understood the message!

The control of air has also been known to be an expressive device in voice disguise. As noted earlier, the Hanunóo of the Philippines carry on extensive courting behavior as well as entertainment, by modifying normal patterns of speech. Speed and glottal tension contribute to vocal disguise. Whispering and falsetto are used; whole conversations are carried on with the direction of the air inward instead of outward. Ingressive speech has also been noted in the courting behavior of the Swiss-German in a custom called Fensterle, in which a village lad talks to a village girl beneath her window.

A variety of sounds not recorded in linguistic studies, but evident when one lets the imagination run free, can be articulated with variations in the manipulation of the air stream. Let the reader experiment! Start by inflating the cheeks and striking them gently with a pencil.

Paralinguistic Acts

Tush, tush, man; never fleer and jest at me
--Leonato, Much Ado About Nothing (V, i)

A complete inventory of the physical elements that might occur in paralanguage was presented in the preceding pages. The following give further examples where these paralinguistic elements are utilized in certain acts which function in communication. The first part of the discussion treats single acts or outcries. The second part deals with mimicry which modifies whole segments of discourse.

Outcries

Exclamations, and simple vocal outcries can be listed as paralinguistic acts. These are very often short, spontaneous outbursts. They may be lexical in nature; that is, they can substitute for language and even be listed in a dictionary, such as grunts for affirmative and negative responses, "yes" and "no"; instructions to hush, "shh"; "huh?" a substitute for "what?"; and "phew!" to indicate a foul odor or a disgusting situation. Outcries may also indicate an emotive or emphatic articulation, such as a wolf whistle, or whee!; an expression of pain, ouch! (or in Spanish ay-ay!);

an expression of contempt, bah! or surprise, oh! They may occur as a result of a sensation, brrrr! They may elicit or give response--pssst! or mmmmm, or hmmmm.

These orthographic representations are only approximations of what one hopes that the reader will understand to be well-known paralinguistic acts. There are no certain ways of writing these items in any language, as one will see, for example, in the various ways which writers have attempted to represent the alveolar mouth click which means commiseration, or "For shame!" It is variously written as tsk tsk, tusk tusk, tisk tisk.

Further difficulty is seen in the representation of these types of sounds in other languages. The famous anthropologist, Sir Edward B. Tylor, made one of the first attempts at writing emotive expressions in other languages. He gave examples of "hush!" in several languages: English <u>whist!</u> <u>hist!</u>; Welch <u>ust!</u>; French <u>chut!</u>; Italian <u>zitto!</u>; Swedish <u>tyst!</u>; Russian <u>st'!</u> (1871, Chapter V). Otto Jespersen, the great scholar of English, also gave attention to this type of emotive language. Other than that, linguists have pretty much ignored these outcries, considering them beyond the dignity of scientific study, and it turns out that almost all of the discussions on these important communicative acts, since Tylor and Jespersen, have come from journalists or popular writers of the day.

<u>Mimicry</u>

Mimicry involves human sounds, or speech mimicry; natural sounds, or noise mimicry; and animal noises, such as animal mimicry and animal calls. <u>Speech mimicry</u> or voice disguise, includes all the variations that a speaker might assume that are outside of his normal idiolect. For example, an older person assuming child language would be talking baby talk (not to be confused with actual child language, which is the natural dialect of that individual).

Speech mimicry is used extensively by comedians who can affect a dialect for entertainment. The dialect assumed might be a foreign accent dialect, a dialect from another status class, higher or lower, an occupational dialect, or anything that would create an atmosphere or set the stage for comedy. Speech mimicry (along with other kinds of mimicry) is used by the story teller, the special effects to hold the attention of the audience, which has already heard the story perhaps. "The Three Bears" gives challenging possibilities for rich paralinguistic effects: a tiny voice, a medium voice, and a deep voice.

Baby talk is distinguished from child language in that it is not a developmental stage of natural language, but a stylized variety used in special situations (See Ferguson for a good summary of baby talk in six languages.) It is a language used to create an atmosphere of a special, exclusive kind of relationship, to establish a status, or nurturant relationship, or to control behavior. In the first instance, it is perhaps more widely recognized and occurs more frequently. Baby talk is used in the following situations:

1. Adult to youngster and youngster to adult
2. Adult to adult within family or intimate circle
3. Between lovers
4. Human being to pet
5. Nurses to patients
6. Personnel to mentally incompetent
7. A person to anyone he feels superior to--anyone of a different race or sex, or working class, a waitress, secretary...
8. In songs, riddles, rhymes...
9. Between persons to insult

There are some differences between the above varieties. For example, a nurse might say to her patient, "How are we today?" "Did we brush our teeth yet?" using the pronoun "we" instead of the direct address, "you." Whereas in baby talk to children, a parent might use the pronoun "her" or a proper name in a similar situation, "Is her do-ing Bye Bye?" for "Are you going for a ride?" and "Let Daddy carry Teddy" in place of "Let me carry you."

Further grammatical analysis of baby talk shows a greater use of nouns than pronouns and verbs. The verb "to be" is often left out. "The baby is funny" becomes "baby funny." A diminutive affix is common in baby talk in many languages. "Doll" becomes "dollie/dolly"; "pants" become "panties"; "pot" becomes "pottie." Other languages, as well as English, also use reduplication in baby talk: Choo-choo, Bye-bye, wee-wee, Boo-hoo. Certain features of pronunciation are evident in baby talk; for example, consonant substitution: "truck" becomes "twuck." In general, the lips are puckered or pouted, imparting labialization to the overall speech. The pitch may be either higher or lower than in normal speech.

New lexical items are created for purposes of baby talk. A train becomes "choo-choo." "Peek-a-boo" is a game for which there is no adult vocabulary. Very often the new terms are family specific, created only for the benefit of and known only to the intimate family circle. Songs of the post-depression era in the United States featured baby talk and were sung with characteristic puckered lips and childish eye and head movement. "How much is that doggie in the window?" "Mares eat oats and does eat oats and little lambs eat ivy." "Boop-boop did-um, dad-um, wat-um ... Choo!"

Noise mimicry imitates sounds and these articulations are sometimes called "sound-imitative" words (Perrin). Again, "The Three Bears" lends itself to a wide variety of paralinguistic behavior, accompanying the verbal story. One can hear the noise of the splash! of water as the bears wash their hands for dinner; the noise of "slurping" the too-hot soup; the noise of the door slamming on the way out to take a walk--plof! in Dutch, bats! in Russian; the rumble of an ox-cart in the distance--mullra-bullra in Swedish; the bang! of a gun as Father Bear hunts chicken hawks and the bump-bump as they fall through the trees; the rrrrrr of an airplane as it flies overhead; the bell ringing in the far-off church steeple--bim-bam in German, cing-e-bing in Albanian, tsil-tsul in Hebrew; the coins clinking as they buy an extra loaf of bread before returning home--žbluňk-žbluňk in Czech, cumberlop-cumberlop in Turkish; the "cruuunch" of the breaking chair; the surprise noises when Goldilocks is found, boo! (bø! in Norwegian). And finally everybody sneezed--atchoo!--at the happy ending: kshu Sanskrit, echiun Chilian, hah-chee Chinese, hepci Czech, atchouin French, apchi Russian, wah Indonesian, gugu Japanese, hatsii Finnish.

Animal mimicry is distinguished from animal calls in that the former tries to approximate what the animals say, and the latter is a "come hither!" cry to the animal. In English cats are called by hollering "kitty-kitty-kitty"; in Spanish, they are called by Bichi-Bichi. Chickens are informed of the distribution of corn by "Here chick-chick-chick-chick!" (high pitched) and in Spanish pio-pio-pio.

Anthropologists have documented the use of animal language by shamans and witch-doctors. The practitioner may imitate the cries and sounds of animals and birds and noises as evidence that he can transform himself at will into a nonhuman (May). Animal calls are used extensively in hunting cultures where the diet is dependent on what the hunter brings home from the forest or the jungle.

At the headwaters of the Amazon jungle, the alligator makes a haunting cry during the mating season that sounds very much like an implosive, suction sound that a human being can make deep down in the throat. An acquaintance was reported to have used this sound as he guided his canoe softly along the edge of a small lake. The story goes that one romantic, moonlit night, a red-blooded, female alligator leaped into the canoe!

Chapter IV: KINESICS--BODY LANGUAGE

That body movement is not random, but has communicative value, has been recognized since the earliest discussions on any of these topics. La Barre used the term "body language" in his much referred-to article in 1947. Goffman (p. 33) speaks of "body idiom"; the term "gesture language" has also been used. "Organ language" refers to the physiological means of communication. The present discussion comprises all kinesic movements resulting from muscular and skeletal shift which are usual among human beings. These include physical or physiological actions, automatic reflexes, gestures, and changes in the physiognomy that occur in the repertory of human behavior. All of these categories make up "body language," an expression popularly used for "kinesic behavior." They all communicate something in the way of response or giving information about emotion or attitude, though perhaps not in the same way that conventional gestures are used. For example, if daughter comes into the room to discuss marriage and father's only answer is to get up and pace the room, we can assume that communication has taken place.

In the following discussions, the term "gesture" will be delimited, more or less, to conventionalized or institutionalized explicit acts, such as a pointing gesture (whether by the lips or the finger), or a hitch-hiker's thumb gesture. In the ways that body language participates in nonverbal acts, it very much parallels paralanguage; i.e., Kinesic Acts may substitute for language, accompany it, or modify it. Facial expressions, for example, affect the language act; sneezing interrupts it; smoking inserts non-linguistic pauses. Body language is somehow different from paralanguage, though, in that none of the elements used in kinesics is used in language--here the analogy ends.

In another way, body language holds a close relationship to paralanguage. The intonational components of paralanguage--pitch, stress, and length--are also seen in body movement in the way of range or extent of movement, intensity of the action, and duration of the movement. Paralinguistic pause, or silence, is immobility in body language and, of course, speaks for itself. The classification of Kinesic Acts is related to function in much the same manner that Paralinguistic Acts can be categorized. Thus, kinesic acts may be lexical or informative and directive in nature, or they may be emotive or emphatic movements. Following are the elements used in kinesics.

Posture

Posture → Bent Knees, Lying Down, Standing
Bent Knees → Sitting (on furniture), Squatting, Kneeling...
Lying Down → ?
Standing → Approach, Withdrawal, Expansion, Contraction...

Studies on postural behavior are significant for their scarcity. The mime and the artist have long been aware of the wide range of communication possible through body stance, but the scholar has only recently begun to make observations on this means of conveying attitude and emotion, eliciting reaction, and articulating response. The vocabulary used in reference to posture gives some idea of its communicative variety: for example, slouching, sprawling, perching, slumping, crouching, lounging, reposing, lolling, stretching out, resting, reclining, leaning, and standing at attention. The analysis of posture indicates three basic positions: Bent Knees, Lying Down, and Standing. It is interesting to note that in the South American language, Chama, the concept of "being" falls into three categories: sitting, lying down, and standing.[25]

Chama verb element ani-	used in expressions such as: "She is [sitting] in the house."
verb element haa-	"The machete is [lying] in the canoe."
verb element neki-	"There is a man [standing] in the trail."

Readers will recall the Sapir-Whorfian hypothesis concerning language and behavior, implicit in this example of world-view.

There are culturally determined styles of posture which are common to all within a particular community or sub-group. Not all cultures use the same postures for the same functions. Most people, perhaps, use Bent Knee position for eating, but the Romans (some of them) ate in the Lying Down position. Only one article on sleeping postures has come to my attention and that is a short description by Prince Peter of Greece and Denmark of the sleeping posture of the Tibetans, which he noted in his travels before World War II. The local men of his caravan slept outside at night, crowding together around the fire, hunched over on their knees with their faces resting in their upturned palms. Elsewhere he noticed that monks slept sitting up in the same position in which they had been praying and telling their beads all day.

Hewes accumulated data on 480 different cultures and subgroups from photographs found in a great variety of sources for Standing and the Bent Knee positions. For example, he found eleven common ways of sitting on chairs or chair-like structures. About 100 positions of Standing and Bent Knee positions are illustrated. Efron (p. 22) discusses the postural changes in Americanized Eastern European Jews and Southern Italians after immigration.

James, in his 1932 study of the expression of bodily posture, recognized the coordinating relationship of facial expression, gesture, and posture. He said that studying them independently was justified for purposes of analysis, but that the total should be recognized as a unit for the function of expression. He abstracted four basic kinds from 347 different postures included in the experiment (pp. 432-3), designating them: approach, withdrawal, expansion, contraction. Approach conveyed such things as attention, interest, scrutiny, and curiosity. Withdrawal involved a drawing back or turning away and indicated negation, refusal, repulsion, and disgust. Expansion referred to the expanded chest, erect trunk and head, and raised shoulders, which conveyed pride, conceit, arrogance, disdain, mastery, self-esteem. Contraction was characterized by forward trunk, bowed head, drooping shoulders, and sunken chest. The figure shrinks, shrivels, cringes, cowers, crouches, droops, and thus indicates that the individual is depressed, abased, downcast, dejected, crestfallen.

Within each of these categories, there are subsets which may overlap in emotional expression. For example, in the posture Approach: with palms up, the approach becomes acceptance, offering, coaxing, supplication, beseeching, humbleness; with palms outward, active repulsion, avoidance, opposition, command, disapproval; with palms down, soothing, calming, blessing.

Besides patterned group behavior, there are also idiosyncratic physical placement configurations of each individual. Studies have identified postural behavior with personality types and ways of life, e.g., (1) Relaxation, (2) Assertiveness, and (3) Restraint; and have noted the correlation of certain kinds of movement in sleeping and waking acts (Sheldon). Posture is situationally defined according to the context and such influences as styles, persons involved, and artifacts concerned. Consider the differences in sitting when the mini-skirt came in style. A century before, young girls had been taught not to cross their legs; wearing the mini-skirt brought about a high occurrence of leg-crossing. Note differences of sitting--on the platform or in crowded circumstances. Tight trousers incase the knee so that, in a sitting position, the feet are extended farther out in front because the knees won't bend.

Consider the stance which is determined by the performance expected or the equipment involved. A firm feet-apart stance is typical of the policeman who must maintain balance with heavy equipment attached to his person. When a static posture is maintained, fatigue is increased, which affects, then, other body movements, especially facial expression. William Austin makes several observations on differences of body placement according to the context of the situation. He comments on German, French, English, and American differences (1972, pp. 152-3):

> ... body stances ... vary according to culture, age, sex and the individual tonus at any particular time. The German male body stance is notoriously stiffer than that of the American, with the shoulders well back, the spine straight, and very little pelvic motion.... English body stance is more similar to the American, but the French stance is something different again, with a greater body limpness than that of the American.

From the few studies available it would appear that

posture is a substantial marker of feminine and masculine behavior. The relationship of posture to sex gestures is obvious in the stereotypes in U.S. advertising. Posture can communicate an invitation to sexual intercourse. Those who attend bars, for example, note that women sit differently depending upon their intentions. In the area of the Buka Passage of the Northern Solomons, a woman who sits with legs stretched out is communicating an invitation. A medical doctor spent considerable time analyzing the postures of his women patients during abdominal or pelvic examination, a "heteroerotic situation attended by essential supine passiveness plus exhibition" (Quackenbos). Apparently no similar study has been made analyzing male postural behavior during a similar type of examination, and one might conclude that women have been overstudied and humans have been understudied.

Posture is an indicator of status and rank. In a study of Roman sculpture and coinage, Brilliant demonstrates that posture identifies the noble and the peasant. Scheflen (1964, p. 329) comments on contemporary rank. Peer relations assume similar postural arrangements, i.e., imitative behavior, when they are interacting. Persons of differing social status may assume quite different postures. Posture is also a marker of etiquette. In Western culture one is taught (or used to be!) to stand when an elderly person enters the room. Among the Navahos, it is considered bad etiquette to remain standing in the hogan for any length of time. With reference to proper behavior in the presence of other persons, Goffman (pp. 26-7) speaks of "limb discipline" as a kind of protective concealment which the male and female are at least subconsciously aware of in sitting circumspectly.

Medical diagnosticians and psychiatrists have long been aware of the significance of posture. Sullivan was known to pay keen attention to postural tonus (La Barre 1947, p. 64). Fromm-Reichmann is said to have imitated her client's posture in order to feel what he or she was experiencing and couldn't say. Deutsch has used postural analysis extensively in psychoanalytic work, and has meaningfully titled a series of articles, "Thus speaks the body." Steig, a psychiatrist, in his hilarious cartoons, gives a humorous perspective to an otherwise painful subject. His line drawings depict the postural feeling reflected in the mental states of schizophrenia, depression, mania, paranoia, and hysteria.

Facial Expression

> Your face, my thane, is as a book where
> men
> May read strange matters.
> --Lady Macbeth (I, vii)

If the face seems to be the most obvious component of body language, it is certainly the most confusing and difficult to understand. Modern studies of facial expression go back to the 19th century, starting with Charles Bell, who in 1806, published Essays on the Anatomy and Philosophy of Expression: As Connected with the Fine Arts. Darwin's work, The Expressions of the Emotions in Man and Animals, 1872, was apparently much influenced by Bell's earlier work. Piderit, in 1867 also brought scientific attention to the face with his now famous model, constructed with exchangeable parts which could portray different emotions (see Boring and Titchener).

A spate of scholarly articles followed. The number of items published since Bell's study on facial expression alone runs in the hundreds. For the most part these earlier works were psychological studies, interested in the emotions involved. Classifications reflect that concern, while still trying to maintain a scientific stance. It is a truism that vocal and bodily expressions are never repeatable in exactly the same proportions and therefore defy experimentation. Like sentences in human language, they are infinite in variety. The application of scientific methods and experimentation is destructive to the spontaneity and communicative value in emotional expression. It changes the data.

The relationship of facial expression to other components of body language and to language itself, is sparsely examined and such observations as have been made are recent. It doesn't take very extensive scientific study to observe that a smiling face makes a sentence sound different from a sentence articulated by a sorrowful, droopy physiognomy. Nevertheless, linguists have pretty much ignored this inextricable relationship and there are still worlds to conquer in this area of human communication.

In the last few decades, classifications of facial expressions have been developing, though by no means is a completely satisfactory model available for discussion of this type of nonverbal communication. In this presentation

I suggest first a physical description of the basic components of facial expression, and then groups of possible results (semantic effect). The physical descriptions, for example, are: Neutral, Relaxed, Tense, Uplifted, Droopy. The Neutral could result in various expressions such as pleasure, mask, respect, thoughtful, and quiet attention. The Relaxed could result in love, pleasure and submission; the Tense, in fear, surprise, determination, contempt, extreme interest, and so forth; the Uplifted could result in happiness, anxiety, rage, religious love, astonishment, attention; and the Droopy, in distress, suffering, grief, dismay, and shock. Further description of the components of facial expression such as eyes and mouth would fill in the detail that would explain the many varieties possible with these five basic abstractions.

The following categories of emotions are suggested from the century of study on these phenomena. Consideration should be given to expanding or telescoping this list as knowledge of universals of expression is gained.

1.	Passive:	the mask, poker-face
2.	Pleasant:	pleasure, happiness, pleased, love, affection, laughing
3.	Fear:	horror, anxiety, alarm, terror, distress, pain, suffering
4.	Determination:	stubborn, firmness, set
5.	Anger:	hate, dislike, rage
6.	Sorrow:	sad, grief, weeping
7.	Reverential:	respect, worship, religious love
8.	Amazement:	astonishment, surprise, bewilderment, dismay, shock
9.	Contempt:	defiance, scorn, sneer, disdain, disgust, rejection, displeased, disapproval, resentment, "extreme Puritan"
10.	Questioning:	doubt, hesitation, quizzical, shame, puzzlement, disbelief
11.	Thoughtful:	pity, sympathy
12.	Interest:	attention
13.	Boredom:	inattention

One of the problems of constructing a theory of emotions that would be universally applied to human beings is that there is not much data available to Westerners on how non-Western people feel and react to life situations. Darwin suggested cross-cultural studies but, a century later, few are available. It is not difficult to investigate round houses, long houses, and houses with no walls and come up with a complete typology of houses around the world. But how does one probe into the innermost being of persons of other languages to find how they feel? It is probable that even Western dictionaries compiled on other languages of the world reflect the West's system of categorizing emotions and the hierarchy of importance and relationship of these abstract entities to behavioral acts.

Facial expression may portray the actual emotion felt and accurately accompany the speech. On the other hand, facial expression, as with other body language and nonverbal components, may contradict the verbal expression, thus giving the real message. One's facial expression may be practiced and may thus be made convincingly to lie, along with the speech act, about one's real feelings. Ethical behavior and the smooth running of society must be considered. One might question whether or not it is necessary for the politician who hates babies to smile and pat them. On the other hand society might crumble if everyone outwardly declared all emotions at all times. Still, there seems to be an unnecessary amount of inhibition in our still-Victorian society. "Cultured" society often looks with disfavor on expressing real and affective emotions such as admiration, grief, dismay, fear.

One widely used but little discussed expression is the "mask": the lack of expression is the expression. The <u>mask</u> is evident to a large degree in the interrelationships of human beings in discriminatory situations. American black people, women, and butlers are well-practiced in the management of the mask. In extreme situations it is a life-saving device. Meerloo (pp. 21-2) tells of World War II prison experiences where the inmates had to be cautious about their facial expressions:

> The Nazis officially recognized and tortured the silent nonconformists among their prisoners. The stubbornness they purported to read on their prisoners' silent faces was called 'physiognomical insubordination.' Prisoners in their strategy of non-cooperation were not allowed silent protest; they had to look stupidly meek and innocent, otherwise the aggressor feared the silent reproach of his victim.

Another interesting use of the mask is in combination with the double-entendre. A sexual innuendo, for example, spoken with a straight face on television may get by, but accompanied by a leering face it is likely to be censored.

The smile often occurs as a component in a mask expression. Thus people know that they have deceived and have been deceived more often by a smile than by an angry expression, and they are more likely to be suspicious of a smile in other situations. The mask smile is a culturally learned rule. One significant difference between the mask smile and the real one may be physical articulation which can be documented. This has yet to be proven, but Haggard's and Isaac's studies show quicker-than-the-eye facial expressions which seem to be transitional expressions occurring between other acceptable expressions on persons in conflict. By running motion picture films at a very slow pace, these short-lived expressions can be seen on the film. It is believed that they occur so rapidly that they are subliminal.

Several of the studies on facial expression have included differential observations on male and female response in the interpretation of facial expression, the assumption being that women, the "more emotional creature," would respond more accurately to the expression of emotion. After reviewing the several investigations, scholars generally conclude that women do not judge any more intuitively or less analytically than do men.

Artists and clowns have effectively exploited facial expressions and gestures as social weapons and entertainment. The caricature, by distortion, can say what the normal figure is not able to convey. Portrait caricature is not known to have existed before the end of the 16th century, but since then has been used to control leaders and to expose social wrongs (Kris and Gombrich). A final comment regards animal behavior: studies on other primates show them to be uncannily similar in facial expression to human beings. The components are the same: eyes, eyelids, eyebrows, ears, mouth, lips. Facial expressions are described as: grin face, lip-smacking face, pout face, and play face, among other things.

Components of the facial expression. Further analysis of the facial expression requires inspection of each of the elements that make up the total expression. I have synthesized the following from many of the important scholarly studies on facial expression.

FOREHEAD/ BROW	normal, raised, lowered, contracted (knit--troubled--vertical furrows), single brow raised, wrinkled brow (horizontal furrows)
EYES	normal (straight ahead), raised, lowered, to side (averted), wide open, narrowed (squint), rolling, wink/blink/closed
NOSE	normal, dilated (expanded, flare--unilateral, bilateral), wrinkled nose, twitching nose
CHEEKS	inflated (puffed), sucked in, trembling, tongue in cheek
MOUTH	normal, relaxed (droopy), tense (set, compressed), corners up, corners down, retracted (withdrawn), pout (puckered, pursed, protruded), open (smiling), open (gapping), curled lip (scornful)
TONGUE	sticking out tongue, rolling tongue, drooling tongue, lip lick
TEETH	clenched teeth, lip bite
CHIN	anterior thrust, lateral thrust, drop (jaw drop), jaw movement (chewing)

The eyes and the mouth, it is generally agreed, carry the heaviest load of communicative and expressive manifestations. Disagreement comes, however, in deciding which is the more important in signalling. When one begins to think of the infinite number of potential situations and individuals that make up the variables, one could very well come to the conclusion that the question of whether the upper or the lower part of the face is more important is either unanswerable or irrelevant.

The Eye

When the eyes of two persons meet there is a special kind of communication. This special communication is not always desirable. In some cultures the Evil Eye, the direct stare, is one of the worst possible social and/or supernatural offenses. The term eye contact is often used to identify this special relationship. Others have spoken of "visual interaction," "visual reciprocity," or "line of regard." The term "eye lock" has been used, and this term seems to imply a more intimate holding. Eye contact is one of the closest possible relationships. It can be used as a "regulator" in conversations in an informal kind of way, and it can be used in a more precise signal, for example, between the chairman of a meeting and a member who is asking for the floor. At the end of a social evening, couples may signal "Let's go!" only by eye contact.

Eye contact occurs as one of the first steps toward a sexual relationship and this kinesic act might well be one of the universals in human behavior. Artifacts again play a part in eye communication acts. A gentleman once observed that among Westerners a woman who looks at someone above the glass while she is drinking is conveying something beside consuming a beverage. And it is said that eye contact is essential in homosexual identification.

Deaf persons are insistent on eye contact in interactions; they depend heavily on kinesic movement to supplement the "conversation." The avoidance of eye contact also signals something meaningful. Looking away contributes to maintaining psychological distance. Goffman calls this "civil inattention," necessary in crowded elevators and in other situations where a relationship must be kept at a distance. The averted gaze, in normal behavior, also means a submissive acknowledgment in the relationship, typical, perhaps of the Biblical woman who knew her place!

While the averted eye is common among normal persons in conversation, particularly with the one speaking, it occurs in non-normal behavior in exaggerated forms. Other eye behaviors are symptoms of abnormalities in human beings, such as excessive blinking, depressed look, dramatic gaze, guarded gaze, and absent gaze (Riemer). The quality and quantity of eye contact is a good measure of discriminatory attitude, and with it, other persons are either excluded or included in the "in" group. The awkwardness of a transition stage in accepting heretofore excluded human beings into an "in" group was poignantly articulated by one of the first female students to enter Princeton University:

> I've found myself a witness to (and, admittedly, a participant in) an awkward but amusing ritual developing on campus throughout these last few days. There are any number of variations, but basically the performance goes something like this: Two students, one male and one female, approximately 50 yards apart and walking toward

> one another on the same path, catch sight of each other. Eye contact lasts for maybe 10 more yards. Then, one or both find something of immense interest (like a tree or a fire hydrant) to contemplate along the way. By Pass-Point minus 15 feet the neck begins to be cramped with side-to-side maneuvers, and the gaze shifts to one's feet. With about four feet to go eye contact is re-established and the eyes then determine whether the remaining distance is to be covered with a smile, a hello, or a silence....[26]

While the physiological eye may be scientifically understood, the perceptual eye is only beginning to be explored. See Hall (1966, Chapter VI, "Visual Space") for an important discussion of his and Gibson's ideas on the perception of the visual world. Hall, who has made significant contributions to the study of space (proxemics), has seen the relationship of space to eye behavior and has defined four distances: intimate, personal, social, and public. In the same book he makes critical cross-cultural observations on the eye behavior of the English and the American, as well as the Arab.

The function of the wink in communication is widespread through time and space. A Chinese novel of the Early Ching period describes a murder hearing where a secretary signaled to the Prefect with a wink, "He realized that the secretary obviously wished to communicate something of importance to him...."[27] Greenwald, in his psychoanalytic study of call girls, describes their language which, in some sense, is also a secret language: "Frequently when they use ordinary words, the inflection or the emphasis or the accompanying winks give them special meaning."[28]

Blinking can also function as a communicative act but here one must think also of automatic reflex and the inherent difficulty of labeling which is which. The blink frequency can be a measure of tension, or even of sobriety as some researchers have concluded (Ponder and Kennedy). Small doses of alcohol increase the number of blinks temporarily and large doses slow the blinking to a dead stop. But there probably are more useful devices than counting the blinks for a wife to discover where her wandering husband has been!

The Mouth

The mouth is a remarkable communicator, both on obvious and subtle levels, but as indicated before, it has hardly been explored by linguists who study sound in language. Nevertheless, the person's mood, position, place in the room (or outside), and distance from the hearer, all contribute to the production and reception of the sound. Shouting outside would require opening up the mouth to an unusual size and shape; this behavior would have to be interpreted as psychotic if such mouth movement took place in a quiet social setting or a library. Besides effecting speech, it is also a ceaselessly twitching, turning, opening organ that often manifests the most subliminal responses of the psyche. In fact, most mouth movement is not associated with sound at all. If the eyes are the "windows of the soul," certainly the mouth is the very door.

The smile has been reported to be the first gesture that a baby makes. The facial movement which produces the smile also affects the cheeks; Darwin speaks of the "smiling cheeks" of a man who meets an old friend. Brannigan and Humphries (p. 44), in their studies on the smile, give three classifications: (1) a simple smile, (2) the upper smile, and (3) the broad smile. Cross-cultural observations on the smile attest that it is not an indication of pleasure alone. The Japanese smile is an often cited example. Klineberg writes (1935, p. 285-6):

> Lafcadio Hearn ... has remarked that the Japanese smile is not necessarily a spontaneous expression of amusement, but a law of etiquette, elaborated and cultivated from early times. It is a silent language, often seemingly inexplicable to Europeans, and it may arouse violent anger in them as a consequence. The Japanese child is taught to smile as a social duty, just as he is taught to bow or prostrate himself; he must always show an appearance of happiness to avoid inflicting his sorrow upon his friends. The story is told of a woman servant who smilingly asked her mistress if she might go to her husband's funeral. Later she returned with his ashes in a vase, and said, actually laughing, 'Here is my husband.' Her White mistress regarded her as a cynical creature; Hearn suggests that this may have been pure heroism.

Other scholars of Japanese culture corroborate that smiling in Japan is "not traditionally associated with good humor or a friendly attitude but rather with embarrassment and social discomfort, or even, in extreme instances, with genuine tragedy and sorrow, or with repressed anger."[29] As a result, the Japanese stewardess on an overseas airline finds irresolvable conflict in greeting passengers with a traditional Japanese polite phrase, which would require a poker face, and at the same time manifesting the warm hospitality of the West, which requires a winning smile.

The <u>grin</u> and the <u>grimace</u> must be distinguished from the smile. Is it the physical components, i.e., the particular muscles and flesh involved, or is it the interpretation that various cultures and sub-cultures put upon the identification of these? One person's smile is another person's grin. The grimace, in contrast to the movement made by a tic, is voluntary and within the control of the person who does it. <u>Pouting</u> is a well-known kinesic act of children. Darwin reports that it could be commonly observed in adult behavior among the Kafirs and in New Zealand among the Maoris.

<u>Sticking out the tongue</u> among the children of Western cultures is a widely-known expression of insult. Adult behavior is more circumscribed; one has to be alone in front of the mirror to stick out the tongue at someone one despises or is frustrated with. Protruding the tongue, however, has other meanings. It is a component of a negative response among the aborigines in Queensland and Gipp's land where a negative is expressed by throwing the head a little backwards and putting out the tongue (Darwin, p. 274). And in other cultures its meaning varies (La Barre 1947, pp. 56-7):

> In Bengali statues of the dread black mother goddess Kali, the tongue is protruded to signify great anger and shock; but the Chinese of the Sung dynasty protruded the tongue playfully to pretend to mock terror, as if to 'make fun of' the ridiculous and unfeared anger of another person. Modern Chinese, in South China at least, protrude the tongue for a moment and then retract it, to express embarrassment at a <u>faux pas</u>.

Eibl-Eibesfeldt has filmed tongue play as a flirt gesture, combined with eyebrow flash among the Waika of Brazil, where it has a more ritualized form than the tongue play which occurs in Europe in flirtation (in Argyle and Exline, p. 13). Tongue movements may take place naturally when one is thinking deeply or preoccupied with writing or silent reading--such behavior when one is alone is known as "autistic behavior."

Jaw movement also occurs in moments of concentration, and in addition when the person is carrying on some activity with an opening-closing motion. It is common for a mother to open her mouth when feeding the baby. Novice barbers have been seen to work their jaw while using the hair clippers or scissors. "Dropping one's jaw" occurs during speechless moments of surprise or horror.

The Nose

In 1672 Ghiradelli commented on the function of the nose in communication (Mantegazza, p. 12). He observed that the nose helps to manifest passion and contempt with various twitches and nostril movement and that when we want to make fun of and mock another, the nose contributes to the communication act. Indeed, it is often associated with distasteful, or negative ideas. In the sign language of the deaf, signs made in proximity to or touching the nose often have reference to derogatory ideas, for example, "lousy, punk, no good." The nose, however, figures in other kinesic acts such as autistic gestures. And as a sign of friendship among the Maori at the turn of the century, one doubled the forefinger of the right hand and placed the projecting second joint on the tip of the nose. A gesture very similar to Western nose thumbing was used by the Todas to mean respect (Klineberg, 1935, pp. 286-7).

The reader is reminded not to think of any of these elements of facial expression as isolated entities, but as parts of the accompaniments and supplements to speech events. They may act as sentence markers, enforcers, or contradictory indications, but all contributing to the message.

Other Body Movement

This category comprises all the rest of body movement which does not fall under posture and facial expression. The hands, of course, are of paramount interest here with a seemingly endless array of possibilities which different cultures utilize in various ways. In some cultures specific hand gestures number in the hundreds, including those with lexical meaning as well as the range of emotive accompaniments used to reinforce speech.

Movement of the head conveys various meanings depending upon the tilt, uprightness, thrust from the body, and side movement. Birdwhistell (1970, p. 100) has abstracted three types of head nods which occur during interaction with another person. The use of these three is a systematic pattern which is responded to by the speaker, in terms of (a) continuing in the same vein of conversation, (b) elaborating a point and increasing the rate of vocalization, or (c) changing the subject. Head nod occurs in regular patterns with the phenomena of hesitation and linguistic stress.

Movement of the legs and feet may seem to be farfetched components of communication, but colleagues who are authorities on the deaf sign language report that the whole body is desirable for communication. One scholar recalled an incident which took place at a conference for the deaf. The non-deaf speaker had interpreters on both sides of the platform in front of the audience. The place for the interpreter had been elaborately rigged up with a large boxlike structure which showed the interpreter's body only from the waist up. The deaf "listeners" objected because they could not get the whole message.

Physiology

Regular Physiological Functions

The category of regular physiological functions includes the necessary acts of locomotion, breathing, eating, drinking, and sleeping, and the functions involved in body elimination and sexual behavior. The physiological systems and the nonverbal communication systems function together, at times overlapping and coinciding. Sometimes one is dominant and another time the other is dominant--but always interdependent--never one without the other. The interpersonal behavior between human beings is very much evident in physiological events and to a great extent determines their style and when and where they will be performed. Lashley, eminent scientist of the preceding generation, acknowledged the relationship between physiology and behavior.

Anthropologists and psychiatrists likewise have recognized the relationship, saying, in effect, that "even the noises which inevitably accompany ... physiologic activities [are] more than just accidental byproducts of behavior" (Ostwald 1963, p. ix).

The many ways in which the regular physiological functions are performed show widely varying stylized differences in various cultures of the world. In order to interpret body language correctly, it is requisite to be familiar with the normal functions in normal behavior. Only then can deviations be correctly identified and understood in communication. In performing bodily functions, what may be deviant behavior in one culture may be straightforward, acceptable behavior in another; what is normal to one people may be unheard of on another continent.

Locomotion includes all the varieties of getting from one place to another, such as walking, running, skipping, and hopping. Although authorities in dance and physical education have studied them extensively, the body movement of walking, for example, has never been successfully analyzed in terms of a general theory that could apply to all cultures, that is, one that would transcend the "culture-induced styles of walking" (La Barre 1964, p. 195). Birdwhistell found that relative to their locomotion, persons can be categorized in three ways: the pusher, the puller, and the balancer (1952, p. 68). He further treats various styles of walking: bent-knee types, straight-knee types, bouncers, gliders, high steppers, foot draggers, shufflers, foot stutterers, dippers, choppy walkers, the flat-footed, the trudger, the toe-point flat-footer, the pigeon-toed, and the practicer of the "duck walk" and the "Indian walk." A recent popular song speaks of the various walks that a single person exhibits in different moods, "There's a kind of walk you walk...." The term "gait" in reference to walking implies rhythm and timing even as in the judging of horses in observing the walk, canter, the cadenced trot, and gallop.

Walking contrasts geographically and temporally even within the same racial constituency. Frances Trollope, a British visitor in the early 1800's, described American women, "They do not walk well, nor in fact, do they ever appear to advantage when in movement.... I fancied I could often trace a mixture of affectation and of shyness in their little mincing step, and the ever changing position of the hands." But a critic of the day in turn described her walk:

"[Mrs. Trollope] might be seen ever and anon, in a green calash, and long plaid cloak draggling at her heels ... walking with those colossean strides unattainable by any but English women."[30]

The act of breathing cannot be considered, of course, apart from control of air movement which was discussed in the previous chapter. In speech and paralanguage, the production of vocal noises is controlled by physiological behavior, with a great deal of interaction. The effects of emotion on breathing result in special effects on language and paralanguage.* Irregular breathing breaks the syllable rhythm of language; holding the breath introduces extra-linguistic pauses; emotional behavior may cause ingressive speech articulation instead of the usual inhaling for breath. The startle reflex usually results in held breath and then an increased rate of breathing, perhaps with irregular rhythms. This says more than the words uttered. Breathing, then, can be described in terms of timing, speed, rhythm, and regularity, as well as noise--quiet to loud. All of these convey various emotional and attitudinal meanings.

Breathing is a sociological as well as a physiological phenomenon (Krout 1942, p. 261):

> Breathing is a simple enough culture trait, socially regarded. Yet the form, as seen when one is faced by an examining committee, when one expects the birth of a baby, when one is in the presence of the dead, or when a trained singer delivers an operatic aria, is obviously complex.

A form of breathing, or sniffing, is a component of affection and/or greeting in some cultures, particularly India (Hopkins). Hall describes Arab communication and its "mutual bathing in the warm moist breath during conversation...." To deny a friend your breath is to act ashamed. But the Arabs are also conscious of bad breath and guard against offending (1966, pp. 148-9).

Various customs stemming from ancient beliefs which connected the breath and soul or spirit may still be seen in some cultures. Some American Indians may cup the hand over the mouth during laughter and cover the mouth before going out into the night air. It was reported long ago, among the Seminoles of Florida, that when a mother was dying, her infant was held over her face to receive her spirit (Tylor, 1873, pp. 16-17). Breath rites were used in cures among the Caddo Indians.[31] Controlled breathing is seen at its best during the performance of an athlete, dancer, auctioneer, or opera singer ... or the astronauts as they approach the moon.

Eating or drinking with much noise may be a matter of good etiquette in some cultures; for example, in China and Japan tea must be drawn in with considerable ingressive friction noise to show appreciation. The same is true of the Navaho people, but in addition, after swallowing, the breath is expelled in an aspirated "aaahh" which indicates appreciation and enjoyment. Older men may exaggerate this supplement. In a recreational, tension-releasing activity, young men in a certain college which is otherwise respectable, hold an annual jello-slurping contest.

Sleeping posture is determined in part by the bed, mat, or hammock, and the number of persons involved. As was noted earlier, there are few descriptions on the normal sleeping habits and postures of human beings. The following are some observations on Navaho sleeping habits (Bailey, pp. 211-2):

> The usual sleeping posture for men and women is on one side, legs either flexed or extended, the head well supported. Occasionally during the daytime a man sleeps on his back, ankles crossed, hands beneath his head, hat over his eyes. Children sleep with little support for the head. If they are put to bed by an adult, they are usually placed on their sides with knees slightly flexed. They often turn to sleep on their backs, arms outflung. No child has been observed sleeping with a hand under the face or head as white children often do. A young child is often put to bed in a nursing position. The mother lies on one side facing the child and cradles him in her arms, patting his buttocks as he nurses. She remains beside him until he falls asleep. One man was observed putting a small boy to sleep by assuming the same nursing position a woman would. The child immediately fell asleep and then the man left him.

Body elimination is more than just a physiological event; it concerns etiquette and other practical matters and customs. The Siriono Indians of Bolivia pick the scabs off their sores and eat them in acceptable behavior. Members of a well-known white-skinned tribe who live on a large body of land between two great waters, blow the waste material from the nose into a white square of cloth, sized according to the sex of the user, and put it in a pocket or bag and carry it around with them all day.

Vomiting is part of the social scene among the Chacobo Indians of Bolivia during their drinking bouts. When they can hold no more they go to the edge of the jungle and vomit, then return to the communal olla and continue drinking. Not to do so is to commit a social breach.

The matter of posture is of concern in body elimination. Depending upon the facilities and customs, male and female may sit, squat or stand to urinate. Peasant women, for example, stand over a hole dug in the ground at a crowded festival in the hinterlands of Europe. Older Navaho women also stand, and African women have been observed standing upright in the village urinating and carrying on a conversation (Samarin, 1969, p. 324). Male postural behavior during urination among the Navahos is differentiated by age groups: young men stand and older men kneel either on one or both knees (Bailey, p. 213).

As an expressive device, youngsters have drawn circles, made crosses, and otherwise run the gamut of possibilities with their streams of water. Young boys use the act as a sign of power--seeing if they can outdo each other in distance reached, "I can do anything better than you can!" Insults are much more potent when articulated by nonverbal means rather than speech. Instead of language, urination toward another, or on another's possessions has been used as an aggressive weapon, "I despise you!" To urinate upon the person of another is an extreme insult in Western cultures. However, such an act may have another meaning. In initiation and curing rituals in Africa, it may indicate a transfer of power (La Barre 1947, p. 56).

The manipulation of flatulent air is much more widely used to communicate than one might suspect. Günter Grass, in a book based on his childhood experiences, describes a particularly hilarious party: "... they're feasting Candlemas with farting and laughter...."[32] Freedman (in Sebeok, Hayes, and Bateson, p. 41) reports farting contests in one of the wards of tuberculosis patients; these "were a principal means of prestige attainment, competition, and communication." This kind of contest apparently occurred in ancient times among the Japanese: "A companion-scroll, The Fart-Battle (He-gassen), is not primarily erotic in nature. It depicts, rather, the ribald account of a legendary 'wind-breaking contest' between two groups of Imperial courtiers."[33] Former military men report that when they were bored with lecture classes they used to amuse themselves and each other by lighting a match to the flatulent gas in a kind of contest to judge the extent and volume of the flame.

Expelling flatus can also be used in an act of insult, as was apparently the intent of the characters in Chaucer's The Miller's Tale. The men of the Royal Air Force found that this was a retort that they could give that was not punishable. Flatulence as an expressive communication of insult or impudence has deep roots in American popular culture. The acceptable public alternative for such an expression is, of course, the Bronx Cheer. A physician reports the behavior of an infant of four months who was frightened by the occurrence of flatulent air until he learned to imitate the sound with his mouth, and thereafter it became a joke (Merrill, p. 222).

Lastly, this physiological act is a pathic means of communication by those who otherwise cannot communicate with other human beings in acceptable manners. Ostwald reports on Patrick, a mentally-retarded youth of twenty-one years: "He also emits audible noises by rectum quite frequently; in fact flatulence constitutes for Patrick an important means for communication since people then notice his stink as well as his noise" (1963, p. 142). Ferenczi (1913) also reports on this practice from emotionally disturbed adult patients. Steig portrays an uninhibited patient in his collection of cartoons, The Lonely Ones.

Sexual functions, again, must be approached with respect to artifacts and posture. The "normal" position and method depends on whichever culture one grew up in. Roheim (p. 228) reports that the Kanakana of Central Australia consider the male in a kneeling position as the natural one. Marriage manuals from India and other non-Western cultures indicate a wide variety of postural behavioral and body movement.

Spontaneous Physiological Acts

Punctiliar physiological acts are of short duration

and may be interjected into speech voluntarily or involuntarily. Spontaneous physiological acts include such things as: coughing, clearing throat, sneezing, spitting, belching, sucking, hiccupping, swallowing, choking, yawning, sighing, scratching, stretching. These have been noted to act as delays in speech in the way of hesitation pauses. In this sense they are extra-linguistic responses in the communication event. They act in conjunction with language and may be interchangeable with the verbal act. Different cultures articulate these physiological acts in various manners. Even within one society various styles can identify status, age, and sex differences. The absence of some of these items, for example, is meaningful. Women don't belch as much as men. Royalty would not be seen scratching in public.

The cough, besides clearing the throat of mucus, may communicate: tension and anxiety, criticism, doubt, surprise, a call to attention, recognition of one's own lies while talking, and various complexes (Feldmen, pp. 239-40). Note the expressions in our language "hesitant cough" and "nervous cough." It has been verified that the cough sounds differently in different cultures. Birdwhistell notes some of these differences (in Sebeok, Hayes, and Bateson, p. 42):

> Take the cough, for instance. The Kutenai Indian could tell the difference between a Kutenai cough and a Shuswap cough. It was a different type of cough and they coughed in a certain way. The Kutenai Indians cough up their nose. This is part of being a decent Kutenai and not to have done so would mean being taken for a damned Shuswap.

Francis Hayes gives a quotation showing the long-established use of the cough in oratory--used by preachers for effect (1957, p. 238).

> The preachers ... looked upon coughing and hemming as ornaments of speech; and when they printed their sermons, noted in the margin where the preacher coughed or hemm'd. This practice was not confined to England, for Oliver Maillard, a Cordelier, and famous preacher, printed a sermon at Brussels in the year 1500, and marked in the margin where the preacher hemm'd once or twice, or coughed [Samuel Butler, *Hudibras*, London, 1907, I, 1, 81-6; editor Henry G. Bohn's note].

The sneeze is well-known in Hungarian folk culture at story-telling time to remind the speaker that the listener is quite aware of the whopper of a lie he is telling! This communicative physiological act was glorified by Kodaly in the folk opera "Háry János" and is probably the only sneeze known to be produced by an orchestra! It is said that during the war, spies could be identified by their sneezes: Germans sneezed with an "atchee!" sound and Americans sneezed with an "atchoo!" sound.

Spitting carries a variety of meanings. It can be used: to seal a bargain (see children's gestures in Chapter VIII); to express contempt or scorn; to express a most intimate relationship, as for example the lovers' exchange of spittle; to express indifference or impotence; or as a component of the ritual that a Japanese gardener partakes in before planting. Guides in Edinburgh point out a place on the pavement near an ancient prison where the prisoners spat in disgust on being released from prison. A more recent example of spitting in disgust was published in a Russian military newspaper, the Red Star, which reported how the Soviet troops reacted when they saw a youth in the Slovak capital of Bratislava kissing his girl friend in public--the Soviet soldiers were "spitting as they watched this scene with disgust."[34] Revulsion is reflected in the English language with such an expression as "to spit out" a vulgar word.

Spitting takes place in religious ceremonies with both negative and positive meanings. A Jewish ceremony was reported to me recently which took place in a private home in order to formally disown the son who married a Christian woman. As the words of rejection were poured forth, the father spit on the picture of his offspring. Spitting has been used by young Caddo Indian boys who were taught never to answer back to father or uncle. When the boy spat, the elder knew he was not listening to the scolding.[35]

Tylor reports on the ancient Roman custom of the nurse touching the lips and forehead of the newborn infant with spittle. In Africa, a medicine man may ritualize a blessing with spit. The Zulus had a religious ceremony which used the spittle collected while dreaming (Tylor, 1873, pp. 525, 233). Among the Navahos, spitting occurs frequently and is done not so much for relief as from habit (Bailey, p. 212):

> The men spit through the teeth in the general di-

> rection of the fire, if indoors. The women lean over and spit onto the ground, using their fingers to wipe the mouth free of saliva. A little dirt is then brushed over the mucus with the fingers to cover it up. Singers lean forward, making ready to spit, and at a suitable moment in the song they spit and continue singing. Though they may miss a word, the song continues on a humming note and there is no break in the rhythm. One singer was timed as spitting every two minutes. Distances vary from two to six feet.

Belching is the acceptable manner of expressing delight in and appreciation of good food in Arabic cultures. It has also been reported among American Indians--without it the hostess is not quite sure that the guests are enjoying the food. In Western cultures belching is not generally accepted as good behavior. Even though we teach our babies to burp when they are learning to eat, we scold them later when they do! An advertisement on television recently declared that "belching cucumbers are out!" and claimed that their product was "burpless pickles." Belching can also be used in sportive spirit for contests; the aforementioned college has an annual "Berger Belch-out," promoted by the dormitory of that name. Medical doctors report belching to be a symptom in certain nervous disorders.

Sucking is an act participated in by: babies, witch-doctors, and the young-in-heart drinking malted milks. Anthropoligists document the sorcerer's practice of pretending to extract objects, such as stones, bones, and balls of hair, from the patient's body by sucking.

Yawning is often interpreted as a sign of boredom in Western cultures, but it is not necessarily so in other societies, where yawning may simply be a spontaneous, natural act.

Automatic Reflex, Instinctive

In order to understand voluntary behavior, the interpreter of body language must be familiar with the range of instinctive behavior which is involuntary. The term "startle pattern" was introduced by Landis and Hunt to refer to the immediate, tense movements characteristic of a fright reaction. This stimulus-response behavior may be instigated by sudden noise, a bright light, an offensive odor, or any sudden movement toward one. Body movements typically include: eye blink, drawing up arms or throwing them out for balance, clenching fists, bending knees, as well as internal reactions concerning the blood pressure, heart rate, sweating, and breathing. The response should be cross-referenced to skin reactions such as blushing, paling, and raising of goose-flesh. Trembling and eye dilatation may occur. Other instinctive responses occur with pain, cold, and heat and these reactions must be differentiated from communicative acts which are voluntary. This is not to say that these responses do not communicate something.

Combinatory--Body Movement and Noise

Except for the physiological noises mentioned previously, the body movement which has been discussed has been a kind of silent language. Besides vocal noise, body language may also produce sounds which communicate. A finger snap, hand clapping, and slapping noises are all produced with one member of the body against another. One can add to this list with a little imagination and some experimentation. Communicative noises are also produced with some member of the body against a by-element such as tapping on the table, stomping feet, playing with keys or bracelets.

German students acknowledge the entrance of the professor by knocking on their desks in unison. At the end of the lecture, they may or may not knock again, depending upon the degree of appreciation for the lecture. A money collector announces the moment to pay by jingling the coins in his pocket or apron--without speech. Indian sign language, which is otherwise a silent language, has some signs which produce noise. One is the sign for "shooting," articulated by one hand hitting against the palm of the other, making a slapping sound. In one evening of performances of Eastern European dancing, I recorded: hand clapping, snapping the fingers, stomping on the floor with feet, and knocking on the floor with knuckles. The exciting noises were produced, sometimes in unison and sometimes in antiphonal response between the dancers.

Kinesic Acts

When Janet Armstrong greeted the public on the day

that her husband, Neill, had just taken those dramatic first steps on the moon, her first communicative message was to raise her hand, crossing her middle finger over the index finger, in the gesture of King's X, meaning "good luck!" The elements used in kinesics which we have just surveyed in the previous pages function in myriads of ways in communicative events.

Some kinesic acts fall into the range of informative or lexical gestures with comparable verbal meaning. Conventional gestures describe or say something either in a pictorial way (such as illustrating a circle or a square with the hands) or in a symbolic way (such as putting two fingers to the mouth for a cigarette). Quantitative gestures showing number, size, and volume give information in this way. Gestures of this type have been called "silent words." These kinesic acts may substitute for the verbal act. The substitute may be a requirement in a society where some verbal items are taboo. Death or a supernatural being may be designated by a gesture rather than speech. Some languages such as Italian and Spanish are extremely rich in vocabulary of the lexical type.

Directive gestures or gestures that elicit a response are kinesic acts which fall into the range of commands (stop!); requests (louder, please); signals (careful!); questions (what?); deictic (over there!); position (down!); response (negation-affirmation). The specific articulation will not be the same in every language, though there may be some near universals, such as "down!" Pointing, for example, is articulated by the lips in some societies where pointing with the finger is taboo.

Another kind of kinesic act is exemplified by emotive movements which express feelings and needs. These may be agreeable or disagreeable; they may be offensive to the point of being obscene, or they may be endearing and affectionate. Some obscene gestures are very old and were previously used to ward off the evil eye or were in some way connected with ancient counter-charms. Though referred to often, offensive gestures have not often been the concern of scholarly studies--no wonder that we understand them so slightly. An exception is a remarkable study by Archer Taylor on the Shanghai gesture, the act of thumbing the nose.

Some kinesic acts are stylized and ritualized. These may be very short as the handshake in greeting behavior.

Or the ritual may carry on for hours or days, as for example, at a rite of passage. They may be personal and social. They may be political, such as the Pledge of Allegiance or the hand sign in oath taking. They may be individual or they may be communal, such as the applause at a public gathering. They may be folk gestures with original meanings lost or they may be contrived for a particular event, such as the V for Victory signal, which burst into wide use during World War II. In any case, kinesic acts figure largely in the interaction between human beings. No society functions without an intricate system of body language.

Tactile Gestures and Movements

A "myth" that dominates U. S. society is that tactile gestures are sexual in nature. There are at least nine other categories of tactile behavior with numerous sub-categories. And undoubtedly more would be found by investigating other cultures. The importance of tactile relationships between human beings has been underestimated because of the inhibitions resulting from the sexual myth. The recent recognition of this importance is sweeping the country now, and Western society is reevaluating tactile communication. Advertisers are in the vanguard, of course. A recent advertisement for clothing says, "Special fringe of very soft brown suede has such pleasant tactility that you can throw away your worry beads!"

The word haptics is used to designate this type of communication in the nonverbal system. Gibson makes a distinction between "active touch" and "passive touch" or being touched. He is particularly interested in the relationship between the tactile and the visual means of communication and has done enough studies and made enough observations to suggest several areas of future research. It is recognized that some cultures use tactile movements more than others. Jourard, for example, gives some startling figures which he gathered during his travels to study this phenomenon. He watched pairs of people conversing in coffee shops in San Juan, Puerto Rico; Paris; London; and in Gainesville, Florida. For one hour he counted the numbers of times the conversants touched. The totals were: San Juan, 180; Paris, 110; London, 0; and Florida, 2.

I have outlined nine general categories where communication is effected by tactile kinesic acts: (1) Greetings and congratulations, (2) Conversation behavior, (3) Ritual and Rites of Passage, (4) Affection, (5) Play, (6) Occupational, (7) Learning or evaluating activity, (8) Manipulation in interpersonal relationships, and (9) Warfare and agression. In greeting behavior, besides the handshake of many varieties, there are many different types, depending upon the times and the places. One can recall the "Kissin' cousins," the abrazo or bear-hug given between Spanish speakers, and the old Hebrew "Greet one another with a holy kiss." The conversation of the Eastern Jews was noted by Efron (p. 90) to be replete with tactile interchange, pulling at each other's sleeves or clothes; "... its extreme case makes itself apparent, in a rather ludicrous way, when the two participants in the gestural fencing become clamped to each other's hands or coat-lapels, and fight out the battle by means of head motions only." The deaf also make more use of tactile communication, though for different reasons, of course. As mentioned previously, they pay acute attention to the face, and thus may call attention by touching to make the person look when they want to talk.

Tactile behavior expresses closeness and special consideration in certain kinds of relationships where affection is exchanged. With infants tactile behavior is thought to be important for their development, especially in speech and cognitive processes. Social grooming is a kind of affectionate communication. The bride receives redundant grooming from her attendants. Combing of hair takes place between close friends and adults and children. American Indians pluck lice from off each other. In South America I have seen them lined up, sometimes in pairs, sometimes three or four in line, picking out the lice and grooming each other outdoors on pleasant days.

The category of "play" comprises a wide range from very informal bantering and exchange to contact sports, though the latter should be at least cross-referenced to the occupational category. Games among children involve much physical contact. Feldman discusses tickling as a special form of communication and notes the differences between touch and tickling. Tickling, for example, is rhythmic, and one doesn't tickle oneself. Studies on tickling go back at least to 1840.

Occupational forms of tactile behavior include the performance of professionals, such as the barber, doctor, dentist, and the therapist, where it is their role to touch.

Business and marketing often require a secret communication which occurs as hand and finger gestures under a cloth, as in a Chinese market or teahouse. Tactile finger communication among the Mongolian horse traders took place inside their long sleeves.

Learning and evaluation activity is enhanced by tactile input. The fingers of children have been called the ten greatest explorers, and teachers have capitalized on this phenomenon by teaching the alphabet in raised letters, or letters with different textures, such as sandpaper or velvet. Style experts touch cloth before buying it; the tobacco buyer walks along the rows of tobacco fingering the leaves to appraise it. Art museums are permitting the public to touch some objects to better appreciate creativity and textures: bronze feels different from crystal.

The manipulation of interpersonal relationships is expedited by tactile expression. Often this relationship involves the need to demonstrate authority. Discipline is more effective with small children by tactile means. In the courtroom the police personnel holds the arm of a young man brought in for trial. Authority is demonstrated in different ways in different societies. Wife beating is expected in some areas of Eastern Europe and among some American Indians. And among the Ulster Scots, wife-beating was not unheard of; in an early account of the Presbyterians, one John Cowen was made to "stand opposite the pulpit, and confess his sins, in the face of the public, of beating his wife on the Lord's Day."[36] Apparently it was all right to beat his wife on any other day! Puberty beatings also define the roles of members of societies. The control of the mentally ill and the apprehension of criminals necessitate tactile acts. Kinesic acts which are tactile are necessary when the verbal event and visual contact are not possible, as in communication with the blind. And the parachutist is touched, or even pushed out, by the person in control of operations. Rescue missions and defensive measures use tactile behavior between persons who otherwise don't touch.

It must be obvious by now, that many of these categories overlap and should be cross-referenced. Human behavior defies classification.

Autistic Gestures and Movements

Walter Midi personified autistic behavior. Autistic gestures are self-directed. They have been said to be "meaningless," but we have already indicated that every movement has some kind of meaning and if observed and analyzed can be seen to be a part of the communication act. Autistic thinking, or day-dreaming, is a means of adapting to the world around us. It is a rehearsal of the past and the future and everyone participates. Autistic behavior is different when one is completely alone, and when one is alone but there is a possibility of another entering the room.

Autistic and tactile gestures and movements are different in kind from other gestures because they affect the optical *and* tactile senses while gestures affect only the optical senses. Another difference in autistic gestures is that they are almost entirely emotive in nature and not lexical or informative. Their function is a release of tension or expression of some kind. We don't go around raising our hand to ask permission to talk to ourselves! Or we don't wave our hand to greet ourselves in the morning!

Laughter is significantly less frequent or even absent in autistic behavior. Laughter is a group activity, a social gesture which does not occur usually with one person (Coser). The relationship can be seen with tickling--one does not tickle oneself; again, some activities are of necessity communal, or at least two-people activities. Therefore the range of autistic behavior is limited by this restriction.

The By-Elements of kinesic behavior, artifacts, clothes, and hair, are particularly significant in autistic activity. Rings, bracelets, watch-chains, beads, and recently, stones, are fondled--even to the point of breaking them! At times, autistic movements are practiced to the extreme. Playing with hair may end up by the disturbed person pulling it out by patches. Scratching, when it doesn't itch, is a manifestation of aggression. Mahl has made six observations on scratching (1968, pp. 314-5):

> (a) It commonly occurs in this context [i.e., aggression] in everyday interaction. (b) The act of scratching the body wall signifies "anger" in the sign language of the deaf (Long, 1944). (c) An occasional instruction in the pantomime literature uses scratching to represent the state of inhibited

anger (e.g., Pardoe, 1931, Pantomime No. 79). (d) We find that Shakespeare used the word "scratch" and hence allied imagery 26 times in his plays. In 16 instances the meaning is "aggression." In one instance (Julius Ceasar, II, i, 237-47), he even has Brutus scratching himself when in a state of inhibited anger. (I wish to thank Steve Ford for his assistance in reviewing Shakespeare's use of scratch). (e) Laura Nader, the anthropologist at the University of California, Berkeley, showed me a film of a young Zapotec-Mexican man standing trial in a village near Oaxaca. At the outset he engaged in prolonged agitated self-scratching. Soon he was leaning across the magistrate's desk, jabbing a pencil at the table-top. Prof. Nader was present at the trial and confirmed my inference that he had changed from a state of inhibited to freely expressed anger. (f) A patient scratched herself as she dreamt of murder.

The autistic behavior of normal people is difficult to study--I find few references--because, by definition, it is impossible to collect data, except from the abnormal who are unaware of another presence, and from oneself. Apparently few scholars are willing to describe their own autistic behavior in print.

Chapter V: SENSORY COMMUNICATION

All the sensory phenomena known to man can serve as channels of communication in informative and expressive behavior. The various modalities generally recognized are:

1. Acoustical
2. Optical
3. Tactual
4. Chemical
5. Electrical

The acoustical channel serves the auditory senses and is the means of carrying language and paralanguage. The optical channel receives communication by kinesic acts. These two, of course, carry the heaviest load of verbal and nonverbal communication. The other modalities can be considered subsidiary. The tactual channel is the means of receiving and sending tactile and autistic gestures and all contact body movement. The optical senses can also receive these kinesic acts. The chemical channel serves the olfactory and gustatory senses, thus permitting response to odors and flavors. The electrical channel carries certain vibrations and sensations that are little understood but widely acknowledged. This kind of communication is referred to as Extra Sensory Communication, among other things.

While all of these contribute to the communicative stream, it isn't clear yet in what ways they coordinate, overlap, emphasize, substitute for, and contradict each other. The explicit relationship of speech to paralanguage and kinesic behavior is of paramount interest to me as a linguist interested in communication. Chemical and electrical modalities also are present when speech occurs, preceding, following, and supplementing the interaction of human beings. But they are different in kind and so far have not been worked into any model of nonverbal behavior coordinate with verbal behavior. Birdwhistell (1964) believes that they are "sub-systems of communication, in some way interdependent with the visual and the auditory modalities and equivalently important to the final comprehension of communication." He speaks of multi-channel redundancy and multi-channel reinforcement. Wiener boldly speaks of "organ language" or "organ jargon" in his discussion of the chemical channels as communicators (pp. 3154-6). He suggests that the alphabet of this language is made up of individual chemicals, and words consist of mixtures of these chemicals. He further hypothesizes on the syntax of this language, the manner in which the words are put together.

It is difficult to imagine any of these modalities articulating in isolation; rather, it is assumed that two or more always operate together. The opera singer's eyebrows may go up with the high notes. Gestures are more expansive with loud speech. Certain odors change the facial expression. A blush accompanies silence which intrudes into the dialogue.

Cultures and individuals utilize the modalities in infinite ways and combinations. Hierarchies are established with varied emphasis according to the behavioral event and the language spoken. The tactual channel ranks high in a love duet and low in a business dialogue. The optical channel ranks high with deaf speakers and is non-existent in telephone conversations. Eye contact, the optical channel receiving and sending, ranks high in some encounters and is taboo in certain relationships, for example some kinship relationships in African societies. American negro men were lynched or castrated for using this modality with white women; white men were not similarly punished for using the same optical channel. Hymes (Gumperz and Hymes, pp. 26, 29fn. 10) cites an example of high tactual rank in a ritual performed by an American Indian witch doctor: the master curer may delegate the verbal act but not the tactile act. The Arab people make more use of the tactual and olfactory channels than Americans (Hall 1966, pp. 2-3). Hall says that people in different cultures "inhabit different sensory worlds." He describes the sensory apparatus in terms of space (pp. 39-47): the distance receptors--those concerned with examination of distant objects, i.e., the eyes, the ears, and the nose; and the immediate receptors--those used to examine the world close up, i.e., the world of touch, the sensations we receive from the skin, membranes, and muscles.

In the discussion of the Model in Chapter II it was seen that the Signal may include certain olfactory experiences such as perfume and incense. These signals, along with others, comprise a group of items which are indirect communication. In space (in another room) and in time (after the crowd has left), they may continue emitting their fragrance, for example, a vase of flowers, or incense left at the temple. In this way they are different from body odors which convey something during speech acts or during silences between them.

In the consideration of the effect of nonverbal phenomena on the structure of language, some intriguing anecdotes would suggest that research would be fruitful in these areas. Wentworth and Flexner state that the basic metaphors depend on the five senses. Would this be the case in all languages?

> The basic metaphors, at any rate, for all levels of language depend on the five senses. Thus rough, smooth, touch; prune, sour puss, sweet; fishy, p.u., rotten egg; blow, loud; blue, red, square. In slang, many metaphors refer to touch (including the sense of heat and cold) and to taste.[37]

In some languages the verbal categories are rich in certain nonverbal events. In India, for example, the yoga system has developed an elaborate postural terminology and rationale, according to Hewes (1955, p. 242), whereas in English, the terminology is sparse: there seems to be only one vocabulary alternative for standing, that is, leaning. In English, the olfactory vocabulary is also deficient to the point of neglect. Wescott calls this "olfactory blindness" (1969, p. 327).

Other sensory phenomena have been noted in certain structural entities, for example the visual, auditory, chemical, and tactile channels of nonverbal communication are represented by a group of verbs: seem, appear, resemble, look, taste, feel, smell, sound. This set of verbs works together in a certain syntactical relationship, as I have pointed out in a previous article (1970). Bolinger (1969) discusses some acoustical and optical verbs in a cross-cultural treatment. The recognition of all the modalities operating in the communication between human beings will surely bring more understanding in the future.

The Olfactory Sense

> I remember my childhood names for grasses and secret flowers ... --how people looked and walked and smelled even. The memory of odors is very rich.
>
> --John Steinbeck[38]

All human beings have an odor and any assumption otherwise simply means that one is used to it and no longer aware of it. Body odors are not necessarily unpleasant. I have poignant memories of the smoky, pungent fragrance of freshly bathed American Indians while sitting around the ground fire making tortillas. The reasons for the different odors of different races and peoples within a race are not clearly understood. The differences have been attributed to diet, tobacco, geography, occupation and other variables. The scent of an individual has been called his "olfactory signature." Mosquitos have known for a long time that some persons smell more delicious than others (Wiener, p. 3155) and that the attractiveness of women varies with the stage of the menstrual cycle, in direct proportion to the rate of excretion of estrogens.

It is an established fact that the olfactory channel ranks high in the sexual interaction among human beings and animals. A recent monograph on insect sex attractants (Wiener, p. 3156) contains 400 references! The olfactory senses are affected in a wide range of sexual involvement--e.g., menstruation, pregnancy, lactation, puberty, and coitus (Fabricant, Kalogerakis, Kloek, Krebs, Wiener, and see others in Wiener's list of references). Róheim describes the sexual life of the Western tribes of Central Australia and refers often to their word aruntijima, which has connotations of kissing, smelling and touching. Smelling is apparently an aspect of adolescent exploration among these people. "The boys described their practice of putting their fingers into a girl's vagina or anus and then smelling them by [aruntijima] ..." (p. 237).

Olfactory emissions signal hate and anger. Olfactory reception of foul odors can change behavior as recorded by Ostwald (1963, pp. 96-102), who noted a tremendous amount of kinesic activity triggered by a vile and irritating smell during an experiment. Olfactory sensations also play an important part in the expression of affection. Many languages have a single word for kiss and smell. Lin Yutang brings to attention the relatively high rank of the olfactory in the hierarchy of sense modalities in the Chinese culture:

> The refined olfactory sense is reflected in the Chinese cuisine and in the fact that, in Peking, one speaks of kissing a baby as 'smelling' a baby, which is what is done actually. The Chinese literary language has also many equivalents of the French odeur de femme, like 'flesh odor' and 'fragrance from marble' (a woman's body).[39]

Hopkins uses the term sniff-kiss which implies this same act in his well-documented study of the varied expressions of affection in ancient India. For example, upon returning from a journey a father sniffs at the head of his children. This token of devotion is used within the family, between friends of the same sex, and by older people to children.

Differences in the use of the olfactory channels by the young and the old have been demonstrated by Moncrieff, and Chalke and Dewhurst. There is a greater tolerance of unpleasant smells with the very old and the very young than with the group in between. There are peaks of liking or disliking at different age levels. Children are less appreciative of flower odors than are adults; children enjoy fruity odors much more than adults do. The odor emitted by schizophrenic patients has been observed by many and studied by a few, for example Smith and Sines. Schizophrenics also appear to have heightened reception to olfactory experiences (Hoffer and Osmond), though there is some disagreement as to whether this is indeed increased sensitivity or olfactory hallucinations, much on the same order as auditory and visual hallucinations.

Another non-normal situation would be the blind person's use of the olfactory channel as an added source of information. The experiences of Helen Keller are worth repeating (Bedichek, Hicks, Wiener, Sebeok 1967):

> The dear odors of those I love are so definite, so unmistakable, that nothing can obliterate them. If many years should elapse before I saw an intimate friend again, I think I should recognize his odor instantly ... [Bedichek, p. 125].

Miss Keller used the term "personality scent" to describe

the body odors of individuals:

> Some people have a vague, unsubstantial odor that floats about, mocking every effort to identify it. It is the will-o'-the-wisp of my olfactive experience. Sometimes I meet one who lacks a distinctive person-scent, and I seldom find such a one lively or entertaining. On the other hand, one who has a pungent odor often possesses great vitality, energy, and vigor of mind [Bedichek, p. 125].

She also notes differences between male and female odors.

A professional perfumer is another kind of "prodigy of smell." It is interesting to note that there is a wide gap between this area of olfactory concern, where it is considered a work of art, and experimental investigation by professional persons who consider it a work of science (Wiener).

Cross-cultural information regarding the use of olfaction in different societies is scarce. A most beautiful description of the intricate involvement of breath-odor-and-friendship among the Arabs is given by Hall (1966, p. 149-50).

The Totonac Indians of central Mexico appear to rank the olfactory channel highly, or at least their language structure would indicate that at one time they might have. A very large vocabulary is concerned with kinds of smell; these single words in Totonac have to be glossed with longer expressions in English. There are eight basic stems for different varieties of smells, and these occur with a number of suffixal formatives. Herman Aschmann has collected the following list:

1.	<u>mú·kɬún</u>	a pleasant smell, as of flowers or food.
	<u>mú·qšún</u>	the smell of corn mush which has too much lime.
	<u>mú·ksún</u>	the smell of mint, parsley, tobacco, Sloan's liniment.
	<u>mú·kún</u>	the smell of raw beans and unripe fruit, with a related meaning of a puckery taste.
2.	<u>púksa</u>	the smell of a skunk, a dead dog, foul meat, manure.
	<u>púqša</u>	the smell of mold or mushrooms.

	pukɬa	the smell of human excrement and rotten things.
3.	haksa	the smell of alcohol, camphor, burnt chile, dust just settled by a rain.
	haqɬa	the smell of urine, certain medicines, and ashes.
	hakša	the smell of citrus fruits, especially the skins.
4.	c̓i·k̓i·n	the smell of perfume, scented soap, sometimes with the definite pejorative implication of a nice smell but in the wrong place, e.g. in speaking of effeminate men who use perfume.
5.	skunka	the smell of metals, mice, fish, and snakes.
	squnqa	the smell of some fish and dirty feet.
	ɬkunka	the smell of grease and fat.
6.	šq̓uta	the smell of leather, sweat, an open sore, and walls that have been damp for a long time.
	šk̓uta	the smell of anything sour, e.g. vinegar.
7.	šk̓iha	the smell of savory, tasty food.
	šq̓aha	the smell of burnt gunpowder, firecrackers, and rockets.
8.	kinkalah	a smell, usually bad, which has permeated an area.[40]

Frazer (1919, Vol. 3, p. 379) relates the use of olfaction in ordeals in Central Africa. In order to discover who has participated in cannibalism, the witch doctor dances up and down in a state of frenzy before the assembled people, smelling their hands to discover the scent of the human flesh they are thought to have consumed. And somewhere I read that in Africa there are some people who are known to "smell their way to water in the desert." Even if the idea is not to be taken literally, it has some significance in the rank importance of modalities among different peoples.

The reference to race odors is often found in the context of discrimination. But the discrimination is not only to race. Where religion was concerned, "The Catholics insisted that they could not live side by side with Protestants because of the heretics' smell. When they accepted each other, the smell mysteriously disappeared."[41]

In the domains of directing human behavior, the institution of advertising in the United States has been highly successful. Advertising has, in some cases, appealed to the olfactory sense--scented writing paper, for example, "to expand his awareness of you, arouse another dimension of your mystique!" Poets and artists have long recognized the value of appeals to the senses. They are particularly sensitive to a wide range of expressive behavior. Walt Whitman is often quoted for his sensitivity to odors; his now-famous armpits, the scent of which is an "aroma finer than prayer." Rupert Brooke's "The Great Lover" is an overflow of sensuous memories.

Cutaneous Response

> I do not remember ever having had the itch; yet scratching is one of the sweetest gratifications of nature, and as ready at hand as any. --Montaigne (1533-1592)[42]

Cutaneous reactions are well known in response to pain and to warmth and cold. To other behavioral effects, the skin also gives evidence. While scientists analyze blushing and paling, perspiring, and horripilation, it is the folklore and literature that tells the behavioral conditions of these expressions of communication. It is often thought that reactions of this type are strictly involuntary. While it isn't clear just how physiology and emotion interact, it is well known that people in different cultures blush and pale for different reasons--what embarrasses one people will not embarrass another. Emotions affect the physiology differently over time and social circumstances even in one culture. Altschule speaks of the 19th-century fevers which affected men and women disappointed in love or ambition who were of delicate breeding, but these fevers were not noted among the peasants. Girls are supposed to blush more than boys, but Feldman says that actually men blush more than women!

Emotional perspiration was recognized in the 16th century by von Elbogen (Altschule, p. 51): "Many an one sweats for fear and thinks he has the English sweat, and when he afterwards hath slept it off acknowledges that it was all nonsense." Scholars now recognize "three general categories of sweat glands: the glands in the palms and soles, which respond well only to psychic stimuli; those of the axillae and forehead, which respond to both thermal and psychic stimuli; and those on the rest of the body, which respond almost entirely to thermal stimuli" (Montagna, p. 364). Hall has examined the work of Barnes on infrared-radiant energy and related these thermal responses to emotional situations, such as differences of temperature of dancing partners and in crowded situations. Hall (1966, pp. 52-57) speaks of "thermal space" and "tactile space" along with his other concepts of visual, auditory, and olfactory space.

The possibilities of communication by cutaneous sensations are further being explored by Geldard and colleagues. Subjects are taught an alphabet much like the Morse Code, and after some training are able to receive messages through the skin.

The act of blushing has received the most varied attention by far, from poet to psychoanalyst. Folklore about women tells us that "Blushing is virtue's color," and on the other hand, psychiatrists have claimed that "Women are ashamed and blush for not being men." Darwin devotes a chapter to the study of blushing. He believed that infants and old people didn't blush. He noted that Laura Bridgman, born deaf and blind, did blush. But all of these studies and observations need to be brought up to date--particularly with regard to blushing in different cultures and races.

Cutaneous phenomena should be cross-referenced with gestures for affection, gestures of defense, children's play, and other obvious interaction of human beings, as well as autistic gestures.

Chapter VI: THE FUNCTION OF SILENCE in Communication[43]

> Silence is the perfectest herald of joy;
> I were but little happy, if I could say how much.
> --Claudio, *Much Ado About Nothing* (II, i)

This chapter is devoted to *silence*--not for silence as an end, but for the *communication* which silence imparts. Silence is not empty; it is filled with meaning, as implied by a recent popular song, "The Sounds of Silence." Silence illustrates again the antitheses of human behavior. It can have quite opposite meanings: consent and no consent; acceptance and rejection; love and hate. The interpretation of these meanings is dependent on the context of situation and motivation of those involved. Silence, as with other elements of nonverbal acts, is culturally defined. Samarin (1965) discusses some cross-cultural differences of the Gbeya people of the Central African Republic. Silence is indulged in freely there with no embarrassment for not filling in the conversation with empty chatter. Silence is looked upon as an effective device in interaction, for the Gbeya believes that it is speech--not silence--which gets a person in trouble! Silence is obligatory while eating, especially while guests are present. Conversation takes place after the meal. Also during "sick calls," silence is expressly adhered to; Gbeya friendship and solidarity with the sick one is communicated by silence.

Silence is often thought of as *nothing*. However, it does communicate *something*--it supplements the speech act, for example. Instead of words, it can convey respect, as in the presence of a great person or an elder, or at a funeral or coronation; comfort, to a distressed loved one who wants to be quiet; companionship, when watching a sunset;

support, when a toddler is learning to tie a shoe; rejection, when a black employee wants to join the office chatter; reprimand, as to a child, or a peer when words would be too embarrassing; consent, as in answer to a challenging statement; and no consent, as an unspoken answer.

A clear distinction must be made in identifying silence in linguistic or verbal structures, and silence in nonverbal acts. Silence is essential to the organization of speech, and in this use is labeled juncture or pause, as discussed in Chapter III. The difference between "I scream" and "ice cream," "night rate" and "nitrate" is that less-than-a-second speck of silence (or juncture) that all native speakers hear without difficulty. In contrast, nonverbal silence or the hesitation phenomenon, as it has already been called, occurs in larger chunks and sometimes at places where linguistic juncture would not occur. The insertion of hesitation phenomena in speech adds another meaning to the communication event. Further contrast between speech and silence must be acknowledged, as for example, the omission of a response (refusing to answer a question) and the absence of anything required.

When making tape recordings, one becomes aware of how extensively silence occurs in conversation. The playback reveals long periods of silence that are not noticed in the face-to-face interaction because they are filled with continuing gestures and facial expressions or other body movement.

Abercrombie (1965, pp. 20, 39) treats the use of silence in "spoken prose" and poetry. He shows that the rhythms of speech are a result of pulse-like movements of the speaker's lung muscles controlling the output of air. These unfilled pulsations he calls "silent stress-pulses." Rhythm, then, is not merely a regulation of the sounds of speech, but rather the use of muscular movements of the speaker. This definition of rhythm suggests an intimate relationship between speech and body movement. And, in fact, other scholars (for example, Watzlawick, Beavin, and Jackson) recognize this relationship by such terms as "postural silence," meaning immobility. By analogy, while cessation of vocal activity results in silence, cessation of kinesic activity results in postural silence or a kinesic freeze. Perhaps we should say near cessation of kinesic activity, because imperceptible, out-of-awareness movement continues that can be recorded by delicate instruments.

Present-day language theories do not make provision for nonverbal components such as silence, paralinguistic, and kinesic acts in the structure of a sentence, even though these nonverbal acts are ubiquitous in the face-to-face interactions between human beings. It would seem that the theoretical work being done today should be called "theories of syntax" or "theories of grammar" rather than linguistic or language theories--recognizing their limitation--by definition, to some syntax--not that which comprises nonverbal entities.

Silence is an integral part of many social acts which take place between or among human beings. It is requisite in the greeting behavior of some American Indians. In Peru and Brazil it is well-known that proper etiquette demands silence for several minutes (or even longer) upon the entrance of a guest among some of the Indian groups. Other ritual behavior exacts silence among people. Mourning behavior is characteristic of silence. Frazer (1919) devotes a whole chapter to The Silent Widow in various cultures of the world, such as some African, some American Indian, aboriginal Australian, and possibly the ancient Hebrew. Sign languages were derived from this role behavior because the mourning periods in some cases extended for months or even a year or two. Mourning is not always expressed by silence, however. Quite the opposite may be true. Where loud expressions of grief are required, professional mourners may participate. In ancient China, there developed a true "language of sorrow" for a funeral, with prescribed gestures and lamentations. The status of a person regulated the amount of silence and speech permitted. A nobleman would speak less during the period of mourning; if a common man maintained silence, he was presuming a status beyond his class--unacceptable in ancient times (Klineberg 1935, p. 284).

Sign language was also developed among religious orders where silence was, and is, considered a higher form of communication with God. The Cistercians continue to use a system of sign language which is hundreds of years old. They even have a dictionary listing the signs. The silence factor is an element of conversation in parts of the world where the clock is not rushing people to shorter and shorter silent (or resting) places within encounters. The American Indians are widely known to make extensive use of comfortable, relaxed silence. I have been a participant in social settings with Indians and have timed the silence periods within a conversation to be as much as five minutes. Try to imagine a social exchange with five minutes of natural, unembarrassed, comfortable, polite silence!

A state of equilibrium is maintained with a patterned amount of silence within a conversation. A non-native, imbued with other rhythms, may break that equilibrium and inject awkwardness into the interaction. These are subtle but meaningful aspects of the communication between human beings. Goffman (p. 103) observed balanced proportions of silence and speech in the Shetland Islands where long winter evenings lengthen the spacing of conversation:

> ... in Shetland Isle, when three or four women were knitting together, one knitter would say a word, it would be allowed to rest for a minute or two, and then another knitter would provide an additional comment. In the same manner a family sitting around its kitchen fire would look into the flames and intersperse replies to statements with periods of observation of the fire. Shetland men used ... the lengthy pauses required for the proper management of their pipes.

Expediency may offer no alternative to silence. In hunting and in war while the action must continue, silence is essential to the performance. In the library and in the hospital, performance is enhanced by silence. Children participate in games of silence to test the endurance of each other. Comedians make magnificent use of silence. Jack Benny says that the biggest laugh he ever got was when he didn't say anything at all! Masters of pantomime bring laughs to the audience by the incongruity of non-synchronizing off-stage sound and silence to accompany their gestures. The best of comedians are masters of the art of timing--the spacing of silence.

An exquisite use of silence is exhibited in the field of drama. A group of dramatists known as the School of Silence dramatized the effects of pauses in the dialogue. Chaitanya quotes Stanislavsky on the subject of silence in the theatre:

> Words are replaced by eyes, facial expression, the sending out of rays, scarcely perceptible movements that carry a hint--all these and many other conscious and unconscious means of communion. They fill out the words. They often act with

> greater intensity, finesse, are more irresistible in silence than when used in conjunction with words. Their wordless conversation can be no less interesting, substantial, and convincing than one carried on verbally.

Besides the social acts which utilize silence as a component in nonverbal behavior, there is the personal use of silence. One may be silent because one has nothing to say, but also because one has too much to say. It is a commonplace that silence is necessary for deep thought--for either the artist or the scientist. The centuries of women's silence might be explained, in part, by the repression caused by not having private periods of productive silence. See, for example, Olsen, "Silences: When writers don't write." Lack of silence, in this respect, can produce silence. On the other hand, silence can be a protection or a means of survival. Prisoners learn the value of silence, or rather the balance of enough but not too much silence. In less extreme encounters not talking back may avoid trouble.

The matter of privacy is an individual concern the world over. In crowded conditions privacy may be established by silence. Hall (1966, p. 148) gives an example from the Arab world where many members of a family live together:

> Since there is no physical privacy as we know it in the Arab family, not even a word for privacy, one could expect that the Arabs might use some other means to be alone. Their way to be alone is to stop talking. ... [A]n Arab who shuts himself off in this way is not indicating that anything is wrong or that he is withdrawing, only that he wants to be alone with his own thoughts or does not want to be intruded upon. One subject said that her father would come and go for days at a time without saying a word, and no one in the family thought anything of it....

Finally, silence may be an element of abnormal behavior or a result of psychological pain too cruel to speak of. Reik (p. 124) tells about a patient who found it difficult to express herself:

> [The patient] who had interrupted her report with a long pause, which she tried in vain to break by

talking about indifferent things, fell back into a long silence. It was obvious that she did not want to talk about a certain experience the memory of which was accompanied by feelings of grief. Finally she said, 'Let's be silent about something else.'

Chapter VII: THE CONTEXT OF SITUATION In a Theory of Communication

This chapter focuses on something that lies behind all of the observations made in this book.[44] The context of situation comprises, briefly, the how, when, and where, the what and the under what circumstances. It involves the choice of channel of communication, such as acoustical, optical, tactual, or chemical; the temporal element and time duration; the location, position, and the space/distance relationship; the description and relationships of the speaker-hearer as well as the non-participants or audience in the surroundings; the physical condition of the surroundings (the amount of light, noise, silence, and artifacts); the Zeitgeist the society is considered to be in; the individual idiosyncracies of the participants; and finally, the style of communication in the medium and genre used. Many of these conditions have been discussed in sociolinguistic studies and in other descriptions of varieties of language. There are large bibliographies surrounding such scholars as Bright, Fishman, Gumperz, Hymes, and Labov.[45]

The dimensions of the context of situation affect and control every communication between human beings. But they are about us so commonly that it isn't always easy to identify them. Einstein asked, "What does a fish know about the water in which he swims all his life?"[46] Birdwhistell (1970, p. 6) drew variations on the fish when he declared, "We cannot study the social behavior of a fish by taking him out of water."

Early recognition of the dimensions of the context of situation obviates lengthy discussions on ambiguity and ungrammaticality in discussions on language. People who use language are not nearly so troubled about ambiguity and ungrammaticalness as linguists who seem to spend an inordinate amount of time niggling about them. The expression,

"I'm looking for a house with green shutters" bothers some, for example, because it can be interpreted as both an inquiry in a real estate office and as a statement while driving around a new housing section looking for a particular address.

The philosopher, J. L. Austin (pp. 33, 62), discusses other potentially ambiguous expressions in terms of constative and performative verbs: "it's yours" either means the bestowing or bequeathing of a gift or is simply a statement that it (already) belongs to the person addressed. "There's a bull in the field" can be either a warning or a constative describing the scenery. "I shall be there" can be either a promise or a statement. If some general features of communication were stated first these expressions could not be considered ambiguous.

The general features which I propose would include, roughly, the <u>context of situation</u>, <u>philosophical</u> categories, <u>psycholinguistic</u> categories, <u>grammatical</u> categories, and <u>nonverbal</u> categories. Most of these are extra-linguistic and have to do with the social contexts or conceptual conditions. Language is not a homogeneous entity and its syntax cannot be described within itself, apparently, as we have witnessed the unsuccessful travail to do so of the last generation of linguists in addition to the deep thinking of previous centuries. In other words, the study of syntax is doomed to sterility unless other extralinguistic features are considered in the analysis. Another way to define extralinguistic features is to acknowledge them as insights provided by other disciplines.

The first of these features, the <u>context of situation</u>, will be the main concern of this chapter. The media would be an important feature to note, for example: [+ written] [+ spoken]. <u>Philosophical</u> categories might include such things as intention, logic, true-false, and other ingredients which the philosopher could contribute to the understanding and description of language. More specifically, the description could include features such as [+ true] [+ legendary] [+ performative] or whatever might be decided by the collaboration of linguists and philosophers. <u>Psycholinguistic</u> categories might include elements such as those concerned with cognitive processes, the "why's" of syntax, developmental stages, individual differences, and second language interference.

<u>Grammatical</u> categories have been discussed by Boas,

Jespersen, Sapir and Swadesh, and Whorf,[47] and more recently by generative grammarians, but the surface has only been scratched. The categories have to do with such things as number, gender, sex, density, age, shape, dimensional, penetrable, positional, status, supernatural, visible, proximate, knowledgeable, animate, and definite. There are others. I approached one of these, the category of sex (not gender) in a recent book on the linguistic behavior of male and female (Key 1975). The nonverbal categories would consist of a set of features that would make statements on posture, facial expression, body movement, and paralinguistic phenomena.

The theoretical framework would specify these dimensions before actual grammatical structures were discussed. The large general features of communication would be stated for every verbal act. Specific features would be stated within each general category. Such a description of a dialogue, of course, would approach a government document in size, but theoretically, such completeness would be desirable for a theory of communication, or of language. The notion of a situational context for language was set forth by Dr. Philipp Wegener in his "Situationstheorie" in 1885 (Firth, pp. 42-3). Gardiner[48] credited Wegener with these notions and Malinowski was the first to use the term "context of situation" widely in English. Firth's writings in the early 1930's reflect his work with Malinowski, and his embracing the concept influenced the London school in their work with language. I have expanded the concept to include a host of ideas.

Malinowski stated clearly that his view was "to correlate the study of language with that of other activities, to interpret the meaning of each utterance within its actual context ... [and] to define meaning in terms of experience and situation" (p. 9). He believed that words do not exist in isolation (p. 22), and he went on to suggest (p. 22) that

> ... it is very profitable in linguistics to widen the concept of context so that it embraces not only spoken words but facial expression, gesture, bodily activities, the whole group of people present during an exchange of utterances and the part of the environment on which these people are engaged.

Sapir and Swadesh, in their discussion of American Indian grammatical categories reiterated the idea that "no language response can be separated from the contextual pattern in which it occurs." Edward T. Hall, the anthropologist who contributed the term "proxemics" (see later in section on Location and Space), stated that "man and his environment participate in molding each other" (1966, p. 4). "Man's relationship to his environment [Hall said] is a function of his sensory apparatus plus how this apparatus is conditioned to respond" (1966, p. 59).

J. L. Austin, in his treatment of performative verbs, took into consideration the "total situation," the "circumstances of the utterance," and the "context of the utterance" (pp. 34, 52, 69, 76, 89, 100). It can be seen that for many of his classes of performative verbs, depending upon these circumstances that he speaks of, nonverbal behavior may substitute for speech, e.g., permission, a head nod; order, by pointing; accepting a bet, a handshake; pronounce guilt, stern facial expression or silence; "out," the umpire's arm gesture; reprimand, a glare; consent, a head nod or a wink (Key 1974). Consideration of extralinguistic evidence, such as context of situation, and nonverbal behavior, is an aid in distinguishing between performative and constative, or statement verbs. For example, "I promise ..." is indeed not a performatory promise when it is spoken between children and the verbal act is accompanied by nonserious behavior, such as giggling and squirming, that indicate it is to be interpreted as a joke.

With a little brain-storming, it is easy to come up with different examples of syntax that could be appropriate expressions in various situations. An example is a greeting form, "Hi!" or "Hello," or "How do you do?" or a hand wave, or a head nod, depending upon the place and persons involved. Or imagine the different syntax used in ordering a sumptuous dinner at a fine restaurant as compared with calling for a hot dog at Greasy Joe's. Trying to determine grammaticality is irrelevant.

Media

The Media determine the channel of communication which can be used: acoustical, optical, tactual, chemical, electrical (see diagram). Written language exemplifies different syntactical structures from spoken language. Written language has to fill in with adjectives and punctuation for the tone of voice and the voice quality which indicate emotion and

COMMUNICATION[49]

Channels: acoustical, optical, tactual, chemical, electrical

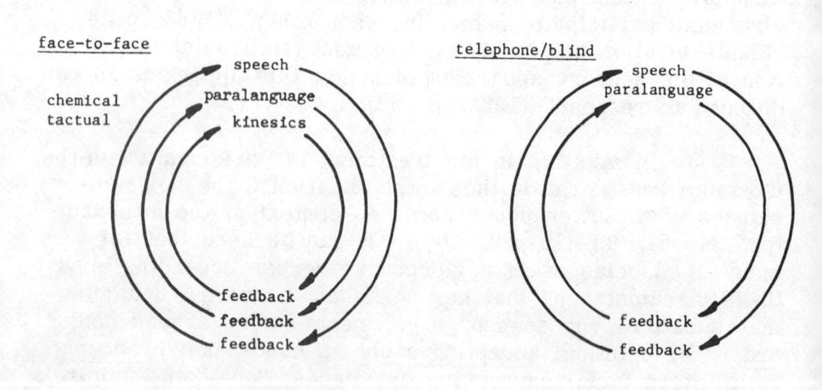

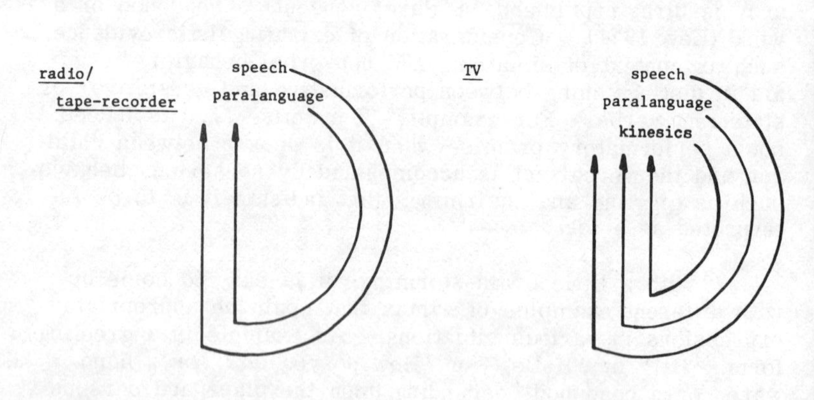

SURROGATES:

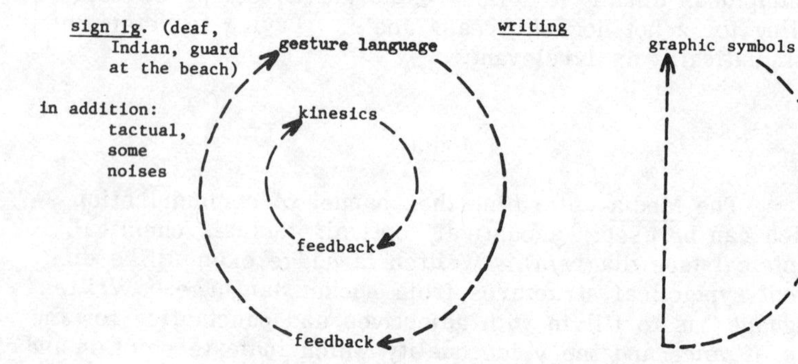

attitude in the message conveyed. Consider the differences in language of an informal penciled note with that on formal, gilt-edged stationery, and those with a quick invitation by telephone. A professor might not lecture in the language he or she publishes in. A reporter does not broadcast the news in the same language he or she writes an editorial in.

Concerning spoken language only, the medium prescribes the particular paralinguistic and gestural acts which can be used in a communicative event. The telephone, for example, permits only paralanguage to accompany the verbal act and precludes any communication by kinesic acts. In a very delicate conversation when feedback is essential, the telephone would not be an appropriate medium. It is not likely that one would ask for a raise by telephone conversation; this kind of dialogue is better handled in a face-to-face situation where the petitioner can lead up to the goal, minutely recording and reacting to the response, which determines whether or not to continue the conversation. Likewise asking for a loan or making a proposal of marriage would not be easily handled by telephone. The appearance of phonevision or picturephone, or whatever it might be called, would change the style of telephone conversations significantly.

Conversation on television without audience response is somewhat altered from a similar type of conversation in front of a live audience. Unless the speaker has wide experience with the medium, he or she may become very awkward and exhibit frustrated expressions because of the lack of response and feedback that one is accustomed to receiving in conversation. The genre also determines which verbal and nonverbal acts may be used. An obscene gesture might be tolerated in a quotation or a recitation from another culture where it wouldn't be in an actual conversation. Things can happen on the stage that wouldn't happen in the home--or vice versa. The mime, jokes, poetry, and all the varieties of literature have their own repertoire of verbal and nonverbal acts.

Time

> "Time interval is a strange and contradictory matter in the mind. It would be reasonable to suppose that a routine time or an eventless time would seem interminable. It should be so, but it

> is not. It is the dull eventless times that have no duration whatever. A time splashed with interest, wounded with tragedy, crevassed with joy--that's the time that seems long in the memory. And this is right when you think about it. Eventlessness has no posts to drape duration on. From nothing to nothing is no time at all."[50]
>
> --John Steinbeck

Temporal aspects affect the communication behavior. The pace differs from event to event. Timing affects paralinguistic acts, which occur as spacing, hesitations, rhythms, durations--which all "say" something beyond the words they surround. Timing is acutely important in the gestural acts of a sports event where the ball would be down the field before one could complete a slow or casual gesture. Consider the deletion and telescoping of communication in a three-minute long distance telephone call. "Mannerisms" or "affectations" displayed can be interpreted, in part, by pinpointing the event or persons from another temporal point of view. For example, one can recall the recital behavior of a pianist or violinist a generation ago and realize that the facial expressions and body movement were much more exaggerated and dramatic than those exhibited today.

Time is ambiguous in the phrase, "I was going to call you Sunday," when taken out of context. Given the context of situation it is clearly understood to be either last Sunday, but an interruption kept me from it, or next Sunday, but since you called me, I won't.

Location and Space

"You have to feel space!"
--Marcel Marceau[51]

Proxemics is a term which Edward Hall coined to discuss the theories and observations on man's use of social and personal space as a specialized elaboration of culture (1966, p. 1). More than anyone else he has made us aware of the communication--or lack of it--which takes place between human beings by the use of space. His cross-cultural discussions are especially insightful. Space and distance are relevant in the choice and use of the channels of communication and the hearer's perception of the message. Eye contact cannot be maintained if the distance is too great.

Olfactory communication is also useless in that circumstance. Tactile communication is not possible beyond arm's reach.

The three facets of intonation: pitch, stress (or loudness), and length (or timing), are adjusted in proportion with space and distance, as well as location indoors or outdoors. Large distance also prescribe careful, precise articulation and judicious choice of words, which would be considered pedantic in the student union. The three elements of intonation mentioned above, pitch, stress, and length, have their counterparts in body movement: shape or design of movement, the muscular contraction effort, and the flow of movement. These, in turn, are affected by space and distance. Extent and deliberation of gesture depend on how well the speaker is seen by the hearer. Behavioral events are distinct from communications that take place out-of-sight, and out-of-hearing--for example, smoke signals, which have been used by the Greeks, Romans, on the Great Wall by the Chinese, and by American Indians, and probably others. Visual communication by signallers too far distant to discern facial expressions takes place by semaphore, flag, and lights. Lifeguards pay acute attention (some, by telescope and binoculars) to facial expression and rate and quality of movement when a swimmer is out-of-hearing.

Ruesch and Kees show pictures of the spacing that human beings assume when they are gathered together, for example waiting for a bus. The discreet spacing strictly adhered to when people queue in Britain is so precisely measured that one can imagine an invisible string keeping people at a certain distance apart. When this pattern is altered, one can be sure that Americans, or lovers, are in the line! An example of inconsistency of behavior is clearly seen in the American use of space. While the American may shove and push to get to the bus first, he maintains a requisite distance while talking to another person. The distance is less in the Spanish culture. Many people have seen a Spanish-speaking person talking an American into actual backward retreat.

The relationship of living space to the number of occupants will qualify the behavior maintained within. Privacy and human dignity are maintained in one-room living all over the world, by other members of the household turning away or averting the eyes. I recall reading in a Chinese novel about the tender way the members of the family turned away from a young man who had just been hit by tragedy so that he could weep "in private" in the single room that they all occupied. Even sexual intercourse can occur "in privacy" in the same room and indeed in the same bed, in cultures where weather or other conditions prohibit going to the edge of the forest or jungle.

The location in which a behavioral event takes place also has its effect on the choice of verbal and nonverbal acts. Consider the variety of different postures that are assumed in a posh office, a narrow corridor in a crowded school between classes, on the beach, in the bathroom, in a rowboat. The high school gym can be transformed with flowers and crepe paper, and in turn transform the behavioral events that take place during the few hours of the Senior Prom. Recognizing that location changes behavior, Barker has as chapter titles: "Structure of the Behavior of American and English Children" and "The Behavior of the Same Child in Different Milieus."

Participants

Description of the speaker and hearer(s) implies age, sex, and race or culture, each having its varying set of behavioral norms. In addition, the status or the power relationship of the participants must be noted in order to interpret the communication between them. The persons involved, of course, display several roles; even in a single day a person may be a father, a teacher, a customer, a patient, a client, a group president, and a chauffeur. "In each case he signals his status by his behavior, his dress, his posture, and his speech style."[52] One can imagine the varied paralinguistic effects and kinesic behavior: casual and relaxed, formal, stiff, controlling, and responsive. The role of the widow in some societies demanded that she be shaved and silenced for a long period of mourning. Earlier in our own society, children used to be seen but not heard. The role of football players in the United States permits extensive tactual behavior--in a society where men shun a male touch in other situations. Partners on the dance floor--even strangers--hold hands, but the same people would not touch each other in other locations.

To interpret the meaning of behavioral events, it is necessary to know the familiarity and desired goals of the participants. Persons well known to each other might exhibit behavior which would be bizarre if they were just acquaintances. Public persons are keenly aware of desired goals in their public appearances: television has added a burden to leaders of society. President Nixon was given extensive exposure during his first inaugural ceremonies. The Sunday evening formal concert was long and not very lively. During one of the numbers the President leaned forward and started to rest his chin on his hand. In mid-gesture he remembered that the President of the United States doesn't lean on his fist in public! He lowered his hand and raised his head to a dignified posture.

Once I attended with several friends that I knew well, a sumptuous reception in the home of an important official. The location, audience, and role-playing triggered highly exaggerated paralinguistic features in the speech of one of the women--so much so that I didn't recognize this voice that I had known well for many years. One can observe the same phenomenon on occasion when a preacher ascends to the pulpit. The pastoral robe and austerity of the ritual may actually change the voice quality. This has been referred to as the "pulpit voice." His voice returns to normal when he gets outside.

Grimshaw[53] points to the different varieties of language spoken in a situation involving various relationships, e.g., when academicians talk to janitors. The language varies when the janitor comes into the office while the academician is: alone, with a senior member of administration, a colleague of peer status, with an undergraduate, with another maintenance man, with the professor's wife, with all-male participants, with parents of students. Similarly the language changes in another physical setting, such as the elevator or the coffee shop. Such descriptions could be made regarding nonverbal behavior.

An individual continues to display nonverbal behavior when he or she is alone. Krout studied austistic gestures. Again the location is relevant; the participants' behavior is modified (though perhaps out-of-awareness) if there is the possibility of an observer's coming on the scene. When two participants are interacting, the possibilities of communication items are of greater number and variety. Some kinesic and paralinguistic acts only occur between two persons: a handshake and other types of greetings, sealing a bargain with the appropriate spat on the ground, a duel, and affection between two loved ones.

Interaction among more than two participants means that at some moments one or more of the participants are also observers--the audience so to speak. Larger gatherings or great audiences again change the repertory of nonverbal acts. In this sense the members of the audience are also participants, and this is important to the performance of the speaker, whether in a formal situation on the stage or informally in a large living room or classroom. Evaluating the performer (for example, evaluations from students of a teacher or a class) is only half of the story. The better the audience, the better the performance! As any actor will testify. The audience does not necessarily have to be actively participating in the event. A child may deliver an exquisite performance of misbehavior at the supermarket but would consider it not worth while at home with only the dog observing.

Even though not allowed to speak, audiences communicate very actively to performers through nonverbal means. Some nonverbal acts lend themselves to larger groups of participants. Applause is no fun done alone. And a single person doesn't throw a hat into the ring. Furthermore, an audience can also limit permitted behaviors. Whispering displaces talking. Boredom can be expressed by coughing, whispering, or averting one's eyes from the performer. Negative response is communicated variously by: booing, hissing, whistling, cat-calling, heckling, laughing, keeping silent, fidgeting or rustling, shuffling feet, whispering, leaving, yelling, grumbling, sleeping, throwing (eggs, tomatoes, bottles, or pillows), and even entering the dialogue of a stage performance if it is thought to be corny. Agreeable response is communicated by: respectful silence, whistling, laughing, waving, smiling, yelling, standing, dancing, screaming, and throwing (coins or flowers). Note that some of these behaviors may occur in either situation, depending on the culture and the circumstances. Cobb discusses the "clappers and the hissers" among various kinds of audiences.

Physical Conditions

Physical conditions, along with social restraints determine which behavior may be used. If in the immediate context there is a noise element which precludes language and paralanguage, the participants are dependent on kinesic acts. Airport personnel use gestures to maneuver aircraft; ushers communicate by gesture during the stage performance; the crane operator is directed by gesture.

The silence factor is somewhat different from the pauses or hesitations which occur in paralinguistic behavior. Here the silence is part of the context--for religious purposes, expediency, or respect, for example in the hospital, the library, the theater, or during a funeral. Frequent reference is made to the gesture language of the Trappist monks who maintain silence. Greetings may take the form of a restrained and prescribed silence in some cultures. Voegelin and Harris[54] discuss the balance of silence and vocal behavior in their statement on language and culture. They refer to the different distribution of talk and silence in different cultures and suggest consideration of nonverbal behavior.

The amount of light and darkness is also of importance in the communication act. In the very dim light of a bar, tactile gestures are of higher incidence where darkness distorts distance perception and also encourages more familiar communication. Artifacts act as signals that elicit different behavioral patterns. An elegant coiffure or a dinner jacket elicits more formal body movement and can seem to change the interpersonal relationship. A policeman's uniform can make giggling teenagers sober up.

Zeitgeist

Another aspect of the context of situation is the attitude and atmosphere of the society at the time of the communication item. Extreme conditions, war, hunger, tragedy, and elation modify the behavior of human beings. The posture in standing and walking becomes radically different when the once proud Minister becomes a refugee and has to hunt through garbage pails for a bite to eat--or the poverty-stricken student has just won a scholarship! The military personnel imprisoned in Korea used obscene gestures when photographed to signal distress. The same men would not participate in this behavior under circumstances without stress.

Consider also the very different degrees of intimacy and consequent behavior of the same group of men at one time floating on a life raft in the Pacific Ocean and again in the office getting out reports. The tactile gestures will be different; the quality of voice covering different forms of address will be different. The behavioral events in a crisis situation will be paced more rapidly than in a humdrum context. The ordering of events may change.

Individual or idiosyncratic conditions must also be acknowledged in the choice of verbal or nonverbal behavior. The degree of fatigue and personal circumstances actually affect syntax. Physical condition alters the voice quality. Women singers, for example, may carefully schedule their performances because of the paralinguistic modification which may occur during the first few days of menstruation, according to Schwalberg.[55]

Style and Function

Finally it remains to consider the aesthetic dimensions and the social approval or acceptance of the communication item. The impact of the message is dependent upon these features of responsibility in communicating. On glancing back at all these determinants of verbal and nonverbal acts it will be seen that there is considerable overlapping and interaction of networks. One aspect cannot be analyzed in isolation, nor as a static condition, because the features change along with the interaction. The context of situation, then, is the controlling influence in the choice in language, from pronunciation features, to syntax, to larger structures and to nonverbal behavior. An analysis without these considerations could only be done in an extremely narrow sense, and this might be almost useless with regard to meaning.

Chapter VIII: DIALECTS OF NONVERBAL BEHAVIOR And Special Message Systems

Patterned Individual Behavior

Each individual in every society exhibits an aura that varies within discernible patterns from day to day and experience to experience. Notice the varied kinds of walking that one individual has--or the variety of sitting postures, depending on the clothes the person is wearing, the location, what he is sitting on, and who he is trying to impress--negatively or positively.

In linguistic studies the term idiolect was coined to refer to the total speech of an individual, including all the varieties in different moods and situations. In the area of gestures, these characteristics are known as "mannerisms." In more technical terms they have been referred to as idiomovements, by analogy to idiolect. The vocal features that distinguish an individual, Trager called voice set (1958, pp. 275-6). This is the background of all other speech--the idiosyncratic, including the physiology of the speaker, resulting in the patterned identification of individuals. Goffman, in The Presentation of Self in Everyday Life,[56] speaks of the characteristics that an individual "gives off."

Nonverbal manifestations which define or reflect personality must be cross-referenced to autistic behavior, at least in the normal sense. Each individual has a unique repertory of paralinguistic and kinesic acts such as clicking noises, twisting the hair or watch, and tapping. Individuals also maintain an idiosyncratic use of the sensory apparatus. It is said that Helen Keller could distinguish the "olfactory signature" of those she knew.

Hymes (1961, pp. 314-6) has reviewed what linguists have said about language in personality--not much. A classic, of course, is Sapir's study of speech as a personality trait. The features which convey individuality are very often paralinguistic and kinesic, and since research in these areas is quite recent, not much could have been said in the way of rigorous scientific descriptions. This is not to say that individual characteristics have not been recognized for a long time. Montaigne (1553-1592) recognized them in himself, as well as in others:[57]

> So I remember that from my tenderest childhood people noticed in me some indefinable way of carrying my body and certain gestures testifying to some empty and stupid pride. I want to say this about it first, that it is not unbecoming to have characteristics and propensities so much our own and so incorporated into us that we have no way of sensing and recognizing them. And of such natural inclinations the body is likely to retain a certain bent, without our knowledge or consent. It was a certain affectation harmonious with his beauty that made Alcxander lean his head a little to one side, and Alcibiades speak softly and with a lisp. Julius Caesar used to scratch his head with one finger, which is the behavior of a man full of troublesome thoughts; and Cicero, it seems to me, was in the habit of wrinkling his nose, which is a sign of a mocking nature. Such gestures can grow on us unperceived.
>
> ...
>
> Among the extraordinary mannerisms, let us not forget the arrogance of the Emperor Constantius, who in public always held his head straight, without turning or bending it this way or that, not even to look at those who saluted him from the side; keeping his body fixed and motionless, without letting himself move with the swaying of his coach, without daring either to spit, or blow his nose, or wipe his face in front of the people.

In defining the idiolect or the idiomovement of an individual it is necessary to establish his or her norm. In pitch, the norm would include a certain range of variation--this might be called the "key" a person speaks in. Speaking above that range would be excited speech, or speech under tension; speaking with a narrower range might mean threat or boredom; speaking with both extra-high and extra-low pitch might be grandiose speech, bragging, or a platform style. Another norm would be in reference to timing. Pauses a bit longer than the pauses of other normal speakers might be the norm of a particular idiolect. Shorter ones--even coinciding with the length of pauses of other normal speakers would mean, for this particular individual, excitement, irritation, tension, or some other extra-reaction to a situation. Slightly longer pauses than the norm might mean only indecision or careful thought. It is obvious that the norm of a person can only be established after observing that person in many situations and responses. This is why, of course, that a loved one or a very well-known acquaintance is a better interpreter of an individual's speech than a trained speech expert, who could only record the physical facts, but without reference to the interpretation of them in the context of situation.

From idiosyncratic nonverbal behavior human beings share group behavior in as small a segment of society as a couple, to larger and larger groups. Many observers have noted the similarities of body movement and paralinguistic habits shared within families or among intimate friends.

Patterned Group Behavior

Turning now to patterned group behavior we see that members of society maintain a range of patterns that are known and responded to by each other. I am using the term "patterned" in two ways: those systems which are coded and those which are non-coded. The non-coded behavior includes all individual and cultural ways of expression through paralinguistics and kinesics, such as styles of speaking and styles of walking. The coded systems range from the extremely limited systems, such as the hand signals used in driving an automobile, to systems with a fairly large number of entities, such as the gestures and vocalizations used in athletics, and on to a seemingly unlimited and complex coded system which is complete enough to substitute for natural language. This would include such systems as sign languages.

Geographic Varieties

Geography determines a certain range of group behavior. There are Eastern and Western dialects; Southern and Northern; mountain and low country; hot country and hill dialects; rural and city dialects. People carry the characteristics of their native area with them when they travel and it is these gestures and body movements, types of walk, as well as vocalizations, that identify a person from another locale, even if the language is essentially the same.

Temporal Varieties

One only has to watch an old movie to become aware of constant change in use of body language. If the concert artist today used the exaggerated movements accepted a generation or two ago, he or she would be laughed off the stage. Though I wouldn't know how to measure the rate of change in the centuries past, it seems as though changes do take place in increasingly shorter periods of time. Amy Vanderbilt (p. 94) explains the change of attitude about pointing that came about with the introduction of the camera. News photographers wanted to get a little action into the picture and thereby the old etiquette rule, "Don't point!" was no longer regarded. Fashion photographers wanted the best view of a woman's legs, so sitting posture, proper, that is, became more varied. Advice from the 1870's included instructions about the nose (quoted by Vanderbilt, p. 98):

> It should never be fondled before company, or, in fact, touched at any time unless absolutely necessary. The nose, like all other organs, augments in size by frequent handling, so we recommend every person to keep his own fingers, as well as those of his friends, or enemies, away from it.

Darwin (p. 32) felt that an educated person's head never itched! "A vulgar man often scratches his head when perplexed in mind...." Schlesinger compiled some do's and don't's of the past:[58] "A lady should gracefully raise her dress a little above her ankle" when crossing the street (p. 35). "Go not singing, whistling or hallooing along the street" (p. 4). "Kill no Vermin as Fleas, lice ticks & in the Sight of Others" (p. 5). The Earl of Chesterfield told his son, "not to indulge in such habits as blowing one's nose without a handkerchief" and averred that "Well-bred people often smile, but seldom laugh" (p. 11). Another book of etiquette (1852), which Schlesinger quoted, catalogued a lot of things a nice person shouldn't do: "balance yourself upon your chair, ... extend your feet on the andirons; ... laugh immoderately; place your hand upon the person with whom you are conversing; take him by the buttons, the collar of his cloak, the cuffs, the waist, etc.; ... beat time with the feet and hands; whirl round a chair on one leg."

A more recent style of group behavior is exemplified by the "playing it cool" lack of expression of the 1960's communicating the loneliness and feelings of isolation prevalent. In addition to the lack of facial expression, hair has been useful to hide behind. Grown over the eyes and full around the face it helps to create the mask which avoids communication. Dark glasses likewise contribute to the mask. The stereotyped politeness of the 1800's and the "play it cool" lack of expression of the 1960's both communicate non-naturalness of human behavior. A poised and confident person has a reasonable repertory of expressions. In this sense animals are interesting creatures to observe because they say what they want to without regard to what the neighbors or the boss will think. Do these temporal changes of styles of behavior indicate that people are not really at home and comfortable with the environment?

State-of-Being Dimensions

Age. Child/Adult Behavior.

"All the world's a stage,
And all the men and women merely players.
They have their exits and their entrances;
And one man in his time plays many parts,
His acts being seven ages. At first the infant,
Mewling and puking in the nurse's arms.
And then the whining school-boy, with his satchel,
And shining morning face, creeping like snail
Unwillingly to school. And then the lover,
Sighing like furnace, with a woeful ballad
Made to his mistress' eyebrow. Then a soldier,
Full of strange oaths, and bearded like the pard,
Jealous in honour, sudden, and quick in quarrel,
Seeking the bubble reputation
Even in the cannon's mouth. And then the justice,
In fair round belly with good capon lin'd,
With eyes severe, and beard of formal cut,
Full of wise saws and modern instances;
And so he plays his part. The sixth age shifts
Into the lean and slipper'd pantaloon,
With spectacles on nose and pouch on side,
His youthful hose, well sav'd, a world too wide

For his shrunk shank; and his big manly voice,
Turning again toward childish treble, pipes
And whistles in his sound. Last scene of all,
That ends this strange eventful history,
Is second childishness and mere oblivion,
Sans teeth, sans eyes, sans taste, sans everything.
From As You Like It, Act II,
Scene vii [emphasis added]:

A second reading of this passage gives one a capsule description of typical paralinguistic and kinesic changes in the various ages of a person. The paralinguistic voice qualities of mewling, whining, sighing, pipes and whistles.... Facial expressions of shining morning face and eyes severe.... The body movement of the creeping walk of the reluctant school boy, the sudden and quick soldier--later slowed down by the shrunk shank.... All noises and movements eventually dwindling off into nothingness. Firth (p. 50) has suggested a language study of the Seven Ages of Man--and I might suggest that the research be extended to include the Nonverbal Behavior in the span of a life time.

Age. Infant's Prelinguistic Behavior. Infant vocalizations are precursors of language. Some vocalizations eventually result in language sounds; some result in paralinguistic phenomena, elements of nonverbal communication. The development of suprasegmentals (intonational features) appears to start within a few days of age. For example, the cry can be described in terms of pitch range, intensity, timing, intervals and rhythm, all elements of adult intonation patterns in every language. These elements are of paramount importance in both the language and paralinguistic systems of the total communication act and are intimately related to motor activity, the precursor of kinesic behavior, among other things.

It is generally conceded that infants respond to paralanguage and kinesic communication long before they understand words. Darwin made many observations on gestures and facial expressions in studying his own children from birth on. Tylor (1878, p. 57) even believed that language is taught by means of gestures. In any case, there is consensus among such notables as Wundt, Krout, and Vygotsky, that nonverbal behavior is crucial in the acquisition of language. Many scholars have noted the close relationship of body language (e.g., gestures, facial expression, and tactile experiences) to the development of speech. Bullowa's studies acknowledge this relationship (p. 198): "It is suggested that the process starts where language and action are united in neuromuscular activity. Eventually language and action become more and more separate until language appears to have a life of its own, as for instance in its written form."

A large portion of the work done on infant vocalizations is concerned with the cry. "Scientific" study of the infant cry goes back at least to 1838 when Gardiner made a musical notation of a child crying (Ostwald 1963, p. 33). Studies of infant vocalizations have proliferated with the advent of sensitive instruments to record and make fine analysis. Summaries of the studies are found in Irwin (in Kaiser) and McCarthy. In the table on the adjoining page, Ostwald, Phibbs, and Fox (p. 69) chart the milestones in the study of infant cry.

The analytical studies isolate three or four different cries. Peter Wolff worked with three types: hunger, anger, and pain. Most of the studies done on infant cries have been done in medical centers where the focus was on diagnostic purposes, for example Karelitz and Fisichelli. Linguists have been interested in the infant's pre-linguistic behavior for the purpose of understanding acquisition of language. Essentially three kinds of analysis have been made of infant vocalizations: instrumental, phonetic or impressionistic descriptions, and distinctive features. It has been established that the newborn infant lacks the anatomical mechanism that is necessary to produce the sounds of human speech (Lieberman and Crelin). The distinctive features analyses were attempted in order to circumvent the problem of matching phonetic symbol to nonspeech sound, though both Gruber, and Ringwall et al. worked with different sets of distinctive features.

Non-cry vocalizations have been studied much less than the cry. Kurtz itemized eighteen sounds which he recorded in the first 24 hours of an infant's life (not all are pre-linguistic sounds) (Ostwald 1963, pp. 16-9):

1.	cry	7.	breath	13.	mutterings
2.	scream	8.	sneeze	14.	squeaks
3.	burp	9.	cough	15.	rises
4.	vomit	10.	hiccup	16.	whimpers
5.	gulp	11.	gargle	17.	lip-puckering sound
6.	laa-sound	12.	whine	18.	flatulence

During the first year of life, the infant experiments with a

(cont. on p. 143)

Table I. Milestones in the Study of Infant Cries.

1838	Gardiner notated musical patterns of crying
1906	Flatau and Gutzman recorded 30 infants; described pitch and phonetic features of cry
1927	Sherman distinguished hunger, anger or pain, and colic cries
1932	Bayley identified 13 causes of crying in 61 infants
1936	Lewis related crying to language development
1936	Searl related screaming to aggression
1942	Fairbanks traced pitch changes of hunger wails for 9 months (1 infant)
1945	Aldrich, Sung and Knop measured amount of crying in nursery and home environments (50 infants)
1946	Brodbeck and Irwin showed that orphanage environment reduces the types and amount of vocalization (94 infants)
1951	Lynip did the first sonagraphic studies of infant vocalization
1954	Stewart related excessive crying (colic) to parental behavior
1955	McCarthy delineated mass motor activity of crying from specific movements which later differentiate to produce speech
1960	Karelitz, Karelitz and Rosenfeld described cries of cretinism, kernicterus, meningitis and Tay-Sachs Disease
1960	Truby differentiated the acoustics of phonation, dysphonation, and hyperphonation
1961	Bosma and Smith reported cineradiographic studies of crying
1962	Ostwald, Freedman and Kurtz described cries of 32 twin infants
1964	Wasz-Höckert and coworkers described the effects of training on ability to differentiate birth, hunger, pain and pleasure vocalizations
1964	Ringel and Kluppel reported normative cry data
1965	Lind et al. described sonagrams of the brain-damaged cry
1965	Sheppard and Lane developed an automated method for sampling the prosodic features of infant's vocalizing
1966	Eisenson described cry-differences between childhood aphasia and apraxia
1966	Vuorenkoski et al. defined spectrographic features of the 'cat cry'
1966	Bayley found early vocalization to be the only clear predictor of later intelligence scores (among girls)
1967	Chase et al. demonstrated infant cry to be unaffected by auditory feedback delays

wide range of noises. In addition to the above:

whistles	finger-lip sounds
snorts	cooing
lip-smacking	humming
tongue clicks (tsk, etc.)	grunts
voiced sigh	sucking noises
voiceless sigh	laughter
fricative turbulence	bubbling spit
tongue games	babbling
throaty sounds	gurgling
Bronx cheer	lallation

Lallation is a necessary stage in the development of speech. The infant makes babbling sounds--hears them--imitates them--hears them--repeats them--and so forth. Without this feedback process the infant cannot continue in the development of language. Deaf children are hampered at this point. To this list should be added other noises which the infant makes with By-Elements: scratching on the sheets, thumping, banging, clapping. The infant is experimenting with sound and resultant control of his or her environment and beginning the patterns of rhythm which are a part of the individual throughout life.

It is probable that intonation is the first linguistic feature of language which the infant acquires. Several investigators have observed early intonation patterns. Lieberman (1968, p. 38) makes a strong case that "the linguistic use of intonation reflects an innately determined and highly organized system." While indeed, there may well be an innate physiologic basis for intonation, it is a commonplace that intonation patterns do vary from language to language, as Lieberman shows later. It is not yet established <u>when</u> these patterns of variation are learned, or begun to be learned. A study of biological rhythms speaks of "fetal activity rhythms" (Anon, <u>Biological Rhythms in Psychiatry and Medicine</u>, p. 36) and further states that time sense and rhythm develop before language (p. 4). Wolff establishes the stability of rhythm in infant cries during the neonatal period (1969, p. 83).

Weir (p. 156) demonstrates the differences of infant intonation configurations of Chinese, Russian, and American infants.

One Chinese infant, recorded first at five-and-one-

> half and then at six-and-one-half months, shows in the second recording a very different pattern from the Russian and American infants. The utterances produced by the Chinese baby are usually monosyllabic and only vocalic, with much tonal variation over individual vowels. A neutral single vowel with various pitches is also typical of another six-month-old Chinese infant, as well as of a still different seven-month-old one. The Russian and American babies, at six and seven months, show little pitch variation over individual syllables....

The elements in rhythm and the force and pitch of crying thus make up the components of intonation in any language. Hungarian scholars, Fónagy and Magdics (p. 316), as mentioned earlier, noted that the "melody of complaint is obviously a stylized form of weeping." Karelitz and Fisichelli (p. 347) note that at three months the infant may display a plaintive quality in the inflectional variations.

Another matter of interest in the acquisition of language is the extent of silences and vocalization periods, i.e. natural vocalizations without artificial stimulus other than normal interaction. The vocal behavior of one of the infants in Bullowa's study (p. 195) indicated that excessive silence was intimately related with retarded vocal development. Until more is known about normal development, it will continue to be difficult to assess "excessive silence." Nevertheless the description of the prelinguistic stages should have some significance in the understanding of cognitive potential and linguistic development. There is no doubt that more investigation is needed to understand the relationships between prelinguistic behavior, the development of language, and the nonverbal correlates. Of concern is the total inventory of vocalization, the extent of use, and the relevance to communication. While cry behavior features the components of intonation, other vocalizations contribute to the development of the air stream mechanisms which control the air stream used in the speech act. This aspect of the development of language seems relatively untouched in the studies reviewed as far as articulatory descriptions are concerned. And even though the vocal cords are not yet developed in the neonate, the infant is using the tongue and other vocal apparatus since birth which eventually produce speech sounds.

With regard to the beginning linguistic stages of child language the child makes ample use of body language. Slobin (p. 6) says that the child uses gestures and context to disambiguate utterances before he has command of the verbal means of communication. Engel gives an example of a three-year-old Italian boy who used facial expression to distinguish two homophones:[59]

> Albertino had one word kappa for both Italian scarpa, 'shoe', and schiaffo, 'slap'. Kappa in the meaning of 'shoe' was unmarked while in the meaning of 'slap' it was consistently accompanied by a stern facial expression, identical to the one his father displayed when telling Albertino that he was preparing to administer this kind of punishment.

As we have seen already, paralinguistic acts may substitute for verbal items within a sentence. In child language this may be a result of incomplete command of the language. Someone gave me an example of a French child learning English who substituted the paralinguistic hmhm 'no' for a negativizer: "I like that hmhm" meaning "I don't like that." It would seem that the understanding of syntax could not be complete without consideration of the nonverbal components.

Age. Children's Nonverbal Behavior. Some of the most delightful expressions of variety of nonverbal behavior are the vocal articulations and movements which occur during the careless pleasures of childhood. The study of human beings would be most fruitful in the early uninhibited and natural years before a person becomes confined to the social customs and restrictions of his experiences. And yet in my search for information, I find that the research is scanty in terms of relating this development to communication.

Some features of child movement can be noted. The body movement, in part, is physiologically defined. For example, a baby can't touch the ear opposite the hand which is reaching. Children's gestures tend to be repetitive--they will make the same movement over and over again. Children's activity may be incongruous in terms of the context of situation. An infant may lift her skirt in public, or children may giggle during a funeral. Children are uninhibited--making faces is a usual event. Children are imitative--for learning purposes and also for annoying and teasing one another. In their imaginative behavior they imitate birds and animals and in their fantasy conversations and visitations they use much speech mimicry. Children's gestures tend to be expansive--whole arm movement, where an adult would use forearm and wrist. Children participate in more tactile communication than adults, and this varies according to cross-cultural and socioeconomic differences.

The By-Elements occurring in children's nonverbal behavior are somewhat different from those of the adult world. Flowers, blades of grass, and dandelions-in-seed are part of the noise and body movement in children's nonverbal events. Among American young people, bobby socks worn a certain way, a penny in a loafer, and a shirt collar left unbuttoned signaled to the opposite sex; among American Indians and European peasants, hair arrangements and ribbons signal the same message.

Children's games and *sports* consume a large part of the study of children's gestures. Many children's gestures and games are *survivals* of earlier magical practices of adult behavior. Others are a result of imitating adults. The "work" of adults is the "play" of children. The constant movement of children is channeled into stylized finger rhymes and songs. Games are the children's first group activity, and pair activity (Call), and provide their first tactile experiences with a community outside their own family. Many children's games are contact games, Blindman's Bluff, London Bridges, Tag, Leapfrog, Tug-of-War. Games that are not contact games often end up that way! At the end of Ashes, Ashes, All Fall Down, the children tumble together in a pile. Rhymes for tickling are another expression of tactile experiences, often tests of endurance.

Margaret Mead describes an unusual kind of child behavior among the Arapesh, which she calls lip-play or lip-bubbling (pp. 58-9):

> Meanwhile, as the child grows older it learns to substitute new delights for its mother's breasts during her ever lengthening absences. It learns to play with its lips. This play it sees all about it among the older children, and the older children also play with the baby's lips and so set the first part of the pattern that fits in so well with the child's temporary loneliness and hunger. Interestingly enough, no Arapesh child ever sucks its thumb or sucks one finger continuously. But it engages in every other conceivable type of lip-play. It flicks its upper lip with its thumb, with its first finger, with its second finger; it blows out its

> cheeks and pounds them; it bubbles its lips with the palm of its hand, with the back of its hand; it tickles the inside of its lower lip with its tongue; it licks its arms and its knees. A hundred different stylized ways of playing with the mouth are present in the play of the older children and gradually transmitted to the developing child.
>
> This lip-play is the thread of behaviour which binds together the child's emotional life, which ties the happy security it felt in its yielding mother's arms to placid enjoyment of the long evenings by the fireside among its elders, and finally to a contented, unspecific sexual life. The Arapesh themselves regard playing with the lips as the symbol of childhood.

A good deal of aggressive behavior is released through nonverbal games, such as "Stare you down!" and "Speak, Monkey, Speak!" Gestures of insult would seem to be universal among children with the nose and tongue taking large shares of the actions, at least among Western peoples. Ritual gestures are matters of serious concern in children's oaths for sealing bargains and keeping secrets. A hair pulled from the head, spit, and blood often figure in these ritual gestures.

Contemporary children use gestures that are centuries old. One sixteenth-century illustration (Moser p. 765) shows a leader of a parade crossing his two index fingers, while a figure near him uses two sticks to make a cross. Another "King's X" example, appropriately gestured by the king himself complete with crown, is shown (see page 148) among old illustrations provided by Fischer (Plate V) (originally from H. R. Paul Schroeder, Geschichte des Lebensmagnetismus und des Hypnotismus, Leipzig, 1899, p. 157). It is likely that there is a relationship between finger crossing and little boys crossing streams of urine in their play-magic encounters (Feldman, p. 273).

Sex. Male/Female Behavior.[60] Male and female differences in human behavior signaling masculinity and femininity are perhaps conveyed more by nonverbal means than any other way. All people walk and talk, but females walk and talk differently from males. When we examine the paralinguistic and kinesic variables of male and female behavior, it is necessary to take into account temporal and cross-

cultural differences throughout history and throughout the world. What may have been considered male behavior at one time may not be considered masculine at a different point in history. Some children's games, for example, were once played by adults; young people courted in this way during the restricted days of Colonial America. During the 1800's businessmen participated in parlor games that have since become games only for children (Newell). One observation concerning female behavior (and this is probably not confined to nonverbal communication but applies to other cultural behavior as well) is that it often coincides with children's behavior. The high pitch and thin quality of a woman's voice may be very like that of a child.

Likewise, characteristics that are said to be feminine behavior in one country may not be thought of as feminine in another country. In order to correctly determine what are feminine and masculine behavior patterns, one must know a great deal about the norms of behavior in many situations of a particular country, or cultural group. As I have searched for descriptions of sex differences in paralanguage and kinesics, I have found surprisingly little that is of substance. The comments made are often subjective and imprecise.

Worse, the descriptions may reflect prejudices and double-standards. Several years ago, a reporter covering the Oscar awards ceremony centered his article on the women's voices and concluded that they sounded "gosh-awful." Here, he wrote, were the ambitious women of America and

Europe, decked out in their best with their hair perfectly coiffured: "Yet, their voices! Holy Eliza Doolittle! What sounds, what nasal sawings, what boorish bleatings, what toneless mumblings, what gratings of brass on tin, what shrill squawks, what jarring scratches, what put-on ladylike breathings assaulted our ears."[61] The male voices, he went on, sounded better on the whole. It would be difficult to honestly assess male and female differences in the atmosphere of that kind of description.

Difficulties in describing male/female paralanguage go back to terminology, subjective judgments, and lack of specific analysis regarding paralanguage itself and the <u>interpretation</u> of these events. My students brought this to my attention one day in class when we were attempting to list all the paralinguistic events we could think of. It was the firm belief of one of the students that "Men yell and women scream"! Other vocabulary differences can be noted when the sex of the speaker is obvious: Men bellow and punch; women purr and slap. The interpretation of events is obscured and distorted by double-standards in reacting to situations. If a female talks or cries into a pillow, it's "muffled sobbing"; if a male does the same, it's "blubbering," with negative connotations.

Added to the difficulties created by double-standards and prejudices, are the difficulties of being scientifically precise and accurate in describing such things as voice quality and movement behavior. The scientific study is in the very early stages of trying to define the discipline and find rigorous, objective ways to describe a "rough/squawky/smooth/sweet/resonant/mellow/brassy-voice."

Nevertheless, a few observations have been made that are worth noting. William Austin (1965) contributes several observations regarding male/female paralinguistic behavior. Women use a higher than usual pitch to indicate innocence, femininity, helplessness, and regression. Males use an exaggerated low pitch to signal masculinity. But, Austin adds, low pitch has become fashionable for women. Teenage boys project toughness with low pitch "O.K., you guys." The distinctive features of oral/nasal sounds are also part of the paralinguistic system even within a language that does not have contrasting nasal vowel sounds. Nasality is a characteristic of the speech of teenage boys and men trying to appear tough. Paralanguage carries a heavy load in courtship language--low and nasal sounds from the male;

high oral and giggling sounds from the female. Only in the final stages is the voice low and nasal with both sexes, but with wide pitch and intensity variation on the part of the female. When intoxicated, both sexes produce nasal quality. Other distinctive features occurring in the paralinguistic system signaling sex roles are laryngealization and extra-aspiration or breathiness. Imitative behavior is exhibited by paralinguistic means. Derogatory imitation, Austin continues, is one of the most infuriating acts of aggression one person can commit on another. A male will imitate a female in high, rapid speech, "Yes dear, I'll be down in a minute" or the female may imitate the male with exaggerated slow and low speech, "Aw, just one more little drink."

Though the information is sparse regarding other cultures of the world, it would appear that male/female behavior patterns are also differentiated by nonverbal means. The Tzeltal women of southern Mexico speak with a very thin, high-pitched quality. George Trager tells me that a Taos Indian woman changes voice quality depending on whom she is speaking with. To the husband and children she uses a special high-pitch, nasalized, twangy quality, with an intense pulsating beat. In Scandinavia, the women but not the men, express agreement by articulating "ja" with air drawn in. The Mazateco whistle speech (Cowan) is articulated almost exclusively by men, though women understand and may respond verbally to a flirtatious approach or to a whistled communication from a son. And note that some females in our own society do not whistle.

"Whistling girls and crowing hens,
Always come to some bad end."

While crying is taboo for American males, in Iran it is the <u>men</u> who weep (A. Hayes; and Pittenger and Smith, p. 73).

Among the Gros Ventre Indians who communicate by sign language, Flannery noticed differences among male and female signers. The Gros Ventre also articulate the "war whoop," which in their case expresses joy and thankfulness, in differing ways: the women "rattle the tongue" and the men break the sound by striking the mouth rhythmically with the palm.[62] In a study of Castilian Spanish[63] it was noted that only the male speakers used the creaky sounds of laryngealized voicing. Note that in English females may use this low, creaky voice in sensuous moods. Austin notes marked linguistic and paralinguistic differences in male/female speech in Japan. The male speech is loud and low, in Samurai movies almost a bark; female speech is soft and high, almost a squeak.

Again, interpretation of nonverbal signals is a delicate process. In Japan, the paralinguistic features which indicate respect and politeness are breathiness, openness, lowered volume, and raised level of pitch. Note that some of these, for example, breathiness, quieter voice, and higher pitch, are female signals to the opposite sex in English. Teachers of English in Japan point out the conflict for Japanese speakers (Cammack and van Buren):

> When the Japanese system is carried over into English, the results are not always as the Japanese speaker would expect. In the case of women's speech (extreme examples of which might be the girls who make announcements over the public address system in department stores, trains, etc.), the English speaker's nearest equivalent is a kind of feminine baby-talk usually associated with lack of intelligence or private male-female relations. On the other hand, female English speakers often sound harsh, raucous, rude, or overly masculine to a Japanese ear.

Voice disguisers--instruments made by stretching a membrane over a hollow--are used in secret ceremonies in Africa and some other areas (Balfour). The voice of the speaker, a male, is disguised by the buzzing membrane, and is thus used to intimidate women and children and gain greater control and discipline.

The falsetto voice is wrongly thought to be a prerogative of male articulation. Among the Gbeya people in the Central African Republic, the speech of women is often modified by falsetto.[64] The uses that were noted seem to have to do with emotions and attitudes, but this is not clear yet. In the United States the use of falsetto is significantly different among some segments of the black population and the white population. Both male and female blacks may use falsetto in ways that are distinct from the use in white Western cultures, though the occurrences are not clearly defined yet. Falsetto occurs frequently with blacks in circumstances of great emotion, either very happy or very angry. It occurs often in story-telling and joking. Both male and female children use it frequently. When black males use it, it does not necessarily have the connotation of femininity. In Western societies falsetto is often used by men to imitate women, but not so in all cultures. Among the Mohave, the male does not change to a falsetto, but using his normal voice, suggests the nuances of female speech (Devereux).

In addition to vocal behavior and speech modification, femininity and masculinity are expressed by body language or movement behavior. Posture is a marked feature and at times communicates things which can not be said. One way to examine postural behavior is to observe the postural configurations in magazines and newspapers. A very common feature that one will discover is that females very often tilt their heads. This head gesture may convey an attitude of coyness or submissiveness, but it is so common that one can almost always find such a head position in any group of women. A recent scientific study with film documented this kinesic behavior. Kendon and Ferber did an extensive study of the greeting behavior which took place at a large birthday party in a garden setting. They analyzed the film by measuring, counting, and showing angles and distances. They categorized five positions of the head during the greetings which took place: erect head, head tilted forward, head tilted back, head cocked to one side, and head held erect or forward. Males favored the forward position: 27 out of 35 occurrences were by males. Females tilted their head to one side significantly more than males: 18 out of 20 times recorded. The head-tilt seemed to be more obvious in male-female greetings. An analysis of children's books showed that the vacuous, "pretty" mother is shown in illustrations "in the classic servant's posture, body slightly bent forward, hands clasped, eyes riveted on the master of the house or the child."[65]

Clothes have an effect on posture. The miniskirt significantly affected the walking and sitting posture of females in recent years. Mark Twain noticed the correlation of clothes and sex in sitting posture in the famous passage where Huck Finn, disguised in a girl's dress, gave himself away when he closed his legs to catch something.

Facial expression is another aspect of kinesic behavior which has rich possibilities for communicating male and female patterns. As we saw earlier, it has been thought that females, who are supposed to be more intuitive, could interpret these aspects of communication better than males.

The research in these matters of sex differences, however, is highly contradictory and ambiguous, with many variables obfuscating the results. In the final analysis, researchers have concluded that no significance can be attributed to sex differences. All we can say is that some males are more sensitive to these features than some females; and some females are more sensitive than some males.

There are some differences in facial expression which do show statistical significance. In interaction, for example, women look at each other more than do males (Argyle et al. 1968). It seems to me, also, in observing the behavior of couples with an established relationship, that the woman looks at her man much more than he looks at her, at least in public appearances.

With regard to differences in the brain, it appears that the visual area also has sex differences. It has been shown that males are superior to females in certain visual-spatial tasks. In the functioning of the right hemisphere of the brain, males tend to have a greater left-visual field superiority for dot location and dot enumeration than females.[66] How much of this innate difference is carried over into the life-style and masculine/feminine behavior of human beings is not at all clear. For just as in sound behavior, females have learned to use their eyes in ways different from males. Beinhauer, a Spanish scholar, noted the many instances throughout the Spanish literature on the references to the glances of women. It would appear to be an endless study!

Another important component of facial expression is the mouth, with all its subtleties of shape and movement even during speech. Study of the smile shows significant differences in male and female use. When females approach males, they smile. In fact, they smile more throughout their lifetime, if they "learned their lesson well"--that females are supposed to be pleasant and create a happy home. A recent observer equates it to the servant shuffle.[67] Recent studies of the chimpanzee may suggest that this submissive gesture is of more than ancient standing. It is uncanny how closely some of the gestural behavior of the chimpanzees resembles that of human beings. In noting the submissive behavior throughout the discussions of chimpanzee life, one is somehow reminded of the smile behavior of female to male human being. In describing the appeasement and submission behavior of one of the low ranking chimpanzees, Lawick-Goodall noted that during such an encounter, he would "pull back the corners of his lips and expose his teeth in a nervous grin."

Submissive and dominant behavior is also evidenced in the manner of touching which male and female exhibit. Henley shows that tactile behavior between the sexes is correlated with status dimensions. Tactile behavior in the autistic realm is also a tension-reliever mechanism. Montagu makes several observations on male/female differences (1971, p. 208) in tension-relievers,

> ... perhaps the most familiar in Western cultures being head scratching in men. Women do not usually behave in this manner; indeed, the sexual differences in the use of the skin are marked. In states of perplexity men will rub their chins with their hand, or tug at the lobes of their ears, or rub their forehead or cheeks or back of the neck. Women have very different gestures in such states. They will either put a finger on their lower front teeth with the mouth slightly open or pose a finger under the chin. Other masculine gestures in states of perplexity are: rubbing one's nose, placing the flexed fingers over the mouth, rubbing the side of the neck, rubbing the infraorbital part of the face, rubbing the closed eyes, and picking the nose. These are all masculine gestures; so is rubbing the back of the hand or the front of the thigh, and pursing of the lips.

The role of the speaker must be considered in describing the inventory of male/female nonverbal events. Silence must be observed by widows in some cultures but is not required of the widower. Male/female nonverbal behavior is closely involved with other dimensions of status and control. Consider for example, the patronizing and conciliating tone of the male department store clerk to a woman asking information, of a male physician to a female physician, or of a government official to a female reporter. He'd better not talk that way to a man! The pattern is reversed when a man becomes ill. The female nurse uses Baby Talk even to mature males who command high executive positions when they are on their feet! A study of Roman art by Brilliant, shows the ranking status depicted in sculpture and coinage. When husband and wife are shown she is in the inferior position.

"Human sounds" have been studied by Ostwald (1960) who also observes sex differentiations among the uses and prohibitions.

> Sexual prejudices and taboos against noise-making by women may account for the fact of so few outstanding female musicians. Traditionally women are expected to be more contained and silent than men, and their instruction in music was limited to such lady-like instruments as lutes and harps. Times change, of course, and during WW II many noisy women were employed as boiler-makers or riveters.

The restrictions and prohibitions surrounding female vocal behavior are of very long standing. Shakespeare recognized them and conveyed this through his characters:

> Her voice was ever soft,
> Gentle and low; an excellent thing in woman [*Lear*, V, iii].

Recently a panel of bachelors described a "feminine" person as "a woman who does not talk loudly."

In order to assess differences of behavior, one is always brought back to consider innate sexual differences. As we saw earlier, there do seem to be some differences in the brains of males and females. Because the research is in very primitive stages, it is not clear yet how these brain differences might affect the nonverbal communicative behavior of male and female. Another physiological difference lies in the vocal cords and this results in higher pitched voices for women. Since pitch is relative, however, some females speak with lower voices than some males. Other than pitch differences, male and female share equal possibilities of articulations for any verbal or paralinguistic communicative act as we observe them in languages of the world. If then, the physiological differences are minimal, why are the culturally learned differences so ubiquitous?

Infants are taught these learned differences at very early ages. We know that infants at the pre-speech age of development respond to male/female differences in intonation patterns (Lieberman 1968, pp. 38-47). Goldberg and Lewis studied early sex differences of infants at six months and again at thirteen months. They found a high correlation between the behavior of mother and resultant response of infant. Their experiment demonstrated that the sex-role behavior patterns are already evident the first year of life. Because of the differential treatment of mothers to sons and daughters, they concluded that parents can be active promulgators of sex-role behavior through reinforcement of sex-role-appropriate responses within the first year.

In adolescent years, and thereafter, paralanguage and kinesics become important in attracting sex partners. Studies on eye movement have indicated that eye communication is a crucial matter in sex response patterns. Pupil dilation occurs in response to the desired sex (Hindmarch, in Argyle and Exline, p. 26).

Birdwhistell (1970, p. 159), who pioneered nonverbal messages of kinesic behavior in a rigorous, scientific way, studied the "courtship dance" among American teen agers:

> We found it quite easy to delineate some twenty-four steps between the initial tactile contact between the young male and female and the coitional act. These steps and countersteps had a coercive order. For instance, a boy taking a girl's hand must await a counter-pressure on his hand before beginning the finger intertwine. The move and countermove, ideally, must take place before he 'casually' and tentatively puts his arm around her shoulders. And each of these contacts should take place before the initial kiss. However, there seems to be no clockable duration necessary for each of these steps. The boy or girl is called 'slow' or 'fast' in terms of the appropriate ordering of the steps, not in terms of the length of time taken at each stage. Skipping steps or reversing their order is 'fast'. Insistence on ignoring the prompting to move to the next step is 'slow'.

Status. Socioeconomic Behavior. Status relationships and class stratification are signalled, among other things, by nonverbal behavior. Such things as tone of voice or the use of silence convey rank. Posture was a marked feature of status among the Romans. A man of high rank was depicted in statues as erect, calmly draped, and in a frontal position. Those without dignity, derelicts, old women, drunkards, servants, and fools are shown as bent figures, tight and tense. The status connections are evident (Brilliant).

The identification of status by nonverbal means influenced the decision at a world-famous trial. According to a titled witness at the trial of Anastasia, the manner in which the defendant sneezed conveyed the information that she was not of royal bearing. She ducked her head under the table at dinner to sneeze. A princess would never have exhibited such bad manners, the duchess claimed![68]

Cultural Dialects

Human beings have devised intricate systems to carry on communication within groups and sub-groups. These are coded systems, arbitrarily chosen, and used for brevity, secrecy, ceremony, or expediency of some kind. It is not as difficult to see the structure of these systems as it is to realize that the non-coded systems are also structured. These systems comprise the gestural and paralinguistic signals used in Rites of Passage, Occupation, Education, and the Arts and Performances. The signals of secret and professional societies, warfare, and religious ritual would also be included in this very large group of cultural systems.

These systems contain formalized gestures and noises (for example the whistles of Cavalrymen) which have been instituted for direct communication. In some cases, as in religious and Rites of Passage body movement, the nonverbal entities don't seem to convey a message, per se, and here we see where nonverbal components merge into etiquette and custom. These systems have the institutional function of maintaining the community and keeping business moving: the auctioneer's and buyer's gestures; the French teacher's gestures to the class; the finger-counting under the cloth in Chinese bargaining; the surgeon's gestures during an operation; the call girl's signals; the referee's exacting arm gestures; the locking of the eyes that leads to population explosion; the secret handshakes of the lodges, fraternities, and teenage gangs; and the animal trainer's almost imperceptible movement to his charges. There are more ... and a chapter or a book could be written about each of these cultural message systems. Curiously enough, very little is found in scholarly or scientific writings that treats these systems. It is as though these varieties of communication are disdainfully considered not worth any high-level thinking. And yet the world moves on just such special message systems as these. Consider a busy metropolitan airport where gestures control hundreds of flights each day--transportation would collapse without them. Consider the economic importance of gesturing in tobacco warehouses and the stock exchange. Consider the helplessness of the television industry if all hand and arm movements outside the camera's eye were paralyzed. Somehow, in some way, these nonverbal components must be considered in a total theory of human communication that goes beyond language.

Language Substitutes

Coded systems which are actual substitutes for the verbal act are derivative of spoken language. They have been created for various practical and circumstantial reasons or have been forced into existence by non-normal conditions. The Lingua Franca of hand signals developed by North American Indians and certain Australian tribes permitted communication between peoples of widely different languages.

Circumstantial reasons such as distance and silence underlie the use of both Gestural and Paralinguistic Languages in some cases. Drum and whistle languages, Australian aborigine and American Indian Sign Languages are reported in use over great distances. Sign Language among the Trappist Monks, in Hindu ceremonial rites, and in Australian tribal rites is reported to be used when silence is desired. It was used by American Indians and Australian tribal people when silence was obligatory, as in hunting or stalking the enemy. Meggitt reports seven categories of use among the Australians, in ceremonies, gossip, love affairs, conversational emphasis, besides hunting or stalking the enemy.

In non-normal situations, such as with the deaf, sign language may be used exclusively. This use is also extended to persons lacking vocalization. In sign languages there is a significant lack of or infrequent use of function words, such as "for, to, am, however, any." In deaf sign language "parents" becomes "mother-father" or "father-mother." Also in deaf sign language, "There's a man in there," becomes "man there" and "there man." Prepositions such as those occurring in adverbials of place or location may be signed, but relational prepositions such as "to" and "of" are not necessarily part of the vocabulary. For example, in deaf sign language, the expression, "I will not be going to discuss...," becomes, "I (negative) (future) discuss...."

Inflections and tense affixes are not signed; basic root forms are expressed by a single sign. Temporal relationships, if not made clear by the context, are expressed by separate forms such as "yesterday" or "now," rather than endings on verbs. In Australian aboriginal sign language a root may occur as either a noun or a verb; for example, a particular sign means "boomerang" as well as the action for throwing the boomerang. In deaf sign language the same sign is used for "car" and "drive" (Stokoe et al. 1965).

There are fewer vocabulary items in sign language than in natural language; synonyms are covered by basic words. The first three signs in William Tomkins' list of synonyms (p. 64) of American Indian sign language illustrate this: Abandoned--divorced, thrown away, displaced, deserted, forsaken; Aboard--sitting down, on top of; Abuse--scold, ill-treat, upbraid, defame, detract. The vocabulary of the American Indian and Australian aboriginal sign languages clearly indicates what things were of interest or of necessity to the people. For example names of animals rank high in the lists.

Descriptions of American Indian sign language, written by those who observed it, in the early encounters of this type of communication, emphasize the fluid articulation of signing. The communication was said to be "a flow of motion," "a smooth flow," "a language of motions and not of positions," "graceful and flowing gestures." Seton (p. xliii) was impressed with the elegant manner of signing: "Many signs are followed by a changeable liaison; that is, by an introduced sweep to join it on to the sign that follows and avoid a jerk or unpleasant movement. This ... is what I call an Indian accent, few whites achieve it." Nevertheless, transition points are observed in sequenced signing. Stokoe (1966, pp. 246-7) speaks of a juncture morpheme, "full stop, period, end of utterance, place to interrupt if you're so minded." Close observation of deaf persons conversing reveals cues for turn-taking, slight body movements, which anticipate change of speaker, fingers itching to respond, or facial expression beginning to interrupt.

Early descriptions of American Indian sign language speak of the dignity and poise with which sign language was articulated between the Indians; few facial movements occurred and the posture was neutral. In contrast, Australian aboriginal signers used facial expression generously and deaf signers depend heavily upon facial expression and posture to carry much of the meaning of the communication. Besides natural expression of the face moving with the communication, the facial expression may be an essential component of the sign. It is, for example, an interrogative marker in a question asked by deaf speakers and has been recorded for American Indian sign language (Mallery, 1881, p. 479) in spite of the usual non-active facial movement mentioned earlier. Bebian, in 1825, used diacritical marks to denote: question, surprise, and reverence in his notation of deaf sign language (Stokoe, 1960, p. 15).

Paralinguistic acts may accompany the sign language though these appear to be very rare. They are expressly forbidden in the Cistercian Order. Paralanguage may occur as a component of the sign as illustrated in the sign for "the Banak tribe": "Make a whistling sound 'phew' (beginning at a high note and ending about an octave lower); then draw the extended index across the throat from the left to the right and out to nearly at arm's length" (Mallery 1881, p. 462). The signs for "raven" and "crow" were similar in the Thompson tribe--the former word signed more slowly--with imitation of the raven croak (krô) and the latter signed with faster movement and the crow cry (kā, kā) (Teit, p. 137). The whistle was used in "whistling elk" (Clark, p. 421) and "sun dance" (Scott, p. 214), in the latter, presumably to represent the instrument used in the dance. Artifacts, such as a blanket, dust, peace-pipe, flint and steel were used as By-Elements in American Indian sign language.

Dialects are said to occur in all the various kinds of sign language. Mallery (1880, pp. 18 ff.) lists seven signs for "chief"; seven signs for "day"; seven signs for "dead, death" and many other examples. Several authors mention the idiosyncratic movement of individual signers. Earl Walpole, in conversation, illustrates the range of variation of one sign by various speakers, much in the concept of emic interpretation.

Deaf sign language is unique in that the verbal act is often articulated along with the signing so that the nondeaf may hear and the deaf may lip-read. Recent discussions of contemporary Indian sign language (Kroeber, p. 1) indicate that an English translation accompanies signing nowadays, but this appears to be a recent invention to entertain the white man!

Sign language is not infallible. Mistakes and misunderstandings occur in signing just as they do in any system where ambiguous constructions are possible. Also, matters of style are conveyed in varieties of articulation. During the Sign Language Conference, sponsored by the Center of Applied Linguistics in 1969, four speakers of sign language illustrated the signs for "mother and father" with varieties of movement which indicated a range of style from formal and reverent to intimate. The English translations offered range from "mama and papa" to "Father-God." In slang expressions (not recorded in his 1965 dictionary, Stokoe tells me!) the tongue may be extended and vibrated, to indicate disgust or rejection in a non-formal manner. Range of emotion was illustrated at the conference by a deaf speaker signing the expression, "I bought a new car," in a variety of moods and attitudes.

Though a recent film on American Indian sign language shows a woman using sign language, early reports such as Dodge's (quoted by Walker, p. 173) never mention women signers. An acquaintance who grew up on a reservation in Montana tells me that the old men used sign language often in conversation, even within the same language community, perhaps for emphasis along with speech, but women seldom used it. However, in Australia reports imply that aboriginal women used sign language the same as men, and possibly even more, because during a long period of mourning, silence was obligatory, and sign language was the means of communication. During this time of mourning, however, when they couldn't talk, they were permitted to laugh!

Drum and whistle languages are generally known to be based on the tonal distinctions which natural speech contain. The whistle language of Gomera in the Canary Islands, however, is based on the phonetic features of Spanish, which of course, is not a tonal language. The most complete description available was done by Classe, who shows that the various vowels and consonants carry certain pitches and thereby can be understood even as arrangements of vowel-consonant represent various words. A feature to be noted is that a "phoneme" which may have two phonetic articulations is actually represented by two different whistles--not one as we might expect the phonemic abstraction to maintain. This should be of interest to those today who hold that languages should be analyzed without the distinction of phonemic and phonetic level.

Chapter IX: SCIENTIFIC METHOD

From previous encounters in daily life or from reading this book, the reader may feel that actually much is known about human communication. However, I would reiterate that the study of human behavior is in a pristine stage and we are only beginning to fathom its magnitude and complexities. There is an urgent need to know more about the nonverbal behavior discussed in this book from cross-disciplinary and cross-cultural points of view. There is an urgent need to know more about the relationship of nonverbal behavior to language in the total communication process.

Concepts and Methodology

The model for nonverbal behavior in Chapter II presupposes that gestures and noises can be grouped into certain definable classes. And this, of course, implies a theoretical basis. At this point it might be well to stop and consider the notion of scientific investigation in studying human behavior. The studies so far seem very anecdotal--no surprise with the givens of human behavior. Nevertheless, linguists have attempted to approach one aspect of behavior, the study of language, with scientific methods. They have tried to describe languages in a way that is (1) consistent (or non-contradictory), (2) exhaustive, and (3) simple. McQuown (1957) discusses his methodology in transcribing a psychiatric interview. He claimed: 1) total accountability, 2) replicability, and 3) verifiability. To a great extent linguists _have_ been successful in assuming a rigorous, scientific stance. The fact remains, though, that human behavior involves so many variables that it is not possible to work in a completely objective manner; the investigator is always part of the behavior or language data. Crystal and Quirk acknowledge the impressionistic nature of working with paralinguistic effects, though they attempt to define the parameters. Inasmuch as possible, one approximates the ideal.

It remains that the study of human communication has only beginning snatches of theory to work with. Much of the work is in the "prescientific stage of collection and classification of interesting facts." In many cases we have only "isolated examples within a theoretical vacuum." In spite of this, there is a certain disdain among those in scholarly circles for gathering data these days and the concern with theory has led researchers away from collecting and observing data. In reading the literature one might conclude that a plethora of theories are flourishing in a paucity of facts. The dichotomizing of theory and application (or data-gathering) is most unfortunate in our search for knowledge and the development of theoretical explanations. The two cannot exist without each other. "Rather than facts crying for a theory, the theory is crying for the facts...." Hockett, a well-known linguist, speaks of "the productive wrong decision," and a review of the history of science will affirm that at times scientists have, indeed, worked for years on the basis of a wrong hypothesis. There is no possible way that this can be avoided altogether, because scientists, as all human beings, are trapped by their environment. Nevertheless, some of these wrong hypotheses could be identified sooner by a closer observation of "non-prestigious" data.

Without a fully developed theoretical framework, it appears that, short of neglecting the study altogether, all we can do is to continue to make descriptions about the nature of human behavior and to look for universals. There must be more of the tedious and time-consuming observations and gathering of data. Darwin's techniques of working, with keen observational ability, are still useful. In a discussion of theory building, a colleague has shown that descriptive research is essential to theoretical advances:

> "Descriptive Research"
>
> There is no more devasting condemnation that the self-designated theorist makes of the researcher than to label his work <u>purely descriptive</u>. There is an implication that associates 'purely descriptive' research with empty-headedness; the label also implies that as a bare minimum every healthy researcher has at least an hypothesis to test, and preferably a whole model. This is nonsense.

> In every discipline, but particularly in its early stages of development, purely descriptive research is indispensable. Descriptive research is the stuff out of which the mind of man, the theorist, develops the units that compose his theories. The very essence of description is to name the properties of things: you may do more, but you cannot do less and still have description. The more adequate the description, the greater is the likelihood that the units derived from the description will be useful in subsequent theory building.[69]

Now, in order to take a serious look at the aspects of human behavior that this study is concerned with, we will use what tools we have, crude as they might be. Tools useful for one piece of work might not be useful to create or develop another. Applying concepts or tools or methodology from one discipline to another must be done with humility and flexibility. If they seem to be giving insight or understanding, we will continue to use them until something better comes along.

Classification is an important device that people use to cope with the environment. To a research worker, the struggle with classification has heuristic value. One is forced to find terminology. A prerequisite of good classification is a comprehensive knowledge of the inventory of items to be explained in the theoretical model. Classification is not a prestige pastime these days. In fact, to be working with data or concerned with classification is to be automatically ostracized to the camp of the "uninteresting," the "trite," or the "trivial"; it even, as one linguist put it, gains "negative prestige." The "hunches" which are the bases of good explanatory theory result from familiarity and struggle with the data. Unexpected findings inevitably show up. One of the surprises I found in dealing with the elements of communication besides verbal language, was that the physiological functions and acts carry such a heavy load of communication.

One conceptual tool that has been useful in analyzing languages is Interpretation. An element that can be described by itself, in isolation, by a completely objective description (assuming that to be possible), has to be "interpreted" as to how it operates in the total system. For example (to take an illustration from language), the sound "t" as heard in the word "top" can be measured and weighed and scrutinized in precise and exact measurements by making a spectrogram and analyzing its exact acoustic proportions. But as far as realizing its function in the total language system, this is inadequate. More important is to discover its behavior in relationship to other elements in the system. For example, in what way is its behavior different from its voiced counterpart "d"? Is the aspiration following it a distinctive feature that must be recognized in the system for communication in the particular language we are investigating? Is it articulated in the same way when it occurs in other positions, for example, finally, as in "tot"? What happens to its behavior when it occurs next to other elements that belong to its same class, for example the consonant "l" as in "little"? We can only understand "t" when we <u>interpret</u> it in terms of response to it in the total system.

An illustration from nonverbal behavior can be offered. Take the event of <u>silence</u> in the hypothetical situation: A young man asks a young woman for a date; she hesitates long before answering. In exploring the "meaning" of the silence, one can postulate several possible answers: (1) she doesn't want to go and doesn't know how to say "no"; (2) she has a date but would rather go with this one; (3) a bystander is near and she feels awkward at this exposure of her private life; (4) she is forbidden to leave the dormitory--can't explain; (5) she wants to go, but her parents have forbidden her to go with this young man; or (6) she is trying to play "hard to get." In order to interpret this event of silence in this behavior situation, it is necessary to know about the relationship of all elements and how they affect each other in time and space.

Another illustration is the event of clearing the throat. One cannot say what this means in isolation; it must be interpreted to determine whether it means: (1) a physiological act of necessity; (2) a signal to call to attention the listener; (3) an intent to interrupt a long-winded speaker; (4) a response--an acknowledgment, where speech might be precluded; or (5) a warning, for example to a child.

Notice that the possible meanings of these acts fall into a range of variation, which in itself is predictable by the participants in the system. To go back to the linguistic illustration of "t": all the variations of this sound are identifiable for a particular language; these illustrations are from English. The sound is articulated with significant aspiration or breath when it occurs initially in an utterance as in "top." The aspiration is significantly diminished when an "s" precedes it as in "stop." It can vary to a flap sound when it occurs between vowels as in "butter." In final position it may be unreleased or released with heavy aspiration as in "tot." The position and articulation of the tongue changes with lateral involvement when it occurs next to "l" as in "little." There is involvement with the glottis when it occurs as in "lightning" or "cotton." There is lengthening when it occurs at a juncture point as in "nighttime." This appears to be a lot of variation for one item! But the varieties themselves fall into patterns--they are all within the "t" range, i.e. they all involve the tip of the tongue and they all occur somewhere in the alveolar area of the mouth cavity. Every native speaker of English responds to and acts in accord with this behavior. This range of possibilities of interpretation would not be the same for another language.

Likewise any nonverbal event would have different ranges of possibilities of interpretation in different cultures or societies. Take, for example, the nonverbal event of sticking out the tongue. In the Aztec drawings of Mexico and in India the tongue protruding from the mouth is a symbol of wisdom. In Tibet it is a component of the gesture for a greeting.

Interpretation, then, is essential when considering nonverbal behavior. There are "infinite variations" in body and facial movement and combinations of all the possible movements, just as there are infinite possibilities of speech acts. We have discussed some of these varieties in the previous chapter. Some are idiosyncratic; some are coded systems of which there would be as many as societies wanted to dream up; some are varieties of chronological age, ever changing; some are sub-culturally defined, the sex and socioeconomic situation giving variation. Some are defined by the particular culture one is reared in. Therefore, in analyzing paralinguistic and kinesic acts, it may not be useful to make a precise recording of each act, but rather deal with descriptions as "representations" of the physical properties of the act and for what purpose it functions.

Segmentation is another concept which is useful in analyzing nonverbal events. First, an illustration from language: The pronunciation of "t" is different in the two words, "tea" and "two," because of the difference of the vowels following. Even before the word begins, the lips are spread in anticipation of pronouncing the [i] in "tea," and the lips are already rounded for the [u] in "two." The spreading and rounding of the lips is only relevant to the vowel sound--not to the "t." How, then, do we segment the different elements of these utterances in order to classify and describe them? A similar difficulty is encountered when attempts are made to classify gestures. When does a gesture begin and when does it end? Which elements of the gesture are reflections of the individual speaker, and which are actually components of the lexical or reinforcement gesture? It isn't easy to separate these. Is it possible? Or even necessary?

Another concept well-known in language study is redundancy. Communication by verbal language would be impossible without redundancy, given the limitations of our systems of senses. Nonverbal behavior also abounds with redundancy. An attitude or emotion is conveyed to another person by what is said, the body placement, the effect of the hands, facial expression, especially the mouth and eyes. Any one of these might be excluded and the communication act still takes place.

Still another concept which must be considered in studying behavioral events is the ordering of these events. In the word "stop" the order of the "s" and the "t" is significant; in fact, the reverse order would be impossible in initial position in English, though not in another language. The ordering of behavioral events also communicates. In greeting friends at the door, the spoken greeting and possibly a handshake occur before the guest is asked to remove his or her coat. The reverse would be an abortive communication--either a joke or mentally disturbed behavior. Some of the order of events is logical, but not all. The order of the courses during a meal is really arbitrary; there is nothing about the digestive system which would preclude eating the soup last; in fact, this is the usual order in a Lithuanian household and in a really elegant, well-ordered Chinese meal. But it is hard to imagine a Westerner tolerating such a change of order in the courses of a meal.

"Serial order" was discussed many years ago by the neuropsychologist, Karl Lashley. He used examples of ordering in language, so well known to linguists, as the introduction to his remarks. He recognized the relationship of physiology to behavior. Ruesch speaks of the cyclical rhythms of life processes and their recursive behavior. He discusses improper timing and the results in disturbed communication (pp. 49 ff.).

Ability to focus is a useful device in the observation of any kind of human behavior. To illustrate from speech: there are many things that happen during a verbal event. Pitch varies, rhythm changes or is steady, quality of vowels changes from syllable to syllable. One cannot accurately hear and describe all these (and more) at once; linguists train themselves to focus on one aspect at a time, "hearing" at one time pitch and only pitch, another time length of sounds and syllables, etc., until they can accurately describe the total by all its parts. A Nonverbal Act is likewise impossible to take in all at once. It is useful to observe or focus on one item at a time: the hands and only the hands, then the face or some part of it (eyes, for example), the stance, ... until the total behavior is described. Right away it is obvious that in order to do this the event must be repeatable. Of course, human behavior is never repeated in exactly the same way. Films and tape recorders are a part of the answer, but only a part, in that they may record too much extraneous material that distracts in careful observation, for example, the rooster crowing or the truck passing, and people change behavior when being recorded. Television provides an observation laboratory. One can't stare in deep concentration at one's acquaintances as one can at the personalities seen on TV, especially extemporaneous talk shows.

A final word of caution concerning interpretation of human behavior. Attributing meaning to gestures and vocalizations is not for amateurs. The dangers are many of interpreting human behavior by speculation or fraudulent character reading in the manner of parlor games. Without regard for the Context of Situation (see Chapter VII) and all the person's previous experience and background, for example cross-cultural contacts, simplistic judgments are tantamount to the cross-examining lawyer who demands "yes" or "no"! Likewise it is somewhat like the psychology test that judges a man effeminate if he chooses to work in a florist shop--when the only alternative is a slaughter house. Too simple generalizations lead to further restrictions and prohibitions that result in inhibited behavior that can cause persons actually not to be able to function in certain areas. Interpretation of human behavior should not be permitted to fall into the hands of a novice.

Applicability of Research

Ultimately the practical value of an academic focus on these matters must be dealt with. Will communication be enhanced between individuals, communities, and nations, by examining the nonverbal subsystems of communication? I think not, contrary to my own first assumptions when I started seriously studying nonverbal communication. In fact, bringing these things to attention, other than for scientific purposes, may even be counterproductive to communication. Flack (1966) speaks of the "limits to sharable meaning." Relationships can be destroyed by knowing too much, or communicating too much--with all the potential for inaccuracies. Or relationships can be destroyed by abortive communication--by trying too hard and bungling. Human beings cannot function with equanimity when too much detail is brought to the level of awareness. The human can cope with only so much. Blind spots are a protection, in a sense. Bringing too much to the attention of a person, about the way he or she fiddles with their hands, or grimaces, or uses over-high pitch too often, will not enhance communication, and may push the individual into isolation.

There is good reason to doubt the much publicized belief held today that the problems between office management and workers, government and people, husband and wife, parent and offspring, are "lack of communication." Rather, the problem may be simply a lack of tolerance or a lack of accepting others as they are. Another reason for not trying to "understand" too insistently is found in the difficulties of interpreting correctly the infinite variety of human behaviors. Without having a complete case history of an individual's background, as well as access to the inner workings of the mind, it is not possible to be able to translate a person's nonverbal behavior into meaningful identifications in all instances. It is a case where a little knowledge could do more harm than good.

It may turn out that trying to understand the other person beyond the usual daily needs is a neurotic tendency. The demand to make the other person communicate and provoking the other person to talk in the name of "better understanding" may be a harmful and neurotic goal. A more productive goal would be to accept human differences.

This is not to say that these things should not be studied by the scientist. It is to say, that we should not expect unmerited results. Studying the digestive system in minute detail will not help digestion. Studying a symphony in excruciating detail will not enhance the listening pleasure. Nonetheless, the academic specialist in communication will most certainly study all the aspects of the communication act in scientific detail.

CHAPTER NOTES

CHAPTER I

1. Robert Coles, "A young psychiatrist looks at his profession," Atlantic Monthly (July 1961); reprinted in The Norton Reader, New York: W. W. Norton, 1965, pp. 32-9.
2. Goethe, Sprüche in Prosa, 1887 Weimar ed., XLII, Part II, p. 118.
3. Alexis de Tocqueville, Democracy in America, 1835, Part I, 1.
4. For example, C. K. Ogden, and I. A. Richards, The Meaning of meaning, New York: Harcourt, Brace and World, 1923.
5. Arthur M. Schlesinger [Sr.], Learning how to behave, New York: Macmillan, 1946, p. 1.

CHAPTER II

6. Albert Einstein, "The fundamentals of theoretical physics," in Leo Hamalian and Edmond L. Volpe, eds., Great essays by Nobel Prize winners, New York: Noonday Press, 1960, p. 219.
7. Joseph Bram, Language and society, New York: Random House [1955] 1966, p. 2.
8. For example, Cherry; also Charles W. Morris, Signs, language, and behavior, New York: Braziller, 1946; Leslie A. White, "The symbol: The origin and basis of human behavior," The science of culture: A Study of man and civilization, 1949, (Indianapolis: Bobbs-Merrill, Reprint Series, Social Sciences A-239).
9. John Lotz, "Linguistics: Symbols make man," in Owen Thomas, ed., The structure of language, New York: Bobbs-Merrill, 1967, p. 11.
10. Philip Rawson, Erotic art of the East: The sexual theme in Oriental painting and sculpture, Intro. by

Alex Comfort, New York: Prometheus Press, 1968, p. 281.

11. Noam Chomsky, *Aspects of the theory of syntax*, Cambridge, Mass.: MIT Press, 1965, p. 201.
12. W. A. White, *Foundations of psychiatry*, New York: Nervous and Mental Disease Pub. Co., 1921, p. 79.
13. Sigmund Freud, *The Standard edition of the complete psychological works of Sigmund Freud*, Vol. 7, London: Hogarth, 1953.
14. Alva Wheeler, "Grammatical structure in Siona," *Lingua* 19 (1967), pp. 60-77.
15. Charles J. Fillmore, "Types of lexical information," NSF Grant GN-534.1 Ohio State University.
16. Jeffrey S. Gruber, "Functions of the lexicon in formal descriptive grammars," Technical Memorandum TM-3770/000/00, System Development Corporation, Santa Monica, Calif., 1967.
17. John Robert Ross, "On declarative sentences," in Roderick A. Jacobs and Peter S. Rosenbaum, eds., *Readings in English transformational grammar*, Boston: Ginn, 1970, pp. 222-72.

CHAPTER III

18. John Henry Hutton, *The Angami Nagas*, New York: Macmillan, 1921, p. 221.
19. James Barke, ed., *Poems and songs of Robert Burns*, London: Collins, 1969, p. 508.
20. I am grateful to Allen Walker Read for this quote by A. E. Ellis, "Refereeing round world," 1954.
21. Roy Andrew Miller, *The Japanese language*, Chicago: University of Chicago Press, 1967, p. 298.
22. Robert Hetzron, *The verbal system of Southern Agaw*, Berkeley: University of California Press, 1969 (University of California Publications, Near Eastern Studies 12), pp. 6-7.
23. Charles Kiel, *Urban blues*, Chicago: University of Chicago Press, 1966, p. 27.
24. Wilfred Powell, *Wandering in a wild country; or, Three years amongst the cannibals of New Britain*, London 1884, p. 252.

CHAPTER IV

25. *Chama pedagogical grammar*, New Tribes Mission, Cochabamba, Bolivia, ca. 1955.
26. "What It's Like to Be a Girl at an Old Boy's School,"

The National Observer, November 3, 1969, p. 10.
27. The dream of the red chamber, trans. by Florence and Isabel McHugh, New York: Pantheon, 1958, p. 35.
28. Harold Greenwald, The call girl: A social and psychoanalytic study, New York: Ballantine Books, 1958, p. 23.
29. Roy Andrew Miller, The Japanese language, Chicago: University of Chicago Press, 1967, p. 288.
30. Frances Trollope, Domestic manners of the Americans [1832], with a history of Mrs. Trollope's adventures in American by Donald Smalley [a contemporary of Mrs. T.], New York: Vintage Books, 1960, pp. 300-1.
31. Elsie C. Parsons, American Anthropologist Memoirs 57 (1941), p. 46.
32. Günter Grass, Dog Years, New York: Fawcett, 1966, p. 14.
33. Rawson, Erotic art of the East [see note 10], p. 305.
34. Los Angeles Herald-Examiner, September 6, 1968.
35. Elsie C. Parsons, American Anthropologist Memoirs 57 (1941), p. 28.
36. James G. Leyburn, The Scotch-Irish: A social history, Chapel Hill: University of North Carolina Press, 1962, p. 145.

CHAPTER V

37. Harold Wentworth, and Stuart Berg Flexner, eds. Dictionary of American slang, New York: Crowell, [1960] 1966, p. xiii.
38. John Steinbeck, East of Eden, New York: Bantam Books, [1952] 1962, p. 1.
39. Lin Yutang, My country and my people, New York: Halcyon House, 1935, p. 27.
40. In Eugene A. Nida, Morphology: The descriptive analysis of words, Ann Arbor: University of Michigan Press, 1949, p. 158.
41. John F. Wharton, "Toward an affirmative morality," Saturday Review (July 12, 1969), p. 12.
42. Michel de Montaigne, Selected essays, New York: Van Nostrand, 1943, p. 337.

CHAPTER VI

43. See also Mary Ritchie Key, "The Silent Woman," Chapter XIII (Key 1975).

CHAPTER VII

44. Most of the material in this chapter was included in a paper, "Nonverbal behavior in speech acts," presented at the conference, "Sociology of language and theory of speech acts," Bielefeld, Germany, April 1973.
45. See especially Dell Hymes, "Models of the interaction of language social setting," in The Journal of Social Issues 23. 2 (April 1967), pp. 8-28.
46. Albert Einstein, Out of my later years, New York: Philosophical Library, 1950, p. 13.
47. Franz Boas, "Introduction," Handbook of American Indian languages BAE-B 40, Part I, Washington, D.C., Smithsonian Institution, pp. 1-83; reprinted in Dell Hymes, Language in culture and society. Otto Jespersen, The philosophy of grammar, New York: W. W. Norton, 1965. Edward Sapir and Morris Swadesh, "American Indian grammatical categories," Word 2 (1946), pp. 103-12; reprinted in Dell Hymes, Language in culture and society. Benjamin Lee Whorf, Language, thought and reality, ed. by John B. Carroll, Cambridge, Mass.: M.I.T. Press and John Wiley, 1956.
48. Sir Alan Gardiner, The theory of speech and language, London: Oxford University Press, 1932, p. 12.
49. I used this diagram in a paper, "Differences between written and spoken language," read at the American Dialect Society, Chicago, 1971.
50. Steinbeck [see note 38], p. 47.
51. Marcel Marceau, on the David Frost television show, February 1970.
52. John Gumperz, "On the ethnology of linguistic change," in William Bright, ed., Sociolinguistics, The Hague: Mouton, 1966, p. 35.
53. Allen D. Grimshaw, "Directions for research in sociolinguistics," Explorations in sociolinguistics, International Journal of American Linguistics 33.4 (October 1967), pp. 191-204.
54. C. F. Voegelin, and Z. Harris, "Linguistics in ethnology," Southwestern Journal of Anthropology 1.4 (1945) pp. 455-65.
55. Carol Schwalberg, "RX: Bel canto," Opera News (December 30, 1967), p. 16.

CHAPTER VIII

56. Erving Goffman; Garden City, N.Y.: Doubleday (Anchor Books), 1959, p. 2.
57. Michel de Montaigne, Selected essays, New York: Van Nostrand, 1943, pp. 128-9.
58. Arthur M. Schlesinger [Sr.], Learning how to behave, New York: Cooper Square Publishers, 1968 [1946].
59. Walburga von Raffler Engel "The LAD, our underlying unconscious, and more on 'Felt sets'," Language Sciences 13 (December 1970), pp. 15-18.
60. The material in this section is taken from my book on the language of male and female (Key 1975).
61. Los Angeles Times, April 25, 1966.
62. Regina Flannery, "Men's and women's speech in Gros Ventre," International Journal of American Linguistics 12.3 (1946), pp. 133-5.
63. Carroll L. Olsen, "Voice register and intonation levels in two dialects of Spanish," paper read at the Modern Language Association, 1972.
64. William J. Samarin, The Gbeya language, Berkeley: University of California Press, 1966, p. 39.
65. Dick and Jane as victims, Princeton, N.J.: Women on Words and Images, 1972, p. 40.
66. Doreen Kimura, "The asymmetry of the human brain," Scientific American (March 1973), pp. 70-8.
67. Shulamith Firestone, The Dialectic of sex, New York: William Morrow, 1970, pp. 101-2.
68. Los Angeles Times, February 18, 1970.

CHAPTER IX

69. Robert Dubin, Theory building, New York: The Free Press, 1969, p. 85.

Part Two

BIBLIOGRAPHY

For additional references see the bibliographies in the following: Barnlund; Birdwhistell 1970; Crystal 1969; Davis; Duncan 1969; Francis Hayes 1957; Hinde; Mahl and Schulze; Sebeok, Hayes, and Bateson.

The following journals are of special interest in the study of nonverbal communication: Semiotica: Journal of the International Association for Semiotic Studies, Thomas A. Sebeok, editor-in-chief, The Hague: Mouton. Sign Language Studies, William C. Stokoe, Jr., editor, The Hague: Mouton.

The following journals published special issues on nonverbal communication: Comparative Group Studies, William Fawcett Hill, editor, "Nonverbal Communication" (special issue) 3.4 (November 1972), Sage Publications, Beverly Hills, California. The Journal of Communication, Randall P. Harrison and Mark L. Knapp, special issue editors, "A special issue on nonverbal communication," 22.4 (December 1972). Langages, A. J. Greimas, editor, "Pratiques et langages gestuels," 10 (June 1968).

Anon
1970 Biological rhythms in psychiatry and medicine, Public Health Service Publication No. 2088, U.S. Government Printing Office, pp. 4, 36-8.

Anon
1926 Regulations of the Order of Cistercians of the Strict Observance, Book VIII, Chapter II, "Of silence" pp. 156-60. "The manner of making the signs used in the Cistercian Order," pp. 317-39. Published by the General Chapter of 1926, Dublin: M. H. Gill and Son.

Abercrombie, David

1956 "Gesture," Chapter 6, Problems and Principles in Language Study, London: Longman, pp. 70-83.

1965 "Conversation and spoken prose," Chapter 1, Studies in Phonetics and Linguistics, Oxford University Press, pp. 1-9.

1967 "Voice quality and voice dynamics," Chapter 6, Elements of General Phonetics, Chicago: Aldine Pub. Co., pp. 89-110. Partially reprinted as "Voice qualities" in Norman N. Markel, ed., Psycholinguistics, Homewood, Ill.: Dorsey Press, 1969, pp. 109-134.

1968 "Paralanguage," British Journal of Disorders of Communication 3.1, pp. 55-9.

Allen, B. V., et al. see Matarazzo, Joseph D., George Saslow [et. al.]

Allen, George D.

1972 "The location of rhythmic stress beats in English: an experimental study: I," Language and Speech 15, Part I (January-March), pp. 72-100; "The location of rhythmic stress beats in English: an experimental study: II," Language and Speech 15, Part 2 (April-June), pp. 179-95.

Allport, Gordon W., and Philip E. Vernon

1933 Studies in Expressive Movement, New York: Macmillan, 269 pages.

Altman, Irwin, and William W. Haythorn

1967 "The ecology of isolated groups," Behavioral Science 12.3 (May), pp. 169-82.

Altschule, Mark D.

1953 "Cutaneous functions," Chapter II, Bodily Physiology in Mental and Emotional Disorders; "Respiration," Chapter III, pp. 61-74, Bodily Physiology in Mental and Emotional Disorders, New York: Grune and Stratton, 228 pages.

Argyle, Michael

1969 Social Interaction, Chicago: Aldine Pub. Co.; London: Methuen, 504 pages. Review by Mark L. Knapp, Journal of Communication 21 (March 1971), pp. 101-02.

________, and Janet Dean
1965 "Eye contact, distance, and affiliation," Sociometry 28.3 (September), pp. 289-304.

________, and Ralph Exline, eds.
1969 NATO Symposium on Non-verbal Communication, Wadham College, Oxford, 45 pages.

________, and Roger Ingham
1972 "Gaze, mutual gaze, and proximity," Semiotica 6, pp. 32-49.

________, and Adam Kendon
1967 "The experimental analysis of social performance," in L. Berkowitz, ed., Advances in Experimental Social Psychology, Vol. 3, New York: Academic Press, pp. 55-91.

________, Mansur Lalljee, and Mark Cook
1968 "The effects of visibility on interaction in a dyad," Human Relations 21.1 (February), pp. 3-17.

Auerbach, Arthur H. see Gottschalk, Louis A.

Austin, Gilbert
1806 Chironomia: or a Treatise on Rhetorical delivery: comprehending many precepts, both ancient and modern, for the proper regulation of the Voice, The countenance, and Gesture: together with an investigation of the elements of gesture, and a new method for the notation thereof: illustrated by many figures, London, 583 pages plus index; reprinted by Southern Illinois University Press, Carbondale, 1966.

Austin, J. L.
1962 How to Do Things with Words: The William James Lectures Delivered at Harvard University in 1955, Cambridge, Mass.: Harvard University Press, 167 pages.

Austin, William M.
1965 "Some social aspects of paralanguage," Canadian Journal of Linguistics 11.1, pp. 31-9; reprinted in Communication Barriers for the Culturally Deprived, USOE, 1966.
1972 "The behavioral components of a two-way conver-

sation," in Lawrence M. Davis, ed., Studies in Linguistics in Honor of Raven McDavid, Jr., University: University of Alabama Press, pp. 231-7.
1972 "Non-verbal communication," Chapter 8, A. L. Davis, ed., Culture, Class, and Language Variety, National Council of Teachers of English, pp. 140-69.

Bailey, Flora L.
1942 "Navaho motor habits," American Anthropologist 44.2 (April-June), pp. 210-34.

Balfour, Henry
1948 "Ritual and secular uses of vibrating membranes as voice-disguisers," Journal of the Royal Anthropological Institute of Great Britain and Ireland 78, pp. 45-69.

Barakat, Robert A.
1973 "Arabic gestures," Journal of Popular Culture 6.4 (Spring), pp. 749-87.

Barker, Larry L., and Nancy B. Collins
1970 "Nonverbal and kinesic research," in Philip Emmert, and William D. Brooks, eds., Methods of research in communication, Boston: Houghton Mifflin, pp. 343-72.

Barker, Roger G., ed.
1963 The Stream of Behavior as an Empirical Problem, New York: Appleton-Century-Croft, pp. 1-22.

Barnes, R. Bowling
1963 "Thermography of the human body: Infrared-radiant energy provides new concepts and instrumentation for medical diagnosis," Science 140.3569 (May 24), pp. 870-7.

Barnlund, Dean C., ed.
1968 "Nonverbal Interaction," Interpersonal Communication: Survey and Studies, Boston: Houghton Mifflin, pp. 511-610.

Bartenieff, Irmgard, and Martha Davis
1965 Effort-Shape Analysis of Movement: The Unity of Expression and Function, New York; reprinted as Research Approaches to Movement and Personality,

New York: Arno Press, 1972.

Basso, Keith H.
1970 "'To give up on words': silence in Western Apache culture," Southwestern Journal of Anthropology 26.3 (Autumn), pp. 213-30.

Bateson, Gregory, et al. see McQuown, Norman A.

Bateson, Mary Catherine
1963 "Kinesics and paralanguage," Science 139, p. 200.

________, and Alfred S. Hayes see Sebeok, Thomas A.

Bäuml, Franz H. [UCLA]
1975 Dictionary of Gestures, Metuchen, N.J.: Scarecrow Press.

Beavin, Janet Helmick, and Don D. Jackson see Watzlawick, Paul

Bedichek, Roy
1960 The sense of smell, New York: Doubleday, 271 p.

Bein, Monte F., and Judith A. Phillis see Markel, Norman N.

Beinhauer, Werner
1934 "Uber Piropos: Eine Studie über spanische Liebessprache," Volkstum und Kultur der Romanen 7.2-3, pp. 111-63 [on women's glances, pp. 133-36 ... quotations from literature...].

Bell, Sir Charles
1806 Essays on the Anatomy and Philosophy of Expression: As Connected with the Fine Arts, London; 6th ed., 1872
1823 On the Motions of the Eye, London: Nicol.

Bellugi, Ursula, and Susan D. Fischer
1972 "A comparison of sign language and spoken language: rate and grammatical mechanisms," Cognition: International Journal of Cognitive Psychology 1.1, pp. 173-200.

________, and Patricia Siple
1971 "Remembering with and without words," Current

Problems in Psycholinguistics, Centre National de la Recherche Scientifique, Paris, France.

Birdwhistell, Ray L.

1952 Introduction to Kinesics: An Annotation System for Analysis of Body Motion and Gesture, Washington, D.C.: Foreign Service Institute; Ann Arbor: University Microfilms, 75 pages.

1964 "Communication without words," P. Alexandre, ed., L'Aventure Humaine, Paris: Société d'Etudes Littéraires et Artistiques.

1965 "Body behavior and communication," International Encyclopedia of the Social Sciences, New York.

1966 "Some relations between American kinesics and spoken American English," Alfred G. Smith, ed., Communication and Culture: Readings in the Codes of Human Interaction, New York: Holt, Rinehart and Winston, pp. 182-9.

1968 "Kinesics," David L. Sills, ed., International Encyclopedia of the Social Sciences, Vol. 8, New York: Macmillan, pp. 379-85.

1970 Kinesics and Context: Essays on Body Motion Communication, Philadelphia: University of Pennsylvania Press, 338 pages. Review by Adam Kendon in American Journal of Psychology 85, 1972, pp. 441-55.

________, et al. see McQuown, Norman A.

Blacker, K. H., and J. A. Starkweather see Hargreaves, W. A.

Blackmur, R. P.

1935 "Language as Gesture," Chapter 1 (pp. 3-24), Language as Gesture: Essays in Poetry, Harcourt, Brace, 440 pages; reprinted in Kerker Quinn and Charles Shattuck, eds., Accent Anthology: Selections from Accent: A Quarterly of New Literature, 1940-1945, 1946, pp. 467-88.

Blake, William Harold

1933 A Preliminary Study of the Interpretation of Bodily Expressions, New York: Teachers College, Columbia University, Contributions to Education No. 574, 54 pages.

Blass, Thomas [University of Maryland]
"A psycholinguistic comparison of speech, dictation and writing."

________, and Benjamin Pope *see* Siegman, Aron Wolfe

Boese, Robert J.
1971 *Native Sign Language and the Problem of Meaning*, University of California, Santa Barbara, Ph.D. thesis.

________ *see* Cicourel, Aaron V.

Bolinger, Dwight L.
1946 "Thoughts on 'Yep' and 'Nope'," *American Speech* 21.2 (April), pp. 90-95.
1965 "Accent and related matters," Part I, *Forms of English: Accent, Morpheme, Order*, Cambridge, Mass.: Harvard University Press.
1969 "The sound of the bell," *Kivung* 2.3 (November), pp. 2-7.
1972 *Intonation*, D. L. Bolinger, ed., Baltimore: Penguin Books.

Boomer, Donald S., and Allen T. Dittman
1964 "Speech rate, filled pause, and body movement in interviews," *Journal of Nervous and Mental Disease* 139, pp. 324-7.

Boring, E. G., and E. B. Titchener
1923 "A model for the demonstration of facial expression," *American Journal of Psychology* 34.4 (October), pp. 471-85. [based on Piderit's model]

Bowen, J. Donald, and I. Silva-Fuenzalida *see* Stockwell, Robert P.

Brandt, John F., and Layne D. Prebor *see* Markel, Norman N.

Brannigan, Christopher R., and David A. Humphries
1972 "Human non-verbal behavior: a means of communication," N. Blurton Jones, ed., *Ethological Studies of Child Behavior*, Cambridge, Eng.: Cambridge University Press, pp. 37-64.

Brannon, Carole, et al. *see* Exline, Ralph V., John Thibaut [et al.]

Brault, Gerard J.
1963 "Kinesics and the classroom: some typical French gestures," The French Review 36.4 (February), pp. 374-82.

Brewer, W. D.
1951 "Patterns of gesture among the Levantine Arabs," American Anthropologist 53.2 (April-June), pp. 232-37.

Brilliant, Richard
1963 Gesture and Rank in Roman Art: The Use of Gestures to Denote Status in Roman Sculpture and Coinage, Memoirs of the Connecticut Academy of Arts & Sciences, Vol. 14, New Haven: The Academy, 238 pages.

Broadbent, D. E. see Ladefoged, Peter

Brophy, John
1963 The Face in Western Art, London: George G. Harrap, 184 pages, 104 plates.

Brosin, Henry W.
1959 "Discussion" of R. L. Birdwhistell's paper: "Contribution of linguistic-kinesic studies to the understanding of schizophrenia" (pp. 99-118), in Alfred Auerbach, ed., Schizophrenia: An Integrated Approach, New York: Ronald Press, pp. 118-23.
1966 "Linguistic-kinesic analysis using film and tape in a clinical setting," American Journal of Psychiatry suppl. 122.12, pp. 33-7.

________, and William S. Condon
1970 "Micro linguistic-kinesic events in schizophrenic behavior," D. V. Siva Sankar, ed., Schizophrenia: Current Concepts and Research, Hicksville, N.Y.: P J D Publications, Ltd.

________, et al. see McQuown, Norman A.

Bruneau, Tom
1973 "Communicative silences: forms and functions," Journal of Communication 23.1 (March), pp. 17-46.

Bugental, Daphne E., Leonore R. Love, and Robert Gianetto
1971 "Perfidious feminine faces," Journal of Personality and Social Psychology 17, pp. 314-8.

Bullowa, Margaret
1970 "The start of the language process," Actes du Xe Congrès International des Linguistes, Bucarest, 1967, Editions de l'Academie de la République Socialiste de Roumanie, pp. 191-200.

Bulwer, John
1644 Chirologia: or The natvrall langvage of the hand. Vol. 2: Chironomia, University Microfilm AC-1, No. 17, 304.

Buren, Hildebert van see Cammack, Floyd M.

Burns, Tom
1964 "Nonverbal communication," Discovery (October), pp. 31-5.

Call, Justin D.
1968 "Lap and finger play in infancy, implications for ego development," International Journal of Psychoanalysis 49.2-3, pp. 375-8.
1970 "Games babies play," Psychology Today (January), pp. 34-7, 54.

Cammack, Floyd M., and Hildebert van Buren
1967 "Paralanguage across cultures: some comparisons between Japanese and English," The English Language Education Council Bulletin 22 (November), Japan, pp. 7-10, 47.

Canfield, D. Lincoln
1946 "The 'rúbrica' of the Hispanic culture pattern," Hispania 29 (November), pp. 527-31.

Canna, D. J., and Eugene Loring
1955 Kineseography: The Loring System of Dance Notation, Academy Press, 57 pages.

Carlsmith, J. M. see Ellsworth, Phoebe C.

Casterline, Dorothy C., and Carl G. Croneberg see Stokoe, William C., Jr.

Cervenka, Edward J. see Saitz, Robert L.

Chaitanya
1968 "The school of silence," Quest: A Quarterly of Inquiry, Criticism and Ideas 59, Bombay, India, pp. 48-51.

Chalke, H. D., and J. R. Dewhurst
1957 "Accidental coal-gas poisoning: loss of sense of smell as a possible contributory factor with old people," British Medical Journal II, pp. 915-7.

Charny, E. Joseph
1966 "Psychosomatic manifestations of rapport in psychotherapy," Psychosomatic Medicine 28.4 (Part I) (July-August), pp. 305-15.

Chatman, Seymour
1966 "Linguistic analysis: A study of James Mason's interpretation of 'The Bishop Orders his Tomb'," Thomas O. Sloan, ed., The Oral Study of Literature, New York: Random House, pp. 94-133.

Cherry, Colin
1957 On Human Communication: A Review, a Survey, and a Criticism, Cambridge, Mass.: M.I.T. Press and John Wiley; reprinted New York: Science Editions, 1961, 333 pages.

Cicourel, Aaron V., and Robert J. Boese
1972 "The acquisition of manual sign language and generative semantics," Semiotica 3, pp. 225-55.
1972 "Sign Language Acquisition and the Teaching of Deaf Children," in Courtney B. Cazden, Vera P. John, and Dell Hymes, eds., Functions of Language in the Classroom, Columbia University: Teachers College Press, pp. 32-62.

Clark, Captain William Philo
1885 The Indian Sign Language: With Brief Explanatory Notes of the Gestures Taught Deaf-mutes in our Institutions for their Instruction: and a Description of some of the Peculiar Laws, Customs, Myths, Superstitions, Ways of Living, Code of Peace and War Signals of our Aborigines, Philadelphia, 443 pages. [Cheyenne, Sioux, Crow, Bannack, Assiniboines, Gros Ventres, Mandans,

Arickarees...]; reprinted by The Rosicrucian Press, San Jose, Cal., 1959.

Classe, André
1957 "Phonetics of the Silbo Gomero," Archivium Linguisticum 9.1, Glasgow, pp. 44-61.
1957 "The whistled language of La Gomera," Scientific American 196.4 (April), pp. 111-20.

Cobb, Jane
1940 "Clappers and hissers," New York Times Magazine (April 21), p. 7.

Cocchiara, Giuseppe
1932 Il linguaggio del gesto, Turin: Fratelli Bocca, 131 pages. Review by F. B., Zeitschrift für Volkskunde 44, p. 299.

Cohen, Einya, et al. see Schlesinger, I. M.

Collins, Nancy B. see Barker, Larry L.

Condon, William S. see Brosin, Henry W.

________, and W. D. Ogston
1966 "Sound film analysis of normal and pathological behavior patterns," Journal of Nervous and Mental Disorder 143.4, pp. 338-46.
1967 "A segmentation of behavior," Journal of Psychiatric Research 5, pp. 221-35.

Conklin, Harold C.
1959 "Linguistic play in its cultural setting," Language 35.4 (October-December), pp. 631-6. Reprinted in Dell Hymes, ed., Language in Culture and Society, 1964, pp. 295-8.

Cook, Mark
1969 "Anxiety, speech disturbances and speech rate," British Journal of Social and Clinical Psychology 8.1, pp. 13-21.
1971 Interpersonal Perception, London: Penguin Books.

________ see Kendon, Adam

________, and Mansur Lalljee see Argyle, Michael

Coser, Rose Laub
1959 "Some Social Functions of Laughter," Human Relations 12, pp. 171-82.

Cowan, George M.
1948 "Mazateco whistle speech," Language 24, pp. 280-86. Reprinted in Dell Hymes, ed., Language in Culture and Society, 1964, pp. 305-11.

Cranach, M. von see von Cranach, M.

Crelin, Edmund S. see Lieberman, Philip

________, and Dennis H. Klatt see Lieberman, Philip

Critchley, Macdonald
1939 The Language of Gesture, London: Edward Arnold, 128 pages. Review by Robert West, Quarterly Journal of Speech 26, 1940, pp. 455-6.

Croneberg, Carl G., and Dorothy C. Casterline see Stokoe, William C., Jr.

Crystal, David
1969 Prosodic Systems and Intonation in English, Cambridge, Eng.: Cambridge University Press, 381 pages. Review by Norman N. Markel, Contemporary Psychology 15.9, September 1970, pp. 547-8.
1971 "Paralinguistics," Thomas A. Sebeok, ed., Current Trends in Linguistics, Vol. 12, The Hague: Mouton.

________, and Randolph Quirk
1964 Systems of Prosodic and Paralinguistic Features in English, The Hague: Mouton, 94 pages. Review by Kerstin Hadding-Koch, International Journal of American Linguistics 33.2 (April 1967), pp. 176-8.

Dabbs, J. M., Jr.
1969 "Similarity of gestures and interpersonal influence," American Psychological Association Proceedings 4, pp. 337-8.

Danehy, John J., and Charles F. Hockett see Pittenger, Robert E.

D'Angelo, Lou
1969 How to Be an Italian, Los Angeles: Price, Stern, Sloan, 93 pages.

Dantzig, Tobias
1930 Number: the language of science; a critical survey written for the cultured non-mathematician, New York: Macmillan; 4th ed. 1959, 340 pages. [Chapter 1 on the hand and counting. Illustrations of finger symbols of 16th century, p. 2. Hayes]

Darwin, Charles R.
1872 The Expression of the Emotions in Man and Animals, New York: Appleton, 1898; Philosophical Library, 1955, introduction by Margaret Mead. University of Chicago Press, 1965, preface by Konrad Lorenz, 372 pages.

Davidson, Levette J.
1950 "Some current folk gestures and sign languages," American Speech 25.1 (February), pp. 3-9.

Davis, Martha
1972 Body Movement: Perspectives in Research, New York: Arno Press. [a series of reprinted works] Evolution of Facial Expression, Facial Expression in Children, Research Approaches to Movement and Personality.
1972 Understanding Body Movement: An Annotated Bibliography, New York: Arno Press, 190 pages.

——— see Bartenieff, Irmgard

Davitz, Joel Robert
1969 "A dictionary of emotional meaning," Chapter 2 (pp. 32-84), The Language of Emotion, New York: Academic Press, 197 pages.

Dean, Janet see Argyle, Michael

DeLong, Alton J.
1972 "Kinesic signals and utterance boundaries in preschool children," Pennsylvania State University, Ph.D. Dissertation.

Deutsch, Felix
1949 "Thus speaks the body: I: An analysis of postural

behavior," Transactions of the New York Academy of Science, New York Academy of Science Series 2, Vol. 12.2, pp. 58-62.

1952 "Thus speaks the body: IV: Analytic posturology," Psychoanalytic Quarterly 21, pp. 196-214.

1966 "Some principles of correlating verbal and non-verbal communication," Louis A. Gottschalk and Arthur H. Auerbach, eds., Methods of Research in Psychotherapy, New York: Appleton-Century-Crofts, pp. 166-9 ["A fragment of a sound filmed psychiatric interview demonstrating Dr. Felix Deutsch's concepts," pp. 170-88.]

Devereux, George

1949 "Mohave voice and speech mannerisms," Word 5.3 (December), pp. 268-72; Dell Hymes, ed., Language in Culture and Society (1964), pp. 267-71.

Devor, S., et al. see Wiener, Morton

Dittmann, Allen T.

1972 Interpersonal Messages of Emotion, New York: Springer.

________ see Boomer, Donald S.

________, and Lynn G. Llewellyn

1967 "The phonemic clause as a unit of speech decoding," Journal of Personality and Social Psychology 6.3, pp. 341-9.

1968 "Relationship between vocalizations and head nods as listener responses," Journal of Personality and Social Psychology 9.1, pp. 79-84.

Duncan, Starkey, Jr.

1969 "Nonverbal Communication," Psychological Bulletin 72.2, pp. 118-37.

1972 "Some signals and rules for taking speaking turns in conversations," Journal of Personality and Social Psychology 23, pp. 283-92.

1973 "Toward a Grammar for Dyadic Conversations," Semiotica 9.1, pp. 29-46.

________, Milton J. Rosenberg, and Jonathan Finkelstein

1969 "The paralanguage of experimenter bias," Sociometry 32.2 (June), pp. 207-219.

_______, and Robert Rosenthal
1968 "Vocal emphasis in experimenters' instruction reading as unintended determinant of subjects' responses," Language and Speech 11.1 (January-March), pp. 20-26.

Dundes, Alan
1968 Every Man his Way: Readings in Cultural Anthropology, Englewood Cliffs, N.J.: Prentice-Hall, 551 pages.

Eco, Umberto
1972 La structure absente, Paris: Mercure de France. [section C on proxemics]

Efron, David
1941 Gesture and Environment: A Tentative Study of Some of the Spatio-Temporal and "Linguistic" Aspects of the Gestural Behavior of Eastern Jews and Southern Italians in New York City, Living Under Similar as well as Different Environmental Conditions, New York: King's Crown Press, sketches by Stuyvesant Van Veen, preface by Franz Boas, 184 pages. Reprinted as Gesto, raza y cultura, Buenos Aires: Ediciones Nueva Vision, 1970; reprinted as Gesture, Race and Culture in Thomas A. Sebeok, ed., Approaches to Semiotics No. 9, The Hague: Mouton, 1972, 226 pages. [with 35 pages of illustrations of gestures added] Review by Mary Ritchie Key, Linguistics, in press.

Eibl-Eibesfeldt, Irenäus
1964 "Experimental criteria for distinguishing innate from culturally conditioned behavior," in F. S. C. Northrop and Helen H. Livingston, eds., Cross-Cultural Understanding: Epistemology in Anthropology, New York: Harper and Row, pp. 297-307.
1969 "Culture-independent invariables in human greeting behavior," in Michael Argyle and Ralph Exline, eds., NATO Symposium on Non-verbal Communication, Oxford.
1970 "The expressive behaviour of the deaf and blind born," in M. von Cranach and I. Vine, eds., Non-verbal Behaviour and Expressive Movements, New York: Academic Press.

Eisenberg, Abne M., and Ralph R. Smith
1971 Nonverbal Communication, Indianapolis: Bobbs-Merrill, 133 pages.

Ekman, Paul
1965 "Communication through nonverbal behavior: a source of information about an interpersonal relasionship," in Silvan S. Tomkins and Carroll E. Izard, eds., Affect, Cognition, and Personality, New York: Springer Press, pp. 390-442.
1972 "Universals and cultural differences in facial expressions of emotion," James Cole, ed., Nebraska Symposium on Motivation, Lincoln: University of Nebraska Press.
1973 Darwin and Facial Expression: A Century of Research in Review, New York: Academic Press.

________, and Wallace V. Friesen
1968 "Nonverbal behavior in psychotherapy research," J. Shlien, ed., Research in Psychotherapy, Vol. 3, Washington, D.C.: American Psychological Association, pp. 179-216 ["The hands," pp. 201-12].
1969a "Nonverbal leakage and clues to deception," Psychiatry: Journal for the Study of Interpersonal Processes 32.1 (February), pp. 88-106.
1969b "The repertoire of nonverbal behavior: categories, origins, usage and coding," Semiotica: Journal of the International Association for Semiotic Studies 1.1, pp. 49-98.
1969c "A tool for the analysis of motion picture film or video tape," American Psychologist 24.3 (March), pp. 240-43.

________, Wallace V. Friesen, and Phoebe C. Ellsworth
1972 Emotion in the Human Face: Guidelines for Research and an Integration of Findings, New York: Pergamon Press, 191 pages.

________, Wallace V. Friesen, and Silvan S. Tomkins
1971 "Facial affect scoring technique: a first validity study," Semiotica 3 (February), pp. 37-58.

________, E. Richard Sorenson, and Wallace V. Friesen
1969 "Pan-cultural elements in facial displays of emotion," Science 164.3875 (April), pp. 86-8. [happiness, anger, fear, disgust, surprise, sadness]

Elkin, A. P.
1953 "The one-leg resting position in Australia," *Man* 53, no. 95 (April), p. 64.

Ellsworth, Phoebe C., and J. M. Carlsmith
1968 "Effects of eye contact and verbal content on affective response to a dyadic interaction," *Journal of Personality and Social Psychology* 10, pp. 15-20.

________, and Wallace V. Friesen *see* Ekman, Paul

________, et al.
1972 "The stare as a stimulus to flight in human subjects," *Journal of Personality and Social Psychology* 21.3, pp. 302-11.

Engel, Walburga von Raffler
1972 "Some phono-stylistic features of Black English," *Phonetica* 25.1 (February), pp. 53-64.

Erickson, Frederick [Harvard]
1971 "Cognitive anthropology, ethnomethodology, and the school counseling interview: a search for a generative grammar of talk about social structure," American Anthropological Association, New York.

Exline, Ralph V.
1972 "Visual interaction: the glance of power and preference," J. K. Cole, ed., *Nebraska Symposium on Maturation*, Vol. 19, Lincoln: University of Nebraska Press.

________ *see* Argyle, Michael

________, D. Gray, and Dorothy Schuette
1965 "Visual behavior in a dyad as affected by interview content and sex of respondent," *Journal of Personality and Social Psychology* 1, pp. 201-9; D. C. Barnlund, ed., *Interpersonal Communication*, Boston: Houghton-Mifflin, 1968.

________, John Thibaut, Carole Brannon, and Peter Gumpert
1961 "Visual interaction in relation to machiavellianism and an unethical act," *American Psychologist* 16.7 (July), p. 396 [abstract]; reprinted in R. Christie and F. Geis, eds., *Studies in Machiavellianism*, New York: Academic Press, 1970.

_______, and L. C. Winters
1965 "Affective relations and mutual glances in dyads," Silvan S. Tomkins and Carroll E. Izard, eds., Affect, Cognition, and Personality, New York: Springer, pp. 319-50.

Fabbri, Paolo
1968 "Considérations sur la proxémique," Langages 10 pp. 65-75.

Fabricant, Noah D.
1960 "Sexual functions and the nose," American Journal of the Medical Sciences 239 (April), pp. 498-502.

Feldman, Sandor S.
1959 Mannerisms of Speech and Gestures in Everyday Life, New York: International Universities Press, 301 pages ("On tickling and ticklishness," pp. 213-25).

Feldstein, Stanley
1972 "Temporal patterns of dialogue: basic research and reconsiderations," A. W. Siegman and B. Pope, eds., Studies in Dyadic Communication, New York: Pergamon Press, pp. 91-113.

_______ see Jaffe, Joseph

Ferber, Andrew see Kendon, Adam

Ferenczi, Sándor
1913 "Flatus as an adult prerogative," Zeitschrift 1, p. 380; reprinted in Further Contributions to the Theory and Technique of Psycho-analysis, London: Hogarth Press, 1926, p. 325.
1915 "Psychogenic anomalies of voice production," Zeitschrift 3.24; reprinted in Ernest Jones, ed., The International Psycho-Analytical Library, No. 11, London: Hogarth Press, 1926, pp. 105-9; reprinted in Further Contributions to the Theory and Technique of Psycho-Analysis, New York: Boni and Liveright, 1927.

Ferguson, Charles A.
1964 "Baby talk in six languages," American Anthropologist 66.6 (December), pp. 103-114; Part 2 in

Special Publication, The Ethnography of Communication.

Finkelstein, Jonathan and Milton J. Rosenberg see Duncan, Starkey, Jr.

Firth, J. R.
1950 "Personality and language in society," Sociological Review: Journal of the Institute of Sociology 42 University of Keele, Straffordshire, pp. 37-52.

Fischer, Herbert
"Heilgebärden," Antaios, Band II. 4, Stuttgart, pp. 318-347 [has King's X, Plate V; crooking/hooking little fingers, Plate VIII].
1960 "Leben und Tod in alter Mittelfingersymbolik," Sonntagsblatt 43, 54 Nr. 462 (30 Oktober).

Fischer, Susan D. see Bellugi, Ursula

Fisichelli, Vincent R. see Karelitz, Samuel

Flack, Michael J.
1966 "Communicable and uncommunicable aspects in personal international relationship," Journal of Communication 16. 3, pp. 283-290.
1967 The Role of Culture in International Operations [translated in French].

Flugel, John Carl
1930 The Psychology of Clothes, New York: International Universities Press [1969 edition], 257 pages.

Fónagy, Ivan, and Judith Fónagy
1966 "Sound pressure level and duration," Phonetica 15. 1, pp. 14-21.

________, and Klara Magdics
1963 "Emotional patterns in intonation and music," Zeitschrift für Phonetik 16, pp. 293-326.

Forrest, William Craig
1969 "Literature as aesthetic object: the kinesthetic stratum," Journal of Aesthetics and Art Criticism 28. 4 (Summer), pp. 455-9.

Fox, S., and R. Phibbs see Ostwald, Peter F.

Frank, Lawrence K.
1957 "Tactile communication," Genetic Psychology Monographs 56.2, pp. 209-55; reprinted in Alfred G. Smith.

Frazer, Sir James George
1919 Folk-Lore in the Old Testament: Studies in Comparative Religion, Legend and Law, New York, 1927 ("Weeping as a salutation," Vol. II, pp. 82-93; "The silent widow," Vol. III, Chapter 17, pp. 71-81).
1961 The New Golden Bough: A New Abridgment of the Classic Work, edited with notes and foreword by Theodor H. Gaster, New York: Anchor Books.

Freedman, Norbert
1972 "The analysis of movement behavior during the clinical interview," A. Siegman and B. Pope, eds., Studies in Dyadic Communication, New York: Pergamon Press.

________, Thomas Blass, Arthur Rifkin, and Frederic Quitkin
1973 "Body movements and the verbal encoding of aggressive affect," Journal of Personality and Social Psychology 26.1, pp. 72-85.

Friesen, Wallace V. see Ekman, Paul

________, and Phoebe C. Ellsworth see Ekman, Paul

________, and Silvan S. Tomkins see Ekman, Paul

________, and E. Richard Sorenson see Ekman, Paul

Frijda, Nico H.
1953 "The understanding of facial expression of emotion," Acta Psychologica 9, pp. 294-362.
1958 "Facial expression and situational cues," Journal of Abnormal and Social Psychology 57, pp. 149-54.
1961 "Facial expression and situational cues: a control," Acta Psychologica: European Journal of Psychology 18.3, pp. 239-44.
1969 "Recognition of emotion," Advances in Experimental Social Psychology 4, New York: Academic Press, pp. 167-223.

_______, and E. Philipszoon
1963 "Dimensions of recognition of expression," Journal of Abnormal and Social Psychology 66, pp. 45-51.

Galanter, Eugene, and Karl H. Pribam see Miller, George A.

Gardner, R. Allen and Beatrice T. Gardner
1969 "Teaching Sign Language to a Chimpanzee," Science 165, pp. 664-72.

Garvin, Paul L., and Peter Ladefoged
1963 "Speaker identification and message identification in speech recognition," Phonetica 9.4, pp. 193-9.

Geldard, Frank
1961 "Cutaneous channels of communication," Walter A. Rosenblith, ed., Sensory Communication: Contributions to the Symposium on Principles of Sensory Communication (1959), Cambridge, Mass.: M.I.T. Press, pp. 73-87.

Gellor, J., et al. see Wiener, Morton

Gibson, James J.
1962 "Observations on active touch," Psychological Review 69.6 (November), pp. 477-91.

Goffman, Erving
1963 Behavior in Public Places: Notes on the Social Organization of Gatherings, New York: Free Press, 248 pages.

Goldberg, Susan, and Michael Lewis
1969 "Play behavior in the year-old infant: early sex differences," Child Development 40.1 (March), pp. 21-31. Reprinted in Judith M. Bardwick, ed., Readings on the Psychology of Women, New York: Harper and Row, 1972, pp. 30-33.

Goldman-Eisler, Frieda
1955 "Speech-breathing activity--a measure of tension and affect during interviews," British Journal of Psychology 46, pp. 53-63.

Gombrich, Ernst see Kris, Ernst

Goodman, Felicitas D.
1972 Speaking in Tongues: A Cross-Cultural Study of Glossolalia, Chicago: University of Chicago Press.

Gottschalk, Louis A.
1974 "The Psychoanalytic study of Hand-Mouth Approximations," Psychoanalysis and Contemporary Science, Vol. 3, New York: Macmillan.

_______, and Arthur H. Auerbach, eds.
1966 Methods of Research in Psychotherapy, New York: Appleton-Century-Crofts.

Gray, D. and Dorothy Schuette see Exline, Ralph V.

Green, Jerald R.
1968 A Gesture Inventory for the Teaching of Spanish, Philadelphia: Chilton Books, 114 pages.
1971 "A focus report: Kinesics in the foreign-language classroom," Foreign Language Annals 5.1 (October), pp. 62-8. ERIC R24- EDRS: ED 055 511.

Gregory, J. C.
1924 The Nature of Laughter, New York: Harcourt-Brace, 241 pages ("Laughter of relief," Chapter III, pp. 20-40; "Laughter and tickling," Chapter IV, pp. 41-51).

Gruber, Jeffrey S.
1966 "Playing with distinctive features in the babbling of infants," Quarterly Progress Report of the Research Laboratory of Electronics, MIT 81 (April), pp. 181-6.

Gumpert, Peter, et al. see Exline, Ralph V., John Thibaut [et al.]

Gumperz, John J., and Dell Hymes, eds.
1964 "The Ethnography of Communication," American Anthropologist 66.6 (December).

Haggard, Ernest A., and Kenneth S. Isaacs
1966 "Micromomentary facial expressions as indicators of ego mechanisms in psychotherapy," Louis A. Gottschalk and Arthur H. Auerbach, eds., Methods of Research in Psychotherapy, New York: Apple-

ton-Century-Croft, pp. 154-65.

Hall, Edward T., Jr.
1959 The Silent Language, New York: Doubleday, 192 pages.
1963 "A system for the notation of proxemic behavior," American Anthropologist 65.5 (October), pp. 1003-26.
1966 The Hidden Dimension, New York: Doubleday, 201 pages.
1968 "Proxemics," Current Anthropology 9.2-3 (April-June), pp. 83-108.

________, and George L. Trager
1953 The Analysis of Culture, Washington, D.C.: American Council of Learned Societies, 62 pages.

Hamp, Eric P.
1957 "Stylistically modified allophones in Huichol," Language 33.2 (April-June), pp. 139-42 [comments on Grimes article, Language 31, 1955].

Hargreaves, W. A., J. A. Starkweather, and K. H. Blacker
1965 "Voice quality in depression," Journal of Abnormal Psychology 70, pp. 218-20.

Harris, Richard M.
1972 "Paralinguistics," Language Sciences (February), pp. 8-11.

________, and Mary Ritchie Key see Kendon, Adam

Harrison, Randall
"Nonverbal communication," Ithiel de Sola Pool, et al., eds., Handbook of Communication, Chicago: Rand-McNally, in press.
1974 Beyond Words: An Introduction to Nonverbal Communication, Englewood Cliffs, N.J.: Prentice-Hall, 210 pages.

Hayes, Alfred S.
1962 "A tentative schematization for research in the teaching of cross-cultural communication," International Journal of American Linguistics 28.1, Part II (January), pp. 155-67.

________, and Mary Catherine Bateson see Sebeok, Thomas A.

Hayes, Francis
1941 "Gesture," Encyclopedia Americana, Vol. 12, 1956, p. 627; 1964, pp. 627a-627d.
1957 "Gesture: a working bibliography," Southern Folklore Quarterly 21.4 (December), pp. 218-317.

Haythorn, William W. see Altman, Irwin

Henley, Nancy
1973a "Power, sex, and nonverbal communication," Berkeley Journal of Sociology 18, pp. 1-26.
1973b "Status and sex: some touching observations," Bulletin of the Psychonomic Society 2.2 (August), pp. 91-3.

Henry, Jules
1936 "The linguistic expression of emotion," American Anthropologist 38.2 (April-June), pp. 250-56.
1965 "White people's time, colored people's time," Trans-Action 2.3 (March-April), pp. 31-4.

Herzog, George
1934 "Speech-melody and primitive music," Musical Quarterly 20.4 (October), pp. 452-66. Abstract in Africa 8, 1935, pp. 375-77.

Hess, Eckhard H.
1959 "Imprinting," Science 130, pp. 133-41.

Hewes, Gordon W.
1955 "World distribution of certain postural habits," American Anthropologist 57.2, Part 1 (April), pp. 231-44.
1957 "The anthropology of posture," Scientific American 196 (February), pp. 123-32.
1973 "Primate communication and the gestural origin of language," Current Anthropology 14.1-2 (February-April), pp. 5-32.

Hicks, Clifford B.
1965 "Your mysterious nose," Today's Health 43 (October), pp. 35-7, 89.

Hill, Archibald A.
1955 "Linguistics since Bloomfield," Quarterly Journal of Speech 41 (October), pp. 253-60; reprinted in Harold B. Allen, ed., Readings in Applied English

Linguistics, 1st ed., 1958, pp. 14-23.
1958 Introduction to Linguistic Structures: From Sound to Sentence in English, New York: Harcourt, Brace, pp. 408-9.

Hinchliffe, M., and F. Roberts
1971 "Depression: defence mechanisms in speech," British Journal of Psychiatry 118 (April).

Hinde, Robert A., ed.
1972 Non-Verbal Communication, Cambridge University Press, 444 pages. Review by Edward O. Wilson, Science 176, (May) pp. 625-7.

Hindmarch, Ian
1973 "Eyes, eye-spots and pupil dilation in nonverbal communication," Ian Vine and M. von Cranach, eds., Social Communication and Movement, New York: Academic Press.

Hockett, Charles F.
1960 "The origin of speech," Scientific American (September), pp. 89-96.

________, and John J. Danehy see Pittenger, Robert E.

________, et al. see McQuown, Norman A.

Hoffer, A., and H. Osmond
1962 "Olfactory changes in schizophrenia," American Journal of Psychiatry 119, pp. 72-5.

Hopkins, E. Washburn
1907 "The sniff-kiss in ancient India," Journal of American Oriental Society 28, pp. 120-34 [kiss/lick/taste/touch/stroke/sniff/smell/breathe in].

Hörmann, Hans, and Sabine Kowal see O'Connell, Daniel

Howard, Kenneth, et al. see Markel, Norman N., Judith A. Phillis [et al.]

Humphries, David A.
1970 "Ethology and linguistic communication," Technology and Society 6.1, pp. 27-33.

________ see Brannigan, Christopher R.

Hunt, Valerie
1964 "Movement behavior: a model for action," Quest 2.1 (April), pp. 69-91.
1968 "The biological organization of man to move," Impulse 1968: Dance, A Projection for the Future, San Francisco: Impulse Publications, pp. 51-63.

Hunt, William A. see Landis, Carney

Hutcheson, Sandy see Laver, John D. M.

Hutt, Clelia
1968 "Etude d'un corpus: Dictionnaire du langage gestuel chez les trappistes," Langage 10, pp. 107-18.

Hutt, Corrine, and Christopher Ounsted
1966 "The biological significance of gaze aversion with particular reference to the syndrome of infantile autism," Behavioral Science 11, pp. 346-56.

Hymes, Dell H.
1961 "Linguistic aspects of cross-cultural personality study," Chapter 10, Bert Kaplan, ed. Studying Personality Cross-culturally, New York: Row, Peterson, pp. 313-59; "The functions of speech," pp. 337-44 of above reprinted in John P. De Cecco, The Psychology of Language, Thought, and Instruction, New York: Holt, Rinehart and Winston, 1967, pp. 78-84; condensed in Norman N. Markel, Psycholinguistics, Homewood, Ill.: Dorsey Press, 1969, pp. 285-317.
1964 Language in Culture and Society: A Reader in Linguistics and Anthropology, New York: Harper and Row.

________ see Gumperz, John J.

Ingham, Roger see Argyle, Michael

Ingram, David
1971 "Transitivity in child language," Language 47.4 (December), pp. 888-910.

Isaacs, Kenneth S. see Haggard, Ernest A.

Izard, Carroll E.
1971 The Face of Emotion, New York: Appleton-Century-Crofts, 468 pages.

Jackson, Don D., and Janet Helmick Beavin see Watzlawick, Paul

Jaffe, Joseph, and Stanley Feldstein
1970 Rhythms of Dialogue, New York: Academic Press, 156 pages.

Jakobson, Roman
1960 "Closing Statement: linguistics and poetics," Thomas A. Sebeok, ed., Style in Language, Cambridge, Mass.: M. I. T. Press [paperback, 1966], pp. 350-77.
1964 "On visual and auditory signs," Phonetica 11, pp. 216-20.
1967 "About the relation between visual and auditory signs," Weiant Wathen-Dunn, ed., Models for the Perception of Speech and Visual Form, Proceedings of a Symposium, 1964, Cambridge, Mass.: M. I. T. Press, pp. 1-7.
1970 "Linguistics," Chapter VI, Main Trends of Research in the Social and Human Sciences: Part 1: Social Sciences, The Hague: Mouton, pp. 419-63.
1972 "Motor signs for 'yes' and 'no'," Language in Society 1.1 (April), pp. 91-6.

James, J. W., and M. G. King see McBride, Glenorchy

James, William T.
1932 "A study of the expression of bodily posture," Journal of General Psychology 7, pp. 405-37.

Johnson, Donald Barton
1970 "Verbs of body position in Russian," The Slavic and East European Journal 14.4 (Winter), pp. 423-35 [sit/set, lie/lay, stand, hang].

Johnson, Kenneth R.
1971 "Black kinesics: some non-verbal communication patterns in the Black culture," The Florida Foreign Language Reporter 9.1-2 (Spring/Fall), pp. 17-20, 57.

Jones, N. G. Blurton
1967 "An ethological study of some aspects of social behaviour of children in nursery school," in Desmond Morris, ed., Primate Ethology, London: Weidenfeld and Nicolson; Chicago: Aldine Pub. Co., pp. 347-68.

Jorio, Andrea De
1832 La mimica degli antichi investigata nel gestire Napoletano, Naples, 384 pages; 21 plates--some colored in "aquatint." See Mallery 1881, which included pictures with explanations.

Josephs, Herbert
1969 Diderot's Dialogue of Language and Gesture, Ohio State University Press, 228 pages.

Jourard, Sidney M.
1966 "An exploratory study of body-accessibility," British Journal of Social and Clinical Psychology 5, pp. 221-31.

Kaeppler, Adrienne L.
1972 "Method and theory in analyzing dance structure with an analysis of Tongan dance," Ethnomusicology 16.2 (May), pp. 173-217.

Kaiser, L.
1957 Manual of Phonetics, Amsterdam: North-Holland Pub. Co., 460 pages.

Kalogerakis, M. G.
1963 "The role of olfaction in sexual development," Psychosomatic Medicine 25, pp. 420ff.

Kaplan, Bernard see Werner, Heinz

Karelitz, Samuel, and Vincent R. Fisichelli
1969 "Infants' vocalizations and their significance," Clinical Proceedings of Children's Hospital 25.11 (December), pp. 345-61.

Kauffman, Lynn E.
1971 "Tacesics, the study of touch: a model for proxemic analysis," Semiotica 4, pp. 149-61.

Kauranne, Urpo see Nummenmaa, Tapio

Kees, Weldon <u>see</u> Ruesch, Jurgen

Kendon, Adam
1967 "Some functions of gaze-direction in social interaction," Acta Psychologica: European Journal of Psychology 26, pp. 22-63.
1972 "The role of visible behaviour in the organization of social interaction," M. von Cranach and Ian Vine, eds., Movement and Communication in Man and Chimpanzee, New York: Academic Press.
1972 "Some relationships between body motion and speech: an analysis of an example," Aron Wolfe Siegman and Benjamin Pope, eds., Studies in Dyadic Communication, Elmsford, New York: Pergamon Press.

________ see Argyle, Michael

________, and M. Cook
1969 "The consistency of gaze patterns in social interaction," British Journal of Psychology 60, pp. 481-94.

________, and Andrew Ferber
1973 "A description of some human greetings," R. P. Michael and J. H. Crook, eds., Comparative Ecology and Behaviour of Primates, London: Academic Press.

________, Richard M. Harris, and Mary Ritchie Key
The Organization of Behavior in Face-to-Face Interaction: The Proceedings of a Pre-Congress Conference, University of Chicago (August 1973), The Hague: Mouton, in press.

________, and J. Schaeffer see Schelfin, Albert E.

Kennedy, W. P. see Ponder, Eric

Key, Mary Ritchie
1970 "Preliminary remarks on paralanguage and kinesics in human communication," La Linguistique 6, pp. 17-36.
1974 "The relationship of verbal and nonverbal communication," International Congress of Linguists (Bologna 1972).
1975 "The nonverbal, extra-linguistic messages," Male/

Female Language, Metuchen, N.J.: Scarecrow Press.

________, and Richard M. Harris see Kendon, Adam

Khan, M. Masud R.
1963 "Silence as communication," Bulletin of the Menninger Clinic 27, pp. 300-17.

King, M. G., and J. W. James see McBride, Glenorchy

Klatt, Dennis H., and Edmund S. Crelin see Lieberman, Philip

Kleck, Robert
1969 "Physical stigma and task oriented interactions," Human Relations 22.1, pp. 53-60.

________ see Lanzetta, John T.

________, and William Nuessle
1968 "Congruence between the indicative and communicative functions of eye contact in interpersonal relations," British Journal of Clinical Psychology 7, pp. 241-6.

Kleinpaul, Rudolf
1888 Das Leben der Sprache und ihre Weltstellung, Vol. I: "Sprache ohne Worte," pp. 158-77; also "Mienen und Gebärden," pp. 277-388, Leipzig, 1888-1893; reprinted in Sprache ohne Worte: Idee einer allgemeinen Wissenschaft der Sprache, Mouton, 1972, 456 pages.

Klineberg, Otto
1935 Race Differences, New York: Harper and Bros., 367 pages ["Emotional expression," Chapter 15, pp. 278-89 discusses "yes" and "no" between races; the Japanese smile].
1938 "Emotional expression in Chinese literature," Journal of Abnormal and Social Psychology 33, pp. 517-20.

Kloek, J.
1961 "The smell of some steroid sex hormones and their metabolites: reflections and experiments concerning the significance of smell for the mutual rela-

tion of the sexes," Psychiatria, Neurologia, Neurochirurgia 64, pp. 309 ff.

Knapp, Mark L.
1972 Nonverbal Communication in Human Interaction, New York: Holt, Rinehart and Winston, 213 pages.

Knapp, Peter H., ed.
1963 Expression of the Emotions in Man, New York: International Universities Press, 351 pages.

Kochman, Thomas, ed.
1972 Rappin' and Stylin' Out, Urbana: University of Illinois Press.

Koivumaki, J., and R. Rosenthal see Scherer, Klaus

Kowal, Sabine see O'Connell, Daniel

________, and Hans Hörmann see O'Connell, Daniel

Krebs, Richard L.
1970 "Mother and child: Interruptus," Psychology Today 3.8 (January), p. 33.

Kris, Ernst, and Ernst Gombrich
1938 "The principles of caricature," British Journal of Medical Psychology 17, pp. 319-42; revised [major changes] and reprinted in Chapter 7, Ernst Kris, Psychoanalytic Explorations in Art, New York: International Universities Press, 1952, pp. 189-203 [on grimace].

Kristeva, Julia
1968 "Le geste, pratique ou communication?", Langages 10, pp. 48-64.

________, Josette Rey-Debove, and Donna Jean Umiker, eds.
1971 Essays in Semiotics/Essais de sémiotique, The Hague: Mouton, 639 pages.

Kroeber, A. L.
1958 "Sign language inquiry," International Journal of American Linguistics 24.1, pp. 1-19; reprinted in Mallery, Sign Language Among North American Indians, Mouton, 1972.

Krout, Maurice H.
1935 "Autistic gestures: an experimental study in symbolic movement," Psychological Monographs 46.4, whole no. 208, pp. 1-126.
1942 Introduction to Social Psychology, New York: Harper.

La Barre, Weston
1947 "The cultural basis of emotions and gestures," Journal of Personality 16.1 (September), pp. 49-68 (Bobbs-Merrill Reprint Series in the Social Sciences S-157); reprinted in D. G. Haring, ed., Personal Character and Cultural Milieu, Syracuse, New York: Syracuse University Press, 1956, pp. 554-61.
1964 "Paralinguistics, kinesics, and cultural anthropology," Thomas Sebeok et al., eds. Approaches to Semiotics, pp. 191-237.

Ladefoged, Peter see Garvin, Paul L.

________, and D. E. Broadbent
1957 "Information conveyed by vowels," Journal of the Acoustical Society of America 29.1 (January), pp. 98-104.

Lallgee, Mansur G., and Mark Cook
1969 "An experimental investigation of the function of filled pauses in speech," Language and Speech 12 (Part I), (January-March), pp. 24-8.

________, and ________ see Argyle, Michael

Landis, Carney, and William A. Hunt
1939 The Startle Pattern, New York; reprinted by Johnson Reprint Corporation, 1968, 168 pages.

Lanigan, Richard L.
1972 Speaking and Semiology, The Hague: Mouton.

Lanzetta, John T., and Robert E. Kleck
1970 "Encoding and decoding of nonverbal affect in humans," Journal of Personality and Social Psychology 16.1, pp. 12-9.

Lashley, K. S.
1951 "The problem of serial order in behavior," Lloyd A. Jeffress, ed., Cerebral Mechanisms in Behavior, New York: Wiley, pp. 112-36; reprinted, New York: Hafner Pub. Co., 1967, pp. 112-46 [with discussion]; reprinted in Frank A. Beach, Donald O. Hebb, and Clifford T. Morgan, eds., The Neuropsychology of Lashley: Selected Papers of K. S. Lashley, New York: McGraw-Hill, 1960, pp. 506-28; reprinted in Sol Saporta, ed., Psycholinguistics: A Book of Readings, New York: Holt, Rinehart and Winston, 1961, pp. 180-98.

Laver, John D. M.
1968 "Voice quality and indexical information," British Journal of Disorders of Communication 3, pp. 43-54.

________, and Sandy Hutcheson, eds.
1972 Communication in Face to Face Interaction, Harmondsworth, Eng.: Penguin Books, 418 pages.

Lawick-Goodall, Jane van see van Lawick-Goodall, Jane

Lawrence, T. Z.
1970 "Regional speech of Texas: a description of certain paralinguistic features," paper read to the Xth International Congress of Linguists, Bucharest, 1967; Editions de l'Academie de la République Socialiste de Roumanie.

Le Mée, Katharine
1967 "Studies in Communication," Chapter 4, Mario Pei, ed., Language Today, New York: Funk and Wagnalls, pp. 98-127.

Levitt, Eugene A.
1964 "The relationship between abilities to express emotional meanings vocally and facially," in Joel R. Davitz, ed. The communication of emotional meaning, New York: McGraw-Hill, pp. 87-100.

Lewis, Michael see Goldberg, Susan

Lieberman, Philip
1968 "Intonation in infant speech," Chapter 3 (pp. 38-47), Intonation, Perception, and Language, Cam-

bridge, Mass.: M.I.T. Press, Research Monograph 38.

_________, and Edmund S. Crelin
1971 "On the speech of Neanderthal man," Linguistic Inquiry 11.2 (Spring), pp. 203-22.

_________, Edmund S. Crelin, and Dennis H. Klatt
1972 "Phonetic ability and related anatomy of the newborn and adult human, Neanderthal Man, and the chimpanzee," American Anthropologist 74.3 (June), pp. 287-307.

_________, and S. B. Michaels
1962 "Some aspects of fundamental frequency, envelope amplitude and the emotional content of speech," Journal of the Acoustical Society of America 34, pp. 922-7.

Lieth, Lars von der, ed.
Nonverbal Kommunikation, No. 4, Copenhagen: Psykologisk Laboratorium, Københavns Universitet.

Lindenfeld, Jacqueline
1971 "Verbal and non-verbal elements in discourse," Semiotica 3.3, pp. 223-33.

Llewellyn, Lynn G. see Dittmann, Allen T.

Lomax, Alan, ed.
1968 Folk Song Style and Culture: A Staff Report on Cantometrics, Washington: American Association for the Advancement of Science Publications, No. 88, 363 pages (includes Norman N. Markel, "The paralinguistic framework," pp. 114-6).

Loring, Eugene see Canna, D. J.

Lyons, John
1972 "Human language," R. A. Hinde, ed., Nonverbal Communication, Cambridge, Eng.: Cambridge University Press.

McBride, Glenorchy, M. G. King, and J. W. James
1965 "Social proximity effects on Galvanic skin responses in adult humans," Journal of Psychology

61 (September), pp. 153-57.

McCarthy, Dorothea
1946 "Language development in children," Chapter 9 in Leonard Carmichael, ed., Manual of child psychology, New York: John Wiley, 1954, pp. 492-630.

McDavid, Raven I., Jr.
1965 "The Cultural matrix of American English," Elementary English (January).

McQuown, Norman A.
1957 "Linguistic transcription and specification of psychiatric interview materials," Psychiatry 20.1 (February), pp. 79-86.

________, ed., with Gregory Bateson, Ray L. Birdwhistell, Henry W. Brosin, and Charles F. Hockett, eds.
1971 The Natural History of an Interview, Microfilm Collection of Manuscripts on Cultural Anthropology, series 15, Chicago: The University of Chicago, Joseph Regenstein Library Department of Photoduplication.

Magdics, Klára
1963 "Research on intonation during the past ten years," Acta Linguistica 13, pp. 133-65.

Mahl, George F.
1956 "Disturbances and silences in the patient's speech in psychotherapy," Journal of Abnormal and Social Psychology 53.1 (July), pp. 1-15.
1961 "Measures of two expressive aspects of a patient's speech in two psychotherapeutic interviews," Louis A. Gottschalk, ed., Comparative Psycholinguistic Analysis of Two Psychotherapeutic Interviews, New York: International Universities Press, pp. 91-114, 174-88.
1963 "The lexical and linguistic levels in the expression of the emotions," Peter Knapp, ed., Expression of the emotions in man, New York: International Universities Press, pp. 77-105.
1968 "Gestures and body movements in interviews," Research in Psychotherapy, Vol. 3, American Psychological Association, pp. 295-346.
1972 "People talking when they can't hear their voices," Chapter 10, A. Siegman and B. Pope, eds.,

Studies in Dyadic Communication, New York: Pergamon Press, pp. 211-64.

________, and Gene Schulze
1964 "Psychological research in the extralinguistic area," Thomas Sebeok, et al., eds., Approaches to Semiotics, The Hague: Mouton, pp. 51-143; partially reprinted in Norman N. Markel, Psycholinguistics, Homewood, Ill.: Dorsey Press, 1969, pp. 318-52.

Malinowski, Bronislaw
1935 The Language of Magic and Gardening, Vol. II: Coral Gardens and their Magic, Bloomington: Indiana University Press, 1965, 350 pages.

Mallery, Garrick
1880 Introduction to the Study of Sign Language among the North American Indians: As Illustrating the Gesture Speech of Mankind, Washington, D.C., Smithsonian Institution--Bureau of Ethnology, 72 pages.
1881 Sign language: among North American Indians: compared with that among other peoples and deaf-mutes, Washington, D.C., Bureau of Ethnology I, 1879-1880, pp. 263-552 [includes pictures from de Jorio with explanations]; reprinted by Mouton, 1972. Review by Mary Ritchie Key, Linguistics, 132 (July 1974) pp. 116-123.

Mantegazza, Paolo
1885 La physionomie et l'expression des sentiments, Paris. English translation, Physiognomy and the Expression of emotions, London, 1890, 327 pages.

Markel, Norman N.
1969 Psycholinguistics: An Introduction to the Study of Speech and Personality, Homewood, Ill.: Dorsey Press, 400 pages.

________, Monte F. Bein, and Judith A. Phillis
1973 "The relationship between words and tone-of-voice," Language and Speech 16, Part 1 (January-March), pp. 15-21.

________, Judith A. Phillis, Robert Vargas, and Kenneth Howard
1972 "Personality traits associated with voice types," Journal of Psycholinguistic Research 1. 3,

pp. 249-55.

________, Layne D. Prebor, and John F. Brandt
1972 "Biosocial factors in dyadic communication: sex and speaking intensity," Journal of Personality and Social Psychology, 23.1, pp. 11-13.

________, and Hayne W. Reese see Ringwall, Egan A.

________, and Gloria L. Roblin
1965 "The effect of content and sex-of-judge on judgments of personality from voice," International Journal of Social Psychiatry 11.4 (Autumn), pp. 295-300.

________, and Clair Ann Sharpless
1972 "Socio-economic and ethnic correlates of dialect differences," Studies in Linguistics in Honor of George L. Trager, The Hague: Mouton, pp. 313-23.

Martin, James G.
1972 "Rhythmic (Hierarchical) versus serial structure in speech and other behavior," Psychological Review 79.6, pp. 487-509.

Matarazzo, Joseph D., George Saslow, Arthur N. Wiens, M. Weitman, and B. V. Allen
1964 "Interviewer head nodding and interviewee speech durations," Psychotherapy: Theory Research and Practice 1, pp. 54-63.

________, and Arthur N. Wiens
1972 The Interview: Research on its Anatomy and Structure, Chicago: Aldine-Atherton, 183 pages.

________, Arthur N. Wiens, Ruth G. Matarazzo, and George Saslow
1968 "Speech and silence behavior in clinical psychotherapy and its laboratory correlates," John M. Shlein, et al., eds., Research in Psychotherapy: Proceedings of the Third Conference, Chicago 1966, Vol. 3, Washington, D.C., American Psychol. Association, pp. 347-94.

Matarazzo, Ruth G., et al. see Matarazzo, Joseph D., Arthur N. Wiens [et al.]

May, L. Carlyle
1956 "A survey of glossolalia and related phenomena in non-Christian religions," American Anthropologist 58.1 (February), pp. 75-96.

Mead, Margaret
1935 Sex and Temperament: In Three Primitive Societies, New York: Dell Pub. Co., 1968.

Meerloo, Joost A. M.
1964 "Psychoanalysis as an experiment in communication," pp. 11-28; "Patterns of silence," pp. 19-23; "A world of smells," pp. 166-69, in Unobtrusive Communication: Essays in Psycholinguistics, Assen, Netherlands: Van Gorcum Ltd.

Meggitt, Mervyn
1954 "Sign language among the Walbiri of Central Australia," Oceania 25.1-2 (September-December), Sydney, pp. 2-16.

Mehrabian, Albert
1968 "Communication without words," Psychology Today 2.4 (September), pp. 52-5.
1972 Nonverbal Communication, Chicago: Aldine-Atherton, 226 pages.

________, and Martin Williams
1971 "Piagetian measures of cognitive development for children up to age two," Journal of Psycholinguistic Research 1.1, pp. 113-26.

Merrill, Bruce R.
1952 "Childhood attitudes toward flatulence and their possible relation to adult character," Yearbook of Psychoanalysis 8, pp. 213-24.

Messing, Simon D.
1960 "The nonverbal language of the Ethiopian Toga," Anthropos 55.3-4, pp. 558-560.

Meyer-Eppler, W.
1957 "Realization of prosodic features in whispered speech," The Journal of the Acoustical Society of America 29.1 (January), pp. 104-6.

Michaels, S. B. see Lieberman, Philip

Miller, George A., Eugene Galanter, and Karl H. Pribam
1960 Plans and the structure of behavior, New York: Holt, Rinehart and Winston.

Moncrieff, R. W.
1965 "Changes in olfactory preferences with age," Revue de laryngologie--otologie--rhinologie, pp. 895-904.

Montagna, William
1956 The Structure and Function of Skin, London, New York: Academic Press, 454 pages.

Montagu, Ashley
1953 "The sensory influences of the skin," Texas Reports on Biology and Medicine 2, pp. 291-301.
1971 Touching: The Human Significance of the Skin, Columbia University Press, 338 pages.

Morris, Desmond
1967 The Naked ape: a zoologist's study of the human animal, New York: McGraw-Hill, 205 pages.

Moser, Oskar
1954 "Zur Geschichte und Kenntnis der volkstümlichen Gebärden," Sonderdruck aus Carinthia I. Mitteilungen des Geschichtsvereines für Kärnten, 144 Jahrgang, Heft 1-3, Klagenfurt, pp. 735-74 [searching through the protocols of the county courts of Carinthia, the years 1570-1670, Moser partially reconstructs the daily life ... provides some illustrations and many descriptions of court gestures, ear-gestures (Ohrfeige), gestures of scorn, insult, greeting, with special emphasis on the sign of the fig which was used both for protection from the evil eye and as an insult"--Comment from Hayes' bibliography].

Newell, William Wells
1883 Games and Songs of American Children. Reprinted, New York: Dover, 1963, 289 pages.

Nielsen, Gerhard
1964 Studies in Self-confrontation: Viewing a Sound Motion Picture of Self and Another Person in a Stressful Dyadic Interaction, Copenhagen: Munks-

gaard; Cleveland: Howard Allen, 221 pages.

Nketia, J. H. Kwabena
1971 "Surrogate languages of Africa," Current Trends in Linguistics, Vol. VII, The Hague: Mouton, pp. 699-732.

Nuessle, William see Kleck, Robert

Nummenmaa, Tapio, and Urpo Kauranne
1958 "Dimensions of facial expression," Reports Department Psychology No. 20, Univ. Jyväskylä, Finland, pp. 91-103.

Nyrop, Christopher
1901 The Kiss: And its History, translated by William Frederick Harvey, London, 188 pages; reissued by Singing Tree Press, Michigan, 1968.

O'Connell, Daniel, and Sabine Kowal
1972 "Cross-linguistic pause and rate phenomena in adults and adolescents," Journal of Psycholinguistic Research 1.2, pp. 155-64.

________, ________, and Hans Hörmann
1969 "Semantic determinants of pauses," Psychologische Forschung 33, pp. 218-23.

Olsen, Tillie
1970 "Silences: when writers don't write," Women: A Journal of Liberation 2.1 (Fall), pp. 43-4.

Osmond, H. see Hoffer, A.

Osser, H., and F. Peng
1964 "A cross-cultural study of speech rate," Language and Speech 7, pp. 120-5.

Ostwald, Peter F.
1959 "When people whistle," Language and Speech 2.3, pp. 137-45.
1960 "Human sounds," Chapter VI (pp. 110-37), Dominick A. Barbara, ed., Psychological and Psychiatric Aspects of Speech and Hearing, Springfield, Ill.: Charles C. Thomas, 756 pages.
1963 Soundmaking: The Acoustic Communication of

Emotion, Springfield, Illinois: Charles C. Thomas, 186 pages. "Baby Sounds," pp. 16-23, 46-8; "Listener responses to baby sounds," Chapter 9, pp. 114-27.

1965 "Acoustic methods in psychiatry," Scientific American 212-3 (March), pp. 82-91.

_______, R. Phibbs, and S. Fox

1968 "Diagnostic use of infant cry," Biologia Neonatorum 13, pp. 68-82.

Ounsted, Christopher see Hutt, Corrine

Paget, Sir Richard A. S.

1930 "Speculation on gestures as antedating language as a means of communication," Chapter I, Babel: Or the Past, Present, and Future of Human Speech, London, 93 pages.

1946 "Gesture as a constant factor in linguistics," Nature 158 (July 6), p. 29.

Peled, Tsiyona, et al. see Schlesinger, J. M.

Peng, Fred C. C. [International Christian University, Tokyo]

"Communicative distance" [unpublished ms.].

"The deaf and their acquisition of the various systems of communication: a speculation against innatism" [unpublished ms.].

_______ see Osser, H.

Perrin, Noel

1962 "Old Macberlitz had a farm," New Yorker (January 27), pp. 28-9.

Peter, H. R. H., Prince of Greece and Denmark

1953 "Peculiar sleeping postures of the Tibetans," Man 53.230 (October), p. 145.

Peterson, Frederick A. see Ritzenthaler, Robert E.

Peterson, Gordon E.

1957 "Breath stream dynamics," L. Kaiser, ed., Manual of Phonetics, Amsterdam: North-Holland Pub. Co., pp. 139-48.

Phibbs, R., and S. Fox see Ostwald, Peter F.

Philipszoon, E. see Frijda, Nico H.

Phillis, Judith A., and Monte F. Bein see Markel, Norman N.

_________, et al. see Markel, Norman N., Judith A. Phillis [et al.]

Phillott, D. C.
1907 "A note on sign-, gesture-, code-, and secret-language, etc. amongst the Persians," Royal Journal of the Asiatic Society of Bengal: Journal and Proceedings, N. S. vol. 3.9 (November), Calcutta, pp. 619-22.

Piderit, Theodor
1867 Mimik und Physiognomik. 2d ed., Wissenschaftliches System der Mimik und Physiognomik, Detmold, 1884. (La mimique et la Physiognomie, 1888.) [Suggests a demonstration model be constructed to reproduce facial expressions by an interchange of a number of mouths, eyes, brows, and noses. See also Boring and Titchener.]

Pike, Evelyn G.
1949 "Controlled infant intonation," Language Learning 2 (January-March), pp. 21-4.

Pike, Kenneth L.
1944 "Marginal Sounds," Chapter I, pp. 5-31; "Nonspeech Sounds," Chapter II, pp. 32-41; and throughout book, Phonetics: A Critical Analysis of Phonetic Theory and a Technic for the Practical Description of Sounds, Ann Arbor: University of Michigan Press, 182 pages.
1945 The Intonation of American English, Ann Arbor, Michigan, 200 pages. [an etic system of voice quality, pp. 99-104]
1960 Language: In Relation to a Unified Theory of the Structure of Human Behavior, 3 vols., Vol. III, Chapters 11-17, pp. 44-55 ["Mode-like emic units and systems," Chapter 13].
1966 "Etic and emic standpoints for the description of behavior," Alfred G. Smith, ed., Communication and Culture: Readings in the Codes of Human In-

teraction, New York: Holt, Rinehart and Winston, pp. 152-63.

Pittenger, Robert E.
1958 "Linguistic analysis of tone of voice in communication of affect," Psychiatric Research, vol. 8, pp. 41-54.

________, Charles F. Hockett, and John J. Danehy
1960 The First Five Minutes: A Sample of Microscopic Interview Analysis, Ithaca, N.Y.: 264 pages. Review by Eric H. Lenneberg, Language 38.1 (1962), pp. 69-73; review by Robert P. Stockwell, International Journal of American Linguistics 28.4 (October 1962), pp. 293-6; review by Helmut Richter, Word 21.3 (December 1965), pp. 483-7.

________, and Henry Lee Smith, Jr.
1957 "A basis for some contributions of linguistics to psychiatry," Psychiatry 20.61-78; reprinted in Alfred G. Smith, ed., Communication and Culture: Readings in the Codes of Human Interaction, Holt, Rinehart and Winston, 1966; reprinted in Bobbs-Merrill Reprint Series in Language and Linguistics L-74; partially reprinted as "Fundamentals of English structure" in Norman N. Markel, Psycholinguistics, Homewood, Ill.: Dorsey Press, 1969, pp. 80-108.

Pollenz, Philippa
1949 "Methods for the comparative study of the dance," American Anthropologist 51.3 (July-September), pp. 428-435 (Has notation for movements and a history of notations).

Ponder, Eric, and W. P. Kennedy
1927 "On the act of blinking," Quarterly Journal of Experimental Physiology 18, pp. 89-110.

Pope, Benjamin see Siegman, Aron Wolfe

Pope, Benjamin, and Thomas Blass see Siegman, Aron Wolfe, Thomas [etc.]

________, and ________ see Siegman, Aron Wolfe, Benjamin [etc.]

Poyatos, Fernando
1972 "The communication system of the speaker-actor and his culture: a preliminary investigation," Linguistics 83 (May), pp. 64-86.
1972 "Paralenguaje y kinésica del personaje novelesco: nueva perspectiva en el análisis de la narración," Revista de Occidente 113-114 (August-September), pp. 148-70.

Prebor, Layne D., and John F. Brandt see Markel, Norman N.

Presser, Bina see Schlesinger, I. M.

________, et al. see Schlesinger, I. M.

Pribam, Karl H., and Eugene Galanter see Miller, George A.

Prost, J. H.
1965 "A definitional system for the classification of primate locomotion," American Anthropologist 67.5 Part 1 (October) pp. 1198-214.
"Expressive posture in humans" [unpublished ms.].
"Varieties of human posture" [unpublished ms.].

Quackenbos, H. M.
1945 "Archetype postures: clinical impressions," The Psychiatric Quarterly 19 (October), pp. 589-91.

Quirk, Randolph see Crystal, David

Read, Allen Walker
1961 "The rebel yell as a linguistic problem," American Speech 36.2 (May), pp. 83-92.

Read, Charlotte Schuchardt
1963/1964 "Communication as 'Contact'," General Semantics Bulletin 30-31, Lakeville, Conn., Institute of General Semantics.

Reese, Hayne W., and Norman N. Markel see Ringwall, Egan A.

Reik, Theodor
1949 "In the beginning is silence," Chapter 12, pp. 121-26; "Conscious and unconscious observations," Chapter 14, pp. 131-43, Listening with the third ear, New York: Farrar, Straus [hearing, sight, touch, smell].

Rey-Debove, Josette and Donna Jean Umiker see Kristeva, Julia

Riemer, Morris D.
1955 "Abnormalities of the gaze--a classification," Psychiatric Quarterly, 659-672.

Ringwall, Egan A., Hayne W. Reese, and Norman N. Markel
1965 "A distinctive features analysis of pre-linguistic infant vocalizations," Klaus F. Riegel, ed., The Development of Language Functions, The University of Michigan, Center for Human Growth and Development, Language Development Program, November, 1965, litho 7 pages.

Ritzenthaler, Robert E., and Frederick A. Peterson
1954 "Courtship whistling of the Mexican Kickapoo Indians," American Anthropologist 56, pp. 1088-9.

Roberts, F. see Hinchliffe, M.

Roblin, Gloria L. see Markel, Norman N.

Róheim, Géza
1958 "The Western tribes of Central Australia: their sexual life," Warner Muensterberger and Sidney Axelrad, eds., Psychoanalysis and the Social Sciences, Vol. V, New York: International Universities Press, pp. 221-45.

Rosenberg, Milton J. and Jonathan Finklestein see Duncan, Starkey, Jr.

Rosenfeld, Howard M.
1966 "Approval-seeking and approval-inducing functions of verbal and nonverbal responses in the dyad," Journal of Personality and Social Psychology 4. 6, pp. 597-605.
1966 "Instrumental affiliative functions of facial and ges-

tural expressions," Journal of Personality and Social Psychology 4, pp. 65-72; reprinted in Dean C. Barnlund, Interpersonal Communication: Survey and Studies, Boston: Houghton-Mifflin, 1968, pp. 587-97.

Rosenthal, Robert
1966 Experimenter Effects in Behavioral Research, New York: Appleton-Century-Crofts.
1967 "Covert Communication in the psychological experiment," Psychological Bulletin 67, pp. 356-67.

________ see Duncan, Starkey, Jr.

________, and J. Koivumaki see Scherer, Klaus

Rubinow, S., et al. see Wiener, Morton

Ruesch, Jurgen
1957 Disturbed Communication: The Clinical Assessment of Normal and Pathological Communicative Behavior, New York: W. W. Norton, 337 pages.

________, and Weldon Kees
1956 Nonverbal Communication: Notes on the Visual Perception of Human Relations, Berkeley: University of California Press, 205 pages.

Saint-Jacques, Bernard
1972 "Quelques aspects du langage gestuel en Japonais," Jacqueline M. C. Thomas and Lucien Bernot, eds., Langues et Techniques, Nature et Société, Festschrift to André G. Haudricourt, Paris: Klincksieck, pp. 391-4.

Saitz, Robert L., and Edward J. Cervenka
1962 Colombian and North American Gestures: A Contrastive Inventory, Bogotá, Centro Colombo Americano; reprinted as Handbook of Gestures: Colombia and the United States, Approaches to Semiotics 31 The Hauge: Mouton, 1972, 164 pages.

Salisbury, Lee H.
1967 "Cross-cultural communication and dramatic ritual," Chapter IV, Lee Thayer, ed., Communication: Concepts and Perspectives, Washington, D.C.:

Spartan Books, pp. 77-95.

Salk, L.
1966 "Thoughts on the concept of imprinting and its place in early human development," Canadian Psychiatric Association Journal 11, pp. 295-305.

Samarin, William J.
1965 "Language of silence," Practical Anthropology 12, pp. 115-9.
1969 "The art of Gbeya insults," International Journal of American Linguistics 35.4 (October), pp. 323-9 [hushed voice, air control, "under one's breath" but yelled at a distance].

Sapir, Edward
1927a "Speech as a personality trait," The American Journal of Sociology 32.6 (May), pp. 892-905; reprinted in: David G. Mandelbaum, ed., Selected Writings of Edward Sapir: In Language, Culture, and Personality, Berkeley: University of California Press, 1949, pp. 533-43; partially reprinted in Norman N. Markel, Psycholinguistics, Homewood, Ill.: Dorsey Press, 1969, pp. 44-56.
1927b "The unconscious patterning of behavior in society," E. S. Dummer, ed., The Unconscious: A Symposium, New York: Knopf, pp. 114-42; reprinted in: David G. Mandelbaum, ed., Selected Writings of Edward Sapir, 1968, pp. 544-59.

Sarles, Harvey B.
1966 "New approaches to the study of human communication," Anthropological Linguistics 8.9 (December), pp. 20-26.
1969 "The study of language and communication across species," Current Anthropology 10.2-3, pp. 211-21.

Saslow, George, et al. see Matarazzo, Joseph D., Arthur N. Wiens [et al.]

________, et al. see Matarazzo, Joseph D., George Saslow [et al.]

Schaeffer, J., and Adam Kendon see Scheflen, Albert E.

Scheflen, Albert E.
1963 "Communication and regulation in psychotherapy," Psychiatry 26.2 (May), pp. 126-36.
1964 "The significance of posture in communication systems," Psychiatry 27.4 (November), pp. 316-31.
1965 "Quasi-courtship behavior in psychotherapy," Psychiatry 28, pp. 245-57.
1973 Communicational Structure: Analysis of a Psychotherapy Transaction, Bloomington: Indiana University Press.

________, Adam Kendon, and J. Schaeffer
1971 "A comparison of video-tape and moving picture film in research in human communication," Milton M. Berger, ed., Videotape Techniques in Psychiatric Training, New York: R. Brunner.

________, and Alice Scheflen
1972 Body Language and Social Order: Communication as Behavioral Control, Englewood Cliffs, N.J.: Prentice-Hall, 208 pages.

Scheflen, Alice see Scheflin, Albert E.

Scherer, Klaus
1970 Non-verbale Kommunikation, Hamburg: Buske.
1972 "Judging personality from voice: a cross-cultural approach to an old issue in interpersonal perception," Journal of Personality 40, pp. 191-210.

________, J. Koivumaki, and R. Rosenthal
1972 "Minimal cues in the vocal communication of affect: judging emotions from content masked speech," Journal of Psycholinguistic Research 1, pp. 269-85.

Schlesinger, I. M.
1971 "The Grammar of Sign Language and the Problems of Language Universals," John Morton, ed., Biological and Social Factors in Psycholinguistics, London: Logos Press, pp. 98-121.

________, and Bina Presser
"Compound Signs in Sign Language," Manuscript, The Hebrew University of Jerusalem, Israel.

________, Bina Presser, Einya Cohen, and Tsiyona Peled
"Transfer of Meaning in Sign Language," Working

Paper #12, The Hebrew University of Jerusalem, Israel.

Schuette, Dorothy and D. Gray _see_ Exline, Ralph V.

Schuler, Edgar A.
1944 "V for victory: a study in symbolic social control," _Journal of Social Psychology_ 19 (May), pp. 283-99.

Scott, Hugh L.
1893 "The sign language of the Plains Indians," _International Folk-Lore Congress 3d_, Chicago, pp. 206-20.

Schulze, Gene _see_ Mahl, George F.

Seaford, H. W.
1966 "The Southern syndrome. A regional pattern of facial muscle contraction," paper delivered at the Annual Meeting of the Pennsylvania Sociological Society, 1966.

Sebeok, Thomas A.
1967 "On chemical signs," _To Honor Roman Jakobson_, Vol. III, pp. 1775-82.

________, Alfred S. Hayes, and Mary Catherine Bateson, eds.
1964 _Approaches to Semiotics: Transactions of the Indiana University Conference on Paralinguistics and Kinesics_, The Hague: Mouton, 294 pages.

Seton, Ernest Thompson
1918 _Sign Talk: A Universal Signal Code, Without Apparatus, for Use in the Army, the Navy, Camping, Hunting, and Daily Life: The Gesture Language of the Cheyenne Indians: With additional Signs used by other tribes, also a few necessary Signs from the code of the Deaf in Europe and America, and others that are established among our Policemen, Firemen, Railroad Men, and School Children, in all 1,725_, prepared with assistance from General Hugh L. Scott, New York: Doubleday, Page, and Co., 700 illustrations, 233 pages.

Sharpless, Clair Ann _see_ Markel, Norman N.

Sheldon, W. H.
1942 _The Varieties of Temperament: A Psychology of Constitutional Differences_, New York, London,

520 pages.

Sherzer, Joel
1973 "Verbal and nonverbal deixis: The pointed lip gesture among the San Blas Cuna," Language in Society 2.1 (April), pp. 117-31.

Shor, R. E.
1964 "Shared patterns of nonverbal normative expectations in automobile driving," Journal of Social Psychology 62, pp. 155-63.

Siegman, Aron Wolfe, Thomas Blass, and Benjamin Pope
1970 "Verbal indices of interpersonal imbalance in the interview," Proceedings of the 78th Annual Convention, American Psychological Association, pp. 525-6.

________, and Benjamin Pope
1966 "Ambiguity and verbal fluency in the TAT," Journal of Consulting Psychology 30, pp. 239-45.

________, and ________, eds.
1972 Studies in Dyadic Communication, Elmsford, N.Y.: Pergamon Press, 336 pages

________, Benjamin Pope, and Thomas Blass
1969 "Effect of interviewer status and duration of interviewer messages on interviewee productivity," Proceedings, 77th Annual Convention, American Psychological Association, pp. 541-2.
1970 "Anxiety and speech in the initial interview," Journal of Consulting and Clinical Psychology 35, pp. 233-8.

Siertsema, B.
1962 "Timbre, pitch, and intonation," Lingua 11, pp. 388-98.

Silva-Fuenzalida, I., and J. Donald Bowen see Stockwell, Robert P.

Sines, Jacob O. see Smith, Kathleen

Siple, Patricia see Bellugi, Ursula

Slobin, Daniel I.
"Universals of grammatical development in children," Working Paper No. 22, Language Behavior Research Laboratory, Berkeley: University of California.

Smith, Alfred G.
1966 Communication and Culture: Readings in the Codes of Human Interaction, New York: Holt, Rinehart and Winston, 626 pages.

Smith, Henry Lee, Jr.
1952 "Linguistic science and pedagogical application," "An outline of metalinguistic analysis," Report of the 3rd Annual Round Table Meeting on Linguistics and Language Teaching, Washington, D.C.: Georgetown University, pp. 59-67.
1969 "Language and the total system of communication," Chapter 9, A. A. Hill, Linguistics Today, New York: Basic Books, pp. 89-102.

________ see Pittenger, Robert E.

Smith, Kathleen, and Jacob O. Sines
1960 "Demonstration of a peculiar odor in the sweat of schizophrenic patients," Archives of General Psychiatry 2 (February), pp. 184-8.

Smith, Ralph R. see Eisenberg, Abne M.

Sommer, Robert
1969 Personal Space: The Behavioral Basis of Design, New York: Prentice-Hall.

Sorensen, E. Richard
1967 "A research film program in the study of changing man," Current Anthropology 8, pp. 443-69.

________, and Wallace V. Friesen see Ekman, Paul

Spencer, Herbert
1860 "On the physiology of laughter," Essays on Education, Etc., New York: E. P. Dutton, 1949, pp. 298-309; reprinted from Macmillan's Magazine, March 1860.

Starkweather, John A.
1967 "Vocal behavior as an information channel of speaker status," in Kurt Salzinger and Suzanne Salzinger, eds., Research in verbal behavior and some neurophysiological implications, New York: Academic Press, pp. 253-65.

________, and K. H. Blacker see Hargreaves, W. A.

Steig, William
1942 The Lonely Ones, New York: Duell Sloan and Pearce, 102 pages; reprinted New York: Windmill Books, 1970, 88 pages.

Stern, Theodore
1957 "Drum and whistle 'languages': An Analysis of Speech surrogates," American Anthropologist 59 (June), pp. 487-506; Bobbs-Merrill Reprint Series in the Social Sciences A-215.

Stockwell, Robert P., J. Donald Bowen, and I. Silva-Fuenzalida
1956 "Spanish juncture and intonation," Language 32, pp. 641-65; reprinted in Martin Joos, ed., Readings in Linguistics: The Development of Descriptive Linguistics in America since 1925, 1957, pp. 406-18 [Section 7, vocalizations, vocal qualifiers, vocal differentiators, vocal identifiers].

Stokoe, William C., Jr.
1960 Sign Language Structure: An Outline of the Visual Communication Systems of the American Deaf, Studies in Linguistics: Occasional papers, No. 8, 78 pages. Review by Herbert Landar, Language 37.2, 1961, pp. 269-71.
1966 "Linguistic description of sign languages," Monograph Series on Languages and Linguistics 17th Annual Round Table, No. 19, Washington, D.C.: Georgetown University, pp. 243-50.
1972 Semiotics and Human Sign Languages, Approaches to Semiotics 21, The Hague: Mouton, 177 pages.

________, Dorothy C. Casterline, and Carl G. Croneberg
1965 A Dictionary: Of American Sign Language on Linguistic Principles, Washington, D.C.: Gallaudet College Press, 346 pages. Review by Sheridan E.

Stasheff, Language Learning 16.3-4, 1966, pp. 228-30.

Taylor, Archer
1956 "The Shanghai gesture," Folklore Fellowship Communications No. 166, Helsinki: Suomalainen Tiedeakatemia, Academia Scientiarum Fennica, 76 pages.
1971 "Gestures in an American detective story," Estudios del folklore 25, Mexico, D. F.: Universidad Nacional Autonoma de Mexico, pp. 295-300.

Tedlock, Dennis
1971 "Silences in spoken narrative," paper, American Anthropological Association, New York, November 1971.
1972 Finding the Center: Narrative Poetry of the Zuni Indians, New York: Dial Press, 298 pages. Review by Stanley Newman, International Journal of American Linguistics 39.4 (October 1973), pp. 261-63.
1972 "Pueblo literature: style and verisimilitude," Alfonso Ortiz, ed., New Perspectives on the Pueblos, Albuquerque: University of New Mexico Press, pp. 219-42.

Teit, James A.
1927/ "The Salishan tribes of the Western Plateaus,"
1928 Franz Boas, ed., Bureau of American Ethnology, 45th Annual Report, Washington, D.C., 1930.

Tervoort, Bernard T.
1968 "You me downtown movie fun?," Lingua 21, pp. 455-65.

Thayer, Lee, ed.
1967 Communication: Concepts and Perspectives, Washington: Spartan Books.

Thayer, Stephen
An Eye for an Ear? Towards a Theory of Social Perception: Nonverbal Communication and Deafness, New York: Deafness Research and Training Center, New York University.

Thibaut, John, et al. see Exline, Ralph V., John

Thibaut [et al.]

Titchener, E. B. see Boring, E. G.

Tomkins, Silvan S.
1962 Affect, Imagery, Consciousness, Vol. 1: The Positive Affects, New York: Springer.
1963 Affect, Imagery, Consciousness, Vol. 2: The Negative Affects, New York: Springer.

________, and Wallace V. Friesen see Ekman, Paul

Tomkins, William
1926 Universal Indian Sign Language, San Diego, Calif., 99 pages; reprinted as Indian Sign Language, New York: Dover Press, 1969, 108 pages.

Trager, George L.
1941 "The theory of accentual systems," Leslie Spier, A. Irving Hallowell, and Stanley S. Newman, eds., Language, Culture, and Personality: Essays in Memory of Edward Sapir, Madison: University of Wisconsin Press, pp. 131-45.
1958 "Paralanguage: a first approximation," Studies in Linguistics 13, pp. 1-12; reprinted in Dell Hymes, ed., Language in Culture and Society, New York: Harper and Row, 1964, pp. 274-9.
1960 "Taos III: paralanguage," Anthropoligical Linguistics 2.2, pp. 24-30.
1961 "The typology of paralanguage," Anthropological Linguistics 3.1, pp. 17-21.
1962 "A scheme for the cultural analysis of sex," Southwestern Journal of Anthropology 18, pp. 114-18.
1964 "Paralanguage and other things," Le Maitre Phonetique 122, pp. 21-3.
1965 "Language," section on "Communication," Encyclopaedia Britannica, Vol. 13, p. 699.
1966 "Language and psychotherapy," Louis A. Gottschalk and Arthur H. Auerbach, eds., Methods of Research in Psychotherapy, New York: Appleton-Century-Crofts, pp. 70-82.

________ see Hall, Edward T., Jr.

________, and Edward T. Hall, Jr.
1954 "Culture and communication: a model and an an-

alysis," Explorations 3 (August), pp. 137-49.

Tylor, Edward Burnett
1871 "The art of counting," Chapter VII, Primitive Culture: Researches into the Development of Mythology, Philosophy, Religion, Language, Art, and Custom, New York: Brentano, 1924, pp. 240ff.
1873 Religion in Primitive Culture, Part II of Primitive Culture, New York: Harper Torchbooks, 1958, 539 pages.
1878 "The Gesture-language," Chapter II; "The Gesture-language (cont.), Chapter III; "Gesture-language and word-language," Chapter IV, Paul Bohannan, ed., Researches into the Early History of Mankind: And the Development of Civilization, Chicago: Phoenix Books, 1964, 295 pages [revised from 1878, 388 pages].

Uldall, Elizabeth
1960 "Attitudinal meanings conveyed by intonation contours," Language and Speech 3, pp. 223-34.
1962 "Ambiguity: question or statement? or 'Are you asking me or telling me?'," Proceedings of the Fourth International Congress of Phonetic Sciences (Helsinki, 1961), Mouton, pp. 779-83.
1964 "Dimensions of meaning in intonation," David Abercrombie, et al., eds., In Honour of Daniel Jones, London: Longmans, Green, pp. 271-9.

Umiker, Donna Jean and Josette Rey-Debove see Kristeva, Julia

Upshur, J. A.
1966 "Cross-cultural testing: what to test," Language Learning 16.3-4, pp. 183-196.

van Buren, Hildebert see Cammack, Floyd M.

Van Lawick-Goodall, Jane
1971 In the Shadow of Man, Boston: Houghton-Mifflin, 304 pages.

Vanderbilt, Amy
1968 "Bad manners in America," The Annals of the American Academy of Political and Social Science

378 (July), pp. 90-8.

Vargas, Robert, et al. see Markel, Norman N., Judith A. Phillis [et al.]

Vaughan, P. W., and M. Hinchliffe
1971 "A study of eye contact changes in depressed and recovered psychiatric patients," *British Journal of Psychiatry* 119 (August).

Vernon, Philip E. see Allport, Gordon W.

Vine, Ian
1970 "Communication by facial-visual signals: a review and analysis of their role in face-to-face encounters," John Harrell Crook, ed., *Social Behaviour in Birds and Mammals; Essays on the Social Ethology of Animals and Man*, New York: Academic Press, pp. 279-354.
1971 "Judgement of direction of gaze: an interpretation of discrepant results," *British Journal of Social and Clinical Psychology* 10, pp. 320-31.
"The significance of facial-visual signalling in human social development," M. von Cranach and Ian Vine, eds., New York: Academic Press, in press.

________ see von Cranach, M.

Voegelin, Carl F.
1958 "Sign language analysis, on one level or two?," *International Journal of American Linguistics* 24.1, pp. 71-7. Reprinted in Garrick Mallery, *Sign Language among North American Indians*, The Hague: Mouton, 1972.

von Cranach, M., and Ian Vine
1970 *Non-Verbal Behaviour and Expressive Movements*, New York: Academic Press.
1973 *Social Communication and Movement*, New York: Academic Press.

Vygotsky, L. S.
1934 *Thought and Language*, ed. and trans., Eugenia Hanfmann and Gertrude Vakar, Cambridge, Mass.: M.I.T. Press, 1969, 168 pages.

Wainerman, Catalina H.
1969 "Estilos de 'tomar el piso': un estudio de hábitos verbales," Revista Interamericana de Psicología 3.4, pp. 259-72.

Walker, Jerell R.
1953 "The sign language of the Plains Indians of North America," Chronicles of Oklahoma 31.2, pp. 168-77.

Ward, J. S. M.
1928 The Sign Language of the Mysteries, London, 2 vols.; reprinted, New York: Land's End Press, 1969.

Watson, O. Michael
1970 Proxemic Behavior: A Cross-cultural Study, The Hague: Mouton, 127 pages. Review by Weston La Barre, Approaches to Semiotics 8, 1970.

Watzlawick, Paul, Janet Helmick Beavin, and Don D. Jackson
1967 Pragmatics of Human Communication: A Study of Interactional Patterns, Pathologies, and Paradoxes, New York: W. W. Norton, 296 pages.

Weeks, Thelma E.
1971 "Speech registers in young children," Child Development 42 (December), pp. 1119-31.

Weir, Ruth H.
1966 "Some questions on the child's learning of phonology," Frank Smith and George A. Miller, The Genesis of Language: A Psycholinguistic Approach, Cambridge, Mass.: M.I.T. Press, 1969, pp. 153-72.

Weitman, M., et al. see Matarazzo, Joseph D., George Saslow [et al.]

Welmers, William E.
1954 "Non-segmental elements in foreign-language learning," Hugo J. Mueller, ed., Report of the 5th Annual Round Table Meeting on Linguistics and Language Teaching, Washington, D.C.: Georgetown University, pp. 130-36.

Werner, Heinz, ed.
1955 On Expressive Language, Clark University Press, 81 pages. Review by Roger Brown, Language 31, 1955, pp. 543-9.

_______, and Bernard Kaplan
1963 Symbol Formation: An Organismic-Developmental Approach to Language and the Expression of Thought, New York: Wiley.

Wescott, Roger W.
1966 "Introducing coenetics: a bio-social analysis of communication," The American Scholar 35.2 (Spring), pp. 342-56.
1967 "Strepital communication: a study of non-vocal sound-production among men and animals," The Bulletin of the New Jersey Academy of Science 12.1 (Spring), pp. 30-34.
1967 "The evolution of language: reopening a closed subject," Studies in Linguistics 19, pp. 67-81 [1. kinesis; 2. strepitus; 3. phasis; 4. echolalia; 5. glossolalia].
1969 The Divine Animal: An Exploration of Human Potentiality, Funk and Wagnalls, 340 pages. "Do we communicate?," Chapter 5, pp. 131-57 (Strepitus); pp. 152-3 (Kinesis and Hapsis); "Olfactory blindness," pp. 327-9.
1971 "Linguistic iconism," Language 47.2 (June), pp. 416-28.

Wiener, Harry
1966 "External chemical messengers, I: Emission and reception in man," New York State Journal of Medicine 66.24 (December 15), pp. 3153-70.

Wiener, Morton, S. Devor, S. Rubinow, and J. Gellor
1972 "Nonverbal behavior and nonverbal communication," Psychological Review 79, pp. 185-214.

_______, and Albert Mehrabian
1968 Language within Language: Immediacy, a Channel in Verbal Communication, New York: Appleton-Century-Crofts, 214 pages.

Wiens, Arthur N. see Matarazzo, Joseph D.

_______, et al. 1964 see Matarazzo, Joseph D., George

Saslow [et al.]

________, et al. 1968 see Matarazzo, Joseph D., Arthur N. Wiens [et al.]

Williams, Martin see Mehrabian, Albert

Winters, L. C. see Exline, Ralph V.

Wolff, Charlotte
1945 A Psychology of Gesture, trans. from the French by Anne Tennant, London: Methuen and Co., 225 pages; reprinted, New York: Arno Press, 1972.

Wolff, Peter H.
1963 "Observations on the early development of smiling," B. M. Foss, ed., Determinants of Infant Behaviour: II, New York: Wiley, pp. 113-38.
1969 "The natural history of crying and other vocalizations in early infancy," B. M. Foss, ed., Determinants of Infant Behaviour: IV, London: Methuen, pp. 81-109.

Worth, Sol
1966 "Film as a non-art: an approach to the study of film," The American Scholar 35.2 (Spring), pp. 322-34.
1968 "Cognitive aspects of sequence in visual communication," AV Communication Review 16.2 (Summer), pp. 1-25.

Wundt, Wilhelm
1911 The Language of Gestures, translated from the German, Völkerpsychologie, intro. by Arthur L. Blumenthal, Approaches to Semiotics, paperback series, 6, The Hague: Mouton.

Yngve, Victor H.
1969 "On achieving agreement in linguistics," Robert I. Binnick, et al., eds., Papers from the Fifth Regional Meeting of the Chicago Linguistic Society, April 1969, University of Chicago, pp. 455-462.

Zwicky, Arnold M.
1971 "In a manner of speaking," Linguistic Inquiry 2.2

(Spring), pp. 223-233.

1972 "On casual speech," Chicago Linguistic Society 8, pp. 607-15.

INDEX

Abercrombie, David 117
acoustical 107, 122, 125-126
acquisition of language 140-141, 144
adult 111, 139
affirmation 71
Africa 47, 48, 113, 118
Agaw (southern) 61
age 139-147; see also adult; child; infant
air (direction, source, amount) 69-71, 150; see also breath
Albanian 74
Allport, Gordon W. 13
Altschule, Mark D. 114
Amahuaca 46
ambiguity/ambiguous 38, 122
American Dialect Society 59, 174
animal call 62, 72, 74-75
animal mimicry 66, 72, 74-75
antithesis 19
Arab/Arabic 31, 44, 46, 93, 99, 108, 112, 120
Arapesh 146-147
Argyle, Michael 57, 90, 153, 156
artifacts 27, 105, 133, 160
arts/artist 114, 157
Aschmann, Herman 112
Asian 29
audience 132
auditory 39, 115
Austin, J. L. 123, 125
Austin, William M. 20, 79, 149-150
Australian 24, 37, 110
autistic 105-106
automatic reflex 99-100
averted eye 86; see also eye
Aztec 49, 166

babbling 143
Baby talk 73, 154
backing 46
Bacon, Lord Francis 65, 67
Bailey, Flora L. 94, 95, 98
Balfour, Henry 65, 151
Barke, James 172
Barker, Roger G. 130
Bateson, Gregory 11, 16, 50, 95, 97
Beavin, Janet Helmick 117
Bedichek, Roy 111-112
behavioral event 20, 22ff., 27, 33, 130
Beinhauer, Werner 153
belch 50, 70, 97, 99
Bell, Sir Charles 81
Bengali 89
bent knee 27, 77
Birdwhistell, Ray L. 10-11, 36, 37, 38, 91, 92, 97, 108, 122, 156

Black 63, 83, 117
blind 17, 111, 126
blink 87
blushing 114-115
Boas, Franz 123, 174
body elimination 91, 94
body language 76-106, 140, 144
body movement 90-91, 100
Bolinger, Dwight L. 35, 109
Boring, E. G. 81
brain 153, 155
Bram, Joseph 23, 171
Brannigan, Christopher R. 88
breath 50, 91, 93, 141, 150, 151; see also air
Brewer, W. D. 31
Bridgman, Laura 17, 115
Bright, William 122, 174
Brilliant, Richard 80, 154, 156
British English 51-52
Brookes, Rupert 114
Bullowa, Margaret 140, 144
Buren, Hildebert van 151
Burns, Robert 53
By-Element 25-29, 36, 64-66, 105, 143, 146, 160

Caddo 94, 98
Call, Justin D. 146
Cammack, Floyd M. 151
Carroll, John B. 174
Cassidy, Frederic 59
Chacobo 28, 95
Chaitanya 119
Chalke, H. D. 111
Chama 77
chemical 39, 107, 122, 125-126
Cherry, Colin 13, 58, 171
child 111, 139-147; see also infant
Chin 55
China/Chinese 21, 23, 43, 47, 48, 64, 69, 74, 89, 94, 104, 111, 118, 129, 143, 157
choking 97
Chomsky, Noam 172
Churchill, Winston 27
Clark, William Philo 29, 160
Classe, André 55, 161
classification 164
clearing throat 50, 97, 165
click 43, 44, 143
clothing 27, 29, 105, 152
Cobb, Jane 132
Coles, Robert 14, 171
Comanche 47
combinatory 24, 100
comedian 119
Comfort, Alex 172
communication item 22, 27
Conklin, Harold C. 66, 69
consonants 42
context of situation 122-134, 168
control of air movement 69-71, 93
Coser, Rose Laub 105
cough 97, 141
Cowan, George M. 55, 150
Crelin, Edmund S. 141
cross-cultural 14, 17, 88, 162
cross-disciplinary 162; see also interdisciplinary
cry 66-69, 140-144
Crystal, David 66, 162
cutaneous 100, 114-115
Czech 45, 50, 74

D'Angelo, Lou 70
Darwin, Charles R. 17, 18, 19, 67, 81, 82, 88, 89, 115, 138, 140, 163
Davitz, Joel Robert 68

deaf 17, 24, 86, 103, 126, 158, 160
descriptive act 29ff.
de Tocqueville, Alexis 16, 171
Deutsch, Felix 80
Devereux, George 62, 152
Dewhurst, J. R. 111
dialect 135-161
direct communication 23
directive 19-20, 101
discourse 37
distance 128, 129, 158
Dittmann, Allen T. 37
drama 119
drinking 91, 94
drum 24, 158, 161
Dubin, Robert 175
Dutch 74

eating 91, 94
education 157
Efron, David 19, 28, 31, 78, 103
Eibl-Eibesfeldt, Irenäus 17-18, 57, 89
Einstein, Albert 22, 122, 171, 174
Ekman, Paul 17, 32, 35
electrical 107, 125-126
elements used in kinesics 77-106
elements used in paralanguage 41-75
Elkin, A. P. 37
embellishment act 29ff.
emotion 82, 114
emotive 101; see also expressive
Engel, Walburga von Raffler 145, 175
English 16, 23, 30, 37, 38, 42, 43, 44, 48, 51, 56, 74
Eskimo 20
Estonian 49
etiquette 157
European 29, 104
exclamation 71; see also interjection
Exline, Ralph V. 57, 90, 156
expressive 19; see also emotive
eye 84-87, 153, 156
eye contact 85-87, 108
eye dilation 156

Fabricant, Noah D. 110
face-to-face 126-127
facial expression 26-27, 32, 81-90, 145, 152-153, 160
falsetto 62, 63, 151
faucalization/faucialization 61
feedback 126-127
Feldman, Sandor S. 54, 97, 103, 114, 147
female 62, 147-156
feminine 148, 152, 153, 155
Ferber, Andrew 152
Ferenczi, Sándor 63, 96
Ferguson, Charles A. 73
Fillmore, Charles J. 38-39, 172
Finnish 74
Firestone, Shulamith 175
Firth, J. R. 124, 140
Fischer, Herbert 147
Fishman, Joshua 122
Fisichelli, Vincent R. 141, 144
Flack, Michael J. 169
Flannery, Regina 150, 175
Flexner, Stuart Berg 109, 173
Flugel, John Carl 29
focus 168
Fónagy, Ivan 45, 52, 69, 144

Fox, S. 141
Frazer, Sir James George 28, 48, 59, 68, 113, 118
Freedman, Norbert 95
French 43, 45, 46, 69, 74
Freud, Sigmund 33, 172
fricative 42
Friesen, Wallace V. 17, 32, 35
Fromm-Reichmann, Frieda 80
fronting and backing <u>see</u> sound placement
function (of communication) 19, 77, 134

Galanter, Eugene 15
Gardiner, Sir Alan 124, 174
Gbeya 70, 116, 151
Geldard, Frank 115
geographic 137
German/Germany 21, 45, 50, 71, 74, 98
Gibson, James J. 102
Goethe 14, 171
Goffman, Erving 57, 76, 80, 86, 119, 135, 175
Goldberg, Susan 155
Gombrich, Ernst 84
Gomera 55
gong 24
grammatical categories 123-124
Grass, Günter 95, 173
Greece/Greek 28, 44, 129
Greenwald, Harold 87, 173
greetings 102-103, 133
Gregory, J. C. 67
Grimshaw, Allen D. 131, 174
grin/grimace 89, 154
group behavior 137
Gruber, Jeffrey S. 39, 141, 172
Gumperz, John J. 46, 108, 122, 174

Haggard, Ernest A. 84
hair 27ff., 105
Hall, Edward T., Jr. 11, 49, 87, 93, 108, 112, 115, 120, 125, 128
Hamalian, Leo 171
hands 90
Hanunóo 69, 71
haptics 102; <u>see also</u> tactile
Harris, Zellig 133, 174
Hayes, Alfred S. 16, 50, 95, 97, 150
Hayes, Francis 21, 97
head 91
head-tilt 152
Hearn, Lafcadio 88
Hebrew 74, 118
Henley, Nancy 154
Herzog, George 63
hesitation 50-51, 91; <u>see also</u> pause
Hess, Eckhard H. 15
Hetzron, Robert 172
Hewes, Gordon W. 78, 109
hiccup 97, 141
Hicks, Clifford B. 111
Hill, Archibald A. 10
Hindmarch, Ian 156
Hindustani 56
Hockett, Charles F. 163
Hoffer, A. 111
Hopkins, E. Washburn 39, 56-57, 93, 111
humming 64, 143
Humphries, David A. 88
Hungarian 45, 52, 55, 69-70, 98, 144
Hunt, William A. 99

Hutton, John Henry 172
Hymes, Dell 46, 108, 122, 135, 174

idiolect 135-137
idiomovement 27, 135-137
idiosyncratic 134, 137
imitative behavior 18, 145, 150
imprinting 15
incidental act 30ff.
India 47, 56, 109
Indian (American) 23, 24, 47, 49, 103, 104, 108, 110, 118, 124, 129, 159
Indian sign language 24
indirect communication 23, 109
individual behavior 134, 135-137
infant 17, 140-145, 155
informative 19, 101
ingressive air 69
innate behavior 17
instinctive 18, 99-100
insult 70, 147
interaction 21, 91, 105, 107, 115-119, 131, 132, 134, 144, 153, 174
interdisciplinary 13, 14, 162
interjection 25; see also exclamation
interpretation 149, 151, 164-166, 168
intonation 25, 36, 51-52, 129, 143; see also suprasegmental
involuntary 99
Iroquois 27
Irwin, O. C. 141
Isaac, Kenneth S. 84
Italy/Italian 21, 30, 37, 70, 145

Jabo 63
Jackson, Don D. 117
Jacobs, Roderick A. 172
Jakobson, Roman 20
James, William T. 34, 78
Japan/Japanese 19, 23, 29, 42, 69, 74, 88, 94, 96, 98, 151
jaw 90
Jespersen, Otto 72, 124, 174
Jews 28, 98, 103
Jonson, Ben 41
Jourard, Sidney M. 102
juncture 50, 117; see also pause

Kafir 89
Kaiser, L. 47, 141
Kalogerakis, M. G. 110
Kanakana 96
Karelitz, Samuel 141, 144
Kees, Weldon 27, 129
Keller, Helen 111, 135
Kendon, Adam 152
Kennedy, W. P. 87
Key, Mary Ritchie 22, 124, 125, 173, 175
Kickapoo 55
Kiel, Charles 63, 172
Kimura, Doreen 175
kinesic act 20, 26, 29ff., 100-106, 166
kinesics 9-10, 24, 76-106
King's X 101, 147
Kiparsky, Paul 39
kiss 56-57, 110
Klineberg, Otto 88, 90, 118
Kloek, J. 110
Krebs, Richard L. 110
Kris, Ernst 84
Kroeber, A. L. 160
Krout, Maurice H. 29, 93, 131, 140

La Barre, Weston 19, 68, 76, 80, 89, 92, 95
labialization 45
Labov, William 122
lallation 143
Landis, Carney 99
language 24, 32, 140
language element modification 45
language sounds 42
language substitutes 158
laryngealization 47, 50, 150
Lashley, Karl S. 91, 167
laugh 50, 66-68, 105, 143
Lawick-Goodall, Jane 153
learned behavior 15, 155
length 48ff., 129
Lewis, Michael 155
lexical act 29ff., 101
Leyburn, James G. 173
Lieberman, Philip 35, 141, 143, 155
light and darkness 133
Lingua Franca 158
linguistic structure 35
Llewellyn, Lynn G. 37
location 128, 130
locomotion 91-93
Lorenz, Konrad 18
Lotz, John 171
lying down 27, 77

McCarthy, Dorothea 141
McDavid, Raven I., Jr. 58
McHugh, Florence 173
McHugh, Isabel 173
McQuown, Norman A. 11, 162
Magdics, Klára 45, 52, 69, 144
Mahl, George F. 105
Maidu 69
male 62, 147-156
Malinowski, Bronislaw 124
Mallery, Garrick 160
Mantegazza, Paolo 90
Maori 68, 89, 90
Marceau, Marcel 128, 174
masculine 148, 152, 153
mask 83, 84
May, L. Carlyle 75
Mazateco 48, 55, 150
Mead, Margaret 16, 146
media 123, 125-127
Meerloo, Joost A. M. 83
Meggitt, Mervyn 158
Mehrabian, Albert 20
men 161; see also male
Merrill, Bruce R. 96
Messing, Simon D. 29
Mexico 23
Miller, George A. 15
Miller, Roy Andrew 172, 173
mimicry 72-75; see also animal, noise, speech mimicry
Mingrelian 28
Mixteco 48
model 22
modifications 25, 45, 60, 64
Mohave 62, 152
Moncrieff, R. W. 111
Montagna, William 115
Montagu, Ashley 154
Montaigne, Michel de 114, 136, 173, 175
Morris, Charles W. 171
Morris, Desmond 18
Moser, Oskar 147
mouth 88-90, 153
muscle construction 46

Naga (India) 47
nasal 43, 149
nasalization 46, 50
Navaho 80, 94, 95, 98

negation 71, 145
Newell, William Wells 27, 57, 66, 148
Nida, Eugene A. 173
noise 100, 132
noise/sound mimicry 74
non-cry vocalization 141
non-language modification 60
non-language sounds 53
nonverbal act 20, 24ff., 168
nonverbal categories 123-124
nonverbal coded language substitutes 24
nonverbal communication 9, 140
Norwegian 74
nose 90, 101, 138
notation systems 141
Nyrop, Christopher 56-57

observation 168
occupation 157
Ogden, C. K. 171
olfactory 109, 110-114, 115, 129
Olsen, Carroll L. 175
Olsen, Tillie 120
optical 107, 108, 122, 125-126; see also visual
order 167
Osmond, H. 111
Ostwald, Peter F. 10, 18, 55, 58, 92, 96, 110, 141, 155
outcries 71
out-of-awareness 15, 16, 117, 131

Pacas Nova 43
palatalization 45
paralanguage 9-10, 24, 41-75, 140, 148
paralinguistic act 20, 26, 29ff., 71-75, 160, 166
Parsons, Elsie C. 173
participants 130
pause 48ff., 117
performative verbs 123, 125
Perrin, Noel 74
Persian 56
personality 135; see also idiosyncratic, individual behavior
Peter, H.R.H. Prince of Greece and Denmark 78
Peterson, Frederick A. 55
pharyngealization 46
Phibbs, R. 141
philosophical categories 123
physical condition 132
physiology 91-100, 114
Piderit, Theodor 81
Pidgin 20
Pike, Kenneth L. 62
pitch 47ff., 129, 144, 149, 151, 155
Pittenger, Robert E. 11, 150
poet/poetry 114, 117, 127
pointing gesture 76
Polanyi, Michael 15
Polish 50
Ponder, Eric 87
posture 26-27, 32, 76-80, 109, 117, 152, 156
pouting 89
Powell, Wilfred 172
prelinguistic 140
Pribam, Karl H. 15
privacy 120, 129
pronominal/pronoun 36, 38
proxemics 128; see also space
psycholinguistic categories 123

Quackenbos, H. M. 80
quantitative 101
quantity see length
Quirk, Randolph 66, 162

rate of speech see speed
Rawson, Philip 171, 173
Read, Allen Walker 58, 172
Rebel Yell 58-59
redundancy 108, 167
reduplication 73
Reik, Theodor 120
reinforcing act 29ff.
relationship of nonverbal act to language 32ff.
religion/religious 114, 157
responsibility 35
rhythm 51, 93, 117, 140, 143-144
Richards, I. A. 171
Riemer, Morris D. 86
Ringwall, Egan A. 141
Rites of passage 102-103, 157
Ritzenthaler, Robert E. 55
Róheim, Géza 110
Romans 78, 80, 98, 129, 154, 156
Rosenbaum, Peter S. 172
Ross, John Robert 39-40, 172
Ruesch, Jurgen 27, 129, 167
Russian 50, 74, 98, 143

Salisbury, Lee H. 20
Salk, L. 15
Samarin, William J. 70, 95, 116, 175
Sanskrit 39, 74
Sapir, Edward 12, 77, 124, 136, 174
Scandinavian 29, 45
Scheflen, Albert E. 36-38, 80
Schlesinger, Arthur M., Sr. 21, 138, 171, 175
Schuler, Edgar A. 20
Schwalberg, Carol 134, 174
science/scientific method 22, 162-170
Scot 58-59, 104
Scott, Hugh L. 160
scratch 97, 105-106, 114
Sebeok, Thomas A. 16, 50, 95, 97, 111
secret language 65, 157
segmental 42
segmentation 166-167
semantic 38
Seminole 93
sensory 107, 115
sentence 25
Seton, Ernest Thompson 159
sex 147, 156
sexual 19, 91, 96, 110, 130
sigh 50, 97, 126
sign language 24, 118, 126, 150, 158-161
signal 22-23, 109
silence 39, 50, 116-121, 133, 144, 154, 158, 165
Sines, Jacob O. 111
Siona 37
Siriono 94
sitting 27, 77
Slavic 45
sleeping 91, 94
Slobin, Daniel I. 144
smile 84, 88, 153
Smith, Henry Lee, Jr. 11, 150
Smith, Kathleen 111
sneeze 97-98, 141, 157
sniff 50, 93

socio-economic 156-157; see also status
Socrates 41
Sorensen, E. Richard 17
sound mimicry see noise mimicry
sound placement 46
space 38, 128, 129; see also proxemics
Spanish 30, 38, 43, 48, 50, 51, 55, 74, 129, 150, 153
spatial 153
speech mimicry 62, 72, 145
speech surrogate 24
speed 51, 93
Spencer, Herbert 67
spit 19, 97-99
spontaneous physiological act 70, 96-99
standing 27, 77
startle reflex 99
status 154, 156-157
Steig, William 80, 96
Steinbeck, John 110, 128, 173, 174
Stern, Theodore 24, 55, 64
Stokoe, William C., Jr. 24, 159, 160, 161
stops 42, 45
stress 48ff., 129
stretch 97
style 134
sucking 97, 99, 143
suprasegmental 48-53, 140
Swadesh, Morris 124, 174
swallowing 50, 97
Swedish 74
Swiss-German 71
syntax 118, 125

tactile/tactual 38-39, 102-104, 105, 107, 122, 125-126, 129, 154
Taos 38, 150
Taylor, Archer 101
Teit, James A. 160
tempo 51
temporal 128, 138, 159; see also time
theory 163
Thomas, Owen 171
tickling 19, 103
time 38, 93, 127, 129; see also temporal
Titchener, E. B. 81
Toda 90
Tomkins, William 159
tongue 89-90, 143, 150
Totonac 112
touch see tactile
Trager, George L. 10-11, 24, 38, 42, 135, 150
Trappist 24
trill 43
Trollope, Frances 92, 173
Turkish 74
turn-taking 159; see also interaction
Twain, Mark 152
Tylor, Sir Edward Burnett 18, 29, 57, 62, 64, 72, 94, 98, 140
Tzeltal 150

Uganda 68
ungrammaticality 122
universals 17
unvoiced/voiceless 47, 143

Vanderbilt, Amy 138
ventriloquism 62
verbal act 20, 24ff., 33, 34
verbal communication 9
Vernon, Philip E. 13
visual 39, 115, 153; see

also optical
Voegelin, C. F. 133, 174
voice disguiser 62, 65, 151
voice quality 60
voice set 135
voiced 47, 143
voiceless/unvoiced 47, 143
Volpe, Edmond L. 171
voluntary 99
vowel 45
Vygotsky, L. S. 140

Waika (Brazil) 89
Walker, Jerell R. 161
walking 92-93
Walpole, Earl 160
warfare 103, 157
Watzlawick, Paul 117
weeping see cry
Wegener, Philipp 124
Weir, Ruth H. 143
Welmers, William E. 10
Wentworth, Harold 109, 173
Wescott, Roger W. 109
Wharton, John F. 173
Wheeler, Alva 172
whisper 47, 48
whistle 24, 53-55, 143, 150, 157, 158, 161
White, Leslie A. 171
White, W. A. 172
Whitman, Walt 114
Whorf, Benjamin Lee 77, 124, 174
Wiener, Harry 108, 110-112
Wilson, Gordon 59
wink 87
Wolff, Peter H. 141, 143
woman 161; see also female
writing 126
Wundt, Wilhelm 140

Xosa 44

yawn 97, 99
yell 57
Yiddish 31, 37
yodel 62
Yutang, Lin 110, 173

Zapoteco 43, 106
Zeitgeist 133
Zulu 98